A Civil War
Road Trip
of A Lifetime

Antietam, Gettysburg and Beyond

John Banks

GETTYSBURG
PUBLISHING

Published by Gettysburg Publishing, LLC
www.gettysburgpublishing.com

Back cover photos clockwise from upper left: Andersonville POW camp at dusk. Confederate spies William Orton Williams and Walter Gibson Peter. Jason Whatley at a Confederate wedding mansion in Columbia, Tennessee. Aaron Sanders with a tray of Civil War artifacts at Thompson's Station, Tennessee. Damon Radcliffe, a USCT soldier descendant, at Fort Harrison in Virginia. A Civil War soldier ID disc unearthed by Richard Clem. Laurie Mack at Antietam's 40-Acre Cornfield holding an image of her great-great-grandfather who died there.

The author and publisher strongly condemn trespassing on any private or National Park property. Please refer to NPS and local laws, rules and regulations.

Library of Congress Cataloging-in-Publication Data

Names: Banks, John, 1959- author.
Title: A Civil War road trip of a lifetime : Antietam, Gettysburg, and
    beyond / John Banks.
Description: First edition. | [Trumbull] : Gettysburg Publishing, [2023] |
    Includes bibliographical references and index.
Identifiers: LCCN 2023020148 (print) | LCCN 2023020149 (ebook) | ISBN
    9781734627671 (paperback) | ISBN 9781734627688 (ebook)
Subjects: LCSH: United States--History--Civil War,
    1861-1865--Battlefields--Guidebooks. | Battlefields--United
    States--Guidebooks. | Historic sites--United States--Guidebooks. |
    United States--Description and travel. | Banks, John,
    1959---Travel--United states.
Classification: LCC E641 .B36 2023 (print) | LCC E641 (ebook) | DDC
    973.7--dc23/eng/20230517
LC record available at https://lccn.loc.gov/2023020148
LC ebook record available at https://lccn.loc.gov/2023020149

Printed and bound in the United States of America

First Edition

To the women who make me smile
– Jessie, Emmy and Mrs. B –
and the journalist who served as
an inspiration, Tony Horwitz

OUR ITINERARY
(Contents)

FOREWORD

THE ROAD LESS TRAVELED

Fresh takes on an event from 160 years ago are elusive and often tortured, especially when that event is the American Civil War—the most poked, prodded, gutted and filleted episode in our nation's past.

In 1861, fate delivered a haymaker to the jaw of our young country. With visceral absurdity, two sides duked it out for reasons that were over the heads of many of the participants. Wars are often like that.

We survived, but ever since the war's conclusion the nation has walked with a limp, an old war wound that never heals. Sometimes we feel this injury when the weather changes, as it did in 1921 in the streets of Tulsa; in 1968 at a Memphis motel; on Boston school buses in 1974; and in many more ways, in the rending of the American fabric so evident in contemporary times. It's 1858 all over again.

Meeting Gettysburg scourge and amputee Dan Sickles well after the war, Mark Twain remarked that the old general "seemed to value the leg he lost more than the one he had left." Likewise, a way of life that was clumsily amputated by the war still hangs in the air today like gun smoke, explaining why many remain so passionate about the Civil War.

Because of this, it seems that no stone has been left unturned in the pursuit of Civil War analysis. The historical record has been written, revised and re-revised. Troop movements have been documented almost to the exact step of every last private. Once upon a time Civil War buffs could tell you every detail of Gettysburg and Antietam. Today they can tell you every detail of Ball's Bluff and Wilson's Creek.

So, now that the Civil War has been so thoroughly parsed in every possible aspect and beaten to a mostly miserable death, where are we to go from here?

As Otter and Boone so eloquently expressed in *Animal House* after their frat house had been ingloriously torn asunder:

"Road trip!"

What John Banks so brilliantly captures is the truth that history is organic, not static. The people who maintain such close ties to the war, and their reasons for doing so, are themselves part of a story now.

In his unholy *tour de force* through the breadth and depth of Civil War country, Banks knits the past to the present, often with unspoken allusions to the course of modern events. As we leap through a mosaic of Civil War sites—some familiar but many that are not—Banks serves as the medium between the ghosts from the 1860s and the living, breathing people of today who, until now, had conversed with these ghosts only in private.

The best storytellers are not only good writers, but they are born with a rare talent for discovering flecks of gold in ordinary streambeds. The chapter "Storming a Rebel Fort With An Englishman" is evidence enough of that.

Banks does not glorify or sugarcoat. His survey of Andersonville, "America's Saddest Place," is a poignant examination of the depths of human depravity that are reached singularly through the stresses of war.

Elsewhere, this work is pure fun, an adventuresome and proudly impulsive Indiana Jones-style romp with some of the most classic characters America has ever produced. And wasn't that, perhaps, the way of the war itself: hours of terror and misery interspersed with weeks or months in which thousands of young men were sitting around in camp looking for ways to amuse themselves. More than a few young men found army life preferable to conditions on their hardscrabble frontier dirt farms.

A Civil War Road Trip Of A Lifetime tells these stories with both reverence and mirth, and from a perspective both modern and historic. We begin to understand that the war cannot be put in proper context without levity, and without considering that we as a people aren't that different today than we were then. This is reason for both optimism and pessimism.

Those who hold to the notion that people who fail to study history are doomed to repeat it overlook the truth that the greatest warriors tend to be history's greatest students. Lee found it a relief that war is so gut-wrenching or we should love it too much. Except that we do love it, even knowing its terrors. War is hell. As Banks demonstrates, war, and remembrance of war, is also fentanyl.

Banks invites us to the war through a door that is seldom entered. It is great fun underlaid with a gentle but important message that unity is at risk when opinions become intractable, beyond the influences of reason and fact. He quotes a young Union soldier who wrote: "There they lay, the blue and the gray intermingled; the same rich, young American blood flowing out in little rivulets of crimson; each thinking he was in the right."

Some things never change.

> **–Tim Rowland, author of *Strange and Obscure***
> ***Stories of the Civil War* and other books**

Acknowledgments And Notes

A story about Red Smith, the Pulitzer Prize-winning *New York Times* sports columnist during the era of black and white TV, is seared into my brain. Asked if writing a newspaper column were a chore, the longtime journalist supposedly deadpanned: "Why, no. You simply sit down at the typewriter, open your veins and bleed."

No blood gushed from my veins during the creation of this book. But my feelings often suffered bruising. Blame Bob Zeller, who for decades toiled as a writer at newspapers, as Smith had. Zeller—"BZ" to me—often pummeled and punched up the prose within these pages and prodded me to do better.

After sending a chapter to Zeller, I'd often find myself staring at my laptop days later, nervously awaiting an email from him about the quality (or lack thereof) of a chapter.

"Until I get a thumbs-up from BZ," I'd tell my wife, "it's all crap!" Thank you, Bob, for your sharp-eyed editing.

My "Rambling" column in *Civil War Times* magazine served as a model for this book. I thank the magazine's longtime editor, fellow Western Pennsylvanian Dana Shoaf, for the opportunity to write for the granddaddy of all Civil War magazines. Several, longer versions of my *Civil War Times* columns appear in these pages.

Tim Rowland, my old West Virginia University journalism pal, wrote the foreword. I owe you.

I also thank the authors, archivists, librarians, historians and others who aided me. The list includes Ron Coddington, Dennis Frye, Lesley Gordon, William Griffing, Michael Hardy, Robert Ireland, Tina Jones, Vicki Lane, Brian Laster, Tom Price, Cliff Roberts, John Schildt, Don Serfass, Rick Warwick and Mark Zimmerman.

Publisher Kevin Drake gave the thumbs-up for my concept of the book. I hope I didn't let you down. Jeff Griffith created the terrific cover design. Tessa Sweigert made the interior look great. Brett Keener expertly proofed the pages and Caroline Stover mastered the rest.

In 1998, Tony Horwitz—the brilliant former *Washington Post* correspondent—published *Confederates In The Attic*, an unforgettable book about the enduring Civil War. His work holds up today as well as ever. Tony died in 2019, leaving the world poorer and less fun. I met him once, at a talk he gave on a wintry night in Litchfield, Connecticut. We laughed about our experiences in Martinsburg, West Virginia, where he reported for his book and my professional journalism career began in 1981.

"Godforsaken town," I believe he called it.

Then I asked him to sign his recently published book about John Brown, the fiery abolitionist, scoundrel and murderer who led the insurrection in 1859 at Harper's Ferry, Virginia. It was a spark that led to war in 1861.

"To John," he wrote, "a fellow hack."

Thank you, Tony, wherever your smiling spirit lurks, for the highest compliment of all.

Over more than a year, I crisscrossed the country reporting for *A Civil War Road Trip Of A Lifetime.* The stories in the book appear in roughly chronological order, with several side trips from previous years weaved in. So I should also thank whoever produced the gas that fueled Banks family vehicles.

CHAPTER 1

A 'LOBSTER CLAW' AND THREE LITTLE DEMONS

On a muggy Middle Tennessee morning, I lean against 82-year-old Sam Huffman's beat-up blue Ford pickup while he explains military maneuvers at the Battle of the West Harpeth—an obscure fight only true Civil War obsessives like us care about. A few feet away, traffic races by on two-lane Columbia Pike. To our left, across the road, are a modern house and an open field with a slight rise; to our right, beyond a fence, sit two huge piles of dirt at a construction site. This sure doesn't look like hallowed ground.

Then the softspoken Huffman, a U.S. Army vet who enjoys reading maps, talks about a "lobster claw." No, he isn't making lunch plans at Crab Fever in Nashville. The former Boy Scout and retired IBM employee pulls from his pickup a copy of a map made shortly after the war. Huffman points to two runs on it branching from a stream, forming that claw. He insists it's compelling evidence that we are standing on the site of the West Harpeth battle between Union cavalry and John Bell Hood's Army of Tennessee rearguard on December 17, 1864.

On that rise in the field across the pike is where Huffman believes the Confederates deployed a rarely used Napoleonic defensive tactic called the "hollow square." Think of it as a giant, square football huddle, only with the "players"—the Rebel soldiers—facing outward. Huffman gestures toward another field across the road, near an electrical transmission tower.

"You ought to get your relic hunting buddies to check that out."

I don't own a metal detector but know a half-dozen people who do. I'm happy simply kicking at the ground to see if anything turns up from 1864.

Huffman's battlefield location revelation is potentially embarrassing for me. Weeks earlier, 2.5 miles *south*, I had led a spirited busload of descendants of Confederate soldiers along a narrow lane on a bridge to the supposed West Harpeth battlefield. It's marked with a historical sign. After my impassioned talk at the site—*"They formed the hollow square right here!"*—I even embraced a descendant of a Rebel soldier.

"There's no lobster claw down that way," Huffman scoffs.

I'm briefly bamboozled but remain undaunted. Mistakes, of course, come with the territory.

Welcome to my Civil War world, where no battlefield is too obscure to investigate; no hill is too steep to climb; no woods are filled with enough ticks, snakes or coyotes to deter an exploration; no clue is too bizarre to pursue; virtually no historical sign is too remote to see; and no road trip is too far to make.

My obsession began decades ago in Gettysburg, as you might suspect. Three one-ounce pieces of lead—*real bullets*—purchased there by my dad, "Big Johnny," on a family vacation in the early 1970s might as well have served as rocket fuel for my sudden passion. These souvenirs have survived moves from Pennsylvania to West Virginia to Maryland to Texas to Connecticut and, finally, to Tennessee.

Those three little demons have led to my purchases of hundreds of Civil War books and scores of magazines; period letters, newspapers, and pho-tographs; and more bullets, as well as the acquisitions of an artillery shell, a soldier's Bible, fort bricks, buttons, bridle rosettes, camp lead, marbles, a killed-in-action Connecticut corporal's schoolbook, a split 1890s albumen of a battlefield monument, a huge framed sketch of Vermont soldier who looks like that evil Vladmir Putin, and the boxed Confederate States of America collection of four Civil War-themed knives made in China.

In our household, Civil War-era, tintypes and albumens of soldiers co-exist in prominent places with photos of our family. In the living room, serious-looking Yankees and Rebels gaze from the covers of dozens of magazines and books. In the garage, hunks of battlefield "witness tree" wood rest next to the car only because my wife won't let me display them in our house. In my mind, family birthdays and my own wedding anniversary get equal play with battle anniversaries.

Over the past four decades, I have traveled thousands of miles—from Arizona to South Carolina—learning about America's greatest conflict. I've teetered on the edge of the creek where young Abraham Lincoln nearly drowned; stared at the site where John Brown's body swayed in the breeze; splashed across the Potomac River at a wartime ford; eaten freshly baked banana coffee cake in the kitchen of the great-granddaughter of celebrated Confederate soldier Sam Watkins; and slithered under barbed-wire fence near a Dairy Queen and the Rooster Cogburn Ostrich Ranch—"The Darndest Place You'll Ever Visit!"—to tramp upon a skirmish site in the desert at Picacho Pass, roughly 40 miles north of Tucson, Arizona.

Supposedly the war's westernmost action, the fight resulted in three dead, all Federals. *Who cares?*

I do.

My Arizona-based mother-in-law—God rest her soul—warned me about the place.

"Watch for *eee-leeeeee-gals*," the Iowa transplant said. "And drug dealers."

I didn't see any evidence of a battle, drug dealers or *eee-leeeeee-gals* on the lunar-like landscape. But I was startled by a pronghorn antelope, something I have never spotted at Devil's Den at Gettysburg.

Closer to home bases, I have also poked about rickety slave cabins with the descendant of Confederate general, slipped about cemeteries in wintry New England examining weather-gnarled gravestones of veterans and unknowingly rummaged through a real Civil War ammunition box filled with live artillery shells.

"Are these shells deactivated?" I asked Earl Roulette, the great-grandson of William Roulette.

William owned the farm that bordered Antietam's infamous Bloody Lane. Earl, an 80-something with a sly sense of humor, lived all his life near the battlefield in Sharpsburg, Maryland.

"Oh, no," Roulette said in his distinctive, high-pitched voice about the artillery shells.

Oh, my God.

Earl died more than a decade ago, not because of the explosive effects of a wartime Hotchkiss shell, but from old age.

Years ago, I connected online with a man whose ancestor, a soldier in the 16th Connecticut, had fought at Antietam's 40-Acre Cornfield. We had agreed to meet at Bonnie's At The Red Byrd in Keedysville, Maryland, a restaurant the locals frequent. It's my favorite haunt near the battlefield.

Midway through our conversation, the man said he had served as a CIA station chief in a European capital.

"That doesn't bother you, does it?" he asked while I devoured my breakfast.

"Of course not."

Then I somehow steered the conversation to the JFK assassination, my other obsession.

I sensed a weird vibe upon my mentions of Lee Harvey Oswald and the name of the CIA station chief in Mexico City in 1963.

I spilled a little coffee. But, alas, my breakfast companion spilled no secrets. The former "agent" said he'd stay in touch, but I never heard from him again. What a missed opportunity—for him and me.

But no matter. On my latest Civil War road trip of a lifetime, I met dozens of characters willing to share their stories. Some are compelling and knowledgeable; others are funny and engaging. Some have all those qualities. A common thread: a tight embrace of all things 1861-65. For them, the Civil War—the good, bad and ugly—still resonates. I'll introduce you to some of them.

On a levee in Arkansas, I gazed with a lawyer into the Mound City Chute, a small lake formed when the Mississippi River changed course more than 100 years ago. Nearby, in late April 1865, the steamboat *Sultana* exploded, resulting in the deaths of nearly 1,200 of her passengers, mostly paroled Union prisoners of war. Survivors clung to trees along the river bank, near where we stood. My new friend is obsessed with the tragedy.

Sam Huffman believes the obscure Battle of the West Harpeth was fought here on December 17, 1864. Others aren't so sure.

In backwoods Mississippi, a devout Christian took me on his ATV over a rugged, unheralded battlefield—*his battlefield*. His great-great-grandparents farmed the ground upon which the armies clashed. Following a brief discussion about moonshine, we spent hours riding on an ATV at his battlefield. I owe him a steak dinner at the Beechwood in Vicksburg, Mississippi, one of *his* favorite haunts.

It was in the historic section of Vicksburg where I met one of the more memorable characters on this road trip of a lifetime—a Black man who owns a remarkable museum filled with more than $1 million worth of Civil War guns, pistols, artillery shells, period photographs and much more. But the artifacts aren't important, he says. The message he aims to deliver to visitors is.

At the infamous prisoner of war camp in Andersonville, Georgia, I walked about the grounds with a park guide after dark. She is the descendant of a Confederate soldier who died at Camp Douglas in Chicago, the equally cruel Union POW camp.

After rainstorms at Andersonville, maggots would crawl over the living and the dead, creating a macabre scene. "The food they got," a Connecticut POW recalled of his fellow Union prisoners, "just past [sic] through them and lay right beside them. Ah, it was horrible."[1]

"I've never found a good word to describe this place," my park guide said.

Even nearly 160 years after the last, bedraggled Union prisoner staggered from America's saddest place, Andersonville sears both our souls.

Along the Valley Pike in Virginia's Shenandoah Valley, I descended into caverns for an inspection of inscriptions made on the walls by soldiers during the war. A local chicken farmer, who explored the place as a kid, said the Union Army stored ammo there underground.

In Sharpsburg, Maryland, I caught up with a friend who is obsessed with Abraham Lincoln. On the wall of the Lincoln Room of her late 18th-century house on Main Street hangs a framed Oreo cookie of the president with his profile in the white frosting. On a frosty morning, we took the cookie from its home base for an adventure in western Maryland and beyond.

---

1. William Nott postwar diary, copy in author's collection

Dripping with sweat on a sweltering Virginia morning, I trudged behind another like-minded obsessive deep into the woods near Richmond, the former capital of the Confederacy.

"Is this remote enough for you?" he asked.

Together, we explored the remains of Rebel earthworks on hallowed ground where 14 U.S. Colored Troops earned the Medal of Honor.

In a small, hippy town in the mountains of western North Carolina, I began my search for a historical sign marking one of the war's little-known tragedies: the massacre of 13 Unionists on a wintry day in January 1863. In a coffee shop in town, I met a self-described "hillbilly guy" who kicked off an excellent adventure.

So, what lessons will I learn on this road trip of a lifetime? Will my Civil War fuel tank ever run empty? Stick with me until the end to find out.

But before we gas up and go, let's meet Mrs. B.

She's my very own Civil War Mission Control.

CHAPTER 2

MISSION CONTROL

I first realized Mrs. B could be The One in 1991, when we attended a JFK assassination symposium together at an upscale hotel in Dallas—an event that included whack jobs, malingerers, hangers-on, egomaniacs and ne'er-do-wells. Mrs. B had never even heard of the single-bullet theory or the "Umbrella Man," so she seemed leery and nervous. But I was in my element because I reveled in assassination conspiracy theories and toiled as an editor for the *Dallas Morning News'* vaunted sports department, which included its own motley collection of oddballs. She and I eventually bonded over our shared love of laughter and sports.

In my mind, Mrs. B is forever the beautiful blonde with big hair, an electric smile and a mostly endearing (and loud) laugh; a sweetheart who could stick it to me as well as I to her—a quality mostly unknown to me in the early 1990s beyond the ball-busting Pittsburgh pals of my youth.

At that time, I was a know-it-all, immature, wise-ass, newspaper-loving, Civil War battlefield-stomping, non-fiction book reading, beer-drinking sports journalist who used hair spray, lacked direction and embarrassed her with stories from my days at West Virginia University.

Somehow, she stuck with me.

On our honeymoon in Germany in May 1992, we tramped together over rubble atop Hitler's bunker in Berlin—a thrill for me, at least. But my love for her became cemented forever on my birthday in 2019, when we walked together in the footsteps of the Irish Brigade on the William Roulette farm at Antietam. As we approached Bloody Lane, I got goosebumps. Mrs. B, feigning interest, simply got sweaty and tired. But she was there, by God, and I loved her more than ever because of it.

Over four decades in journalism, my jobs have taken me from amateur baseball games in Paw Paw, West Virginia to Super Bowls throughout the United States as well as to the Olympics at such far-flung places as Lillehammer, Norway; Nagano, Japan; and Sydney, Australia.

But as my interest in sports waned, I became even more obsessed with the real-life conflicts on home soil more than 150 years ago—at obscure places such as Saltville, Virginia; Shepherdstown, West Virginia; New Hope Church, Georgia; and Denmark, Tennessee, as well as the more well-known battlefields at Gettysburg, Cold Harbor and beyond. Of the 10,000 places the armies clashed, it feels as if I've tramped upon half.

Mrs. B seems pleased whenever I depart on my early morning road trips into Civil Wardom.

"Go have fun," she usually tells me—an odd thing to say, perhaps, before a visit to a killing field.

But the Civil War is not her thing. She's an Iowan with a gift for gab, a pragmatist who looks ahead instead of behind. Smart and funny, Mrs. B would rather not descend into the muck of civil war. Who could blame her? It was awful. Thankfully, slavery ended. But our country's divisions, unfortunately, never have.

Like you, perhaps, I go to battlefields partly to ponder the unfathomable.

How could that 19-year-old kid from Massachusetts crouch behind that stone wall and ram a one-ounce lead ball into a pipe to propel it into the brain of that 19-year-old from Georgia standing on that bluff?

Why, God, why?

While she rarely travels to a battlefield with me, Mrs. B is often drawn into my historical (and often hysterical) orbit.

At my Civil War talks, she serves as audio-visual expert and subject of her husband's bad jokes. She has heard and seen it all at these events— from an elderly man snoring loudly while I talk of bullet-riddled bodies at Burnside Bridge to my repeated references to a brilliant, 37-year-old professor from Connecticut named Newton Manross, who told his wife upon enlisting: "You can better afford to have a country without a husband than a husband without a country."[1] On the march, the beloved 16th Connecticut captain was known to carry the muskets of tired subordinates.

At the 40-Acre Cornfield at Antietam, Manross—who embodies the tragedy of war for me—suffered a mortal wound. Mrs. B knows him, too. After rolling the trash can into our garage every Tuesday night, she deftly places it so as not to harm the rickety window frame from Manross' boyhood home in Bristol, Connecticut. Years ago, the homeowner gave the bizarre relic to me—another example of how deep I'm into this stuff.

At a brief Civil War talk I gave years ago in Avon, Connecticut—our hometown then—papier-mâché and craft paper cows on the walls glared at Mrs. B., me and the scant audience. Afterward, a woman dressed in an 1860s-style hoop skirt warned the few attendees that the subsequent, Civil War-themed play could be a real tear-jerker.

"There are boxes of Kleenexes next to your seats," she said earnestly.

But the faux cows made the play more comical than cry worthy.

Afterward, we burst out laughing. Still do, in fact, every time the subject comes up.

"When discussing the Civil War," I often tell her, "sometimes it's OK to laugh through the pain."

Now depending on whom she's talking with, Mrs. B goes by either "Carol," her maiden name "Danker" or "Mamz," my favorite nickname. Mrs. B—the mother of our two opinionated, adult daughters—is not so much my best friend as she is my adviser, teacher and life coach. I'm the forever freshman at "Husband University," where my domestic skills will never be refined to Mrs. B's exacting standards. She calls me "Bozo," "Jackass," "Jamz" and names my publisher doesn't want to see in this space.

Always eager to provoke Mama Bear, I constantly threaten to renew our wedding vows. But Mrs. B refuses because it may jinx the odd thing we have going. All the couples she knows who have renewed their commitments are divorced.

---

1. Blakeslee, Bernard F., *The History of the Sixteenth Connecticut*, Hartford, Conn.: The Case, Lockwood & Brainard Co. Printers, 1875, Page 20

Carol Banks—the beloved "Mrs. B"—keeps me laughing. I am at right.

For all Civil War road trips, Mrs. B serves as my ATM as well as my very own Mission Control.

"Do you have your wallet?

"Are you wearing deodorant?"

"Did you pack underwear?"

"Is Murray's parking brake on?"

"Murray" is what Mrs. B calls her Murano, which I have often borrowed for road trips while my own vehicle was sidelined with a smashed side panel. Tired and ornery, I accidentally rammed my car into a fence post at the Widow Pence farm at the Cross Keys battlefield in Virginia's Shenandoah Valley. I blamed angry cows, who appeared threatening. Mrs. B blamed me.

From the road, I often call Mrs. B to check in, once at 5 a.m. (Butt dial.) Sometimes she even answers my calls. I didn't even get in a word one time as she proclaimed: "If you lose your car keys in a cornfield on this trip, don't come home." That's never actually happened, but she fears someday it might.

Besides serving as de facto family leader, Mrs. B works magic with family finances as our chief financial officer. That's mainly because I haven't been good with numbers since … well, forever.

Mrs. B and I have a tacit understanding that I'm not to spend over a certain amount—*psst, it's $75*—without running it past her. So, if you spot me at a Civil War shop or military show furiously texting or gabbing on the phone, I'm probably communicating with Mrs. B. Those communications are often remarkable for their brevity.

"I want to buy a 100-pound artillery shell."

"No."

"I like this World War I Browning machine gun. The guy calls it a 'Potato Digger'."

"How much does it cost?"

"$25K."

"No."

"They have a real Civil War cigar out here at the Franklin Show."

"No."

"I'm here at The Horse Soldier in Gettysburg. Just spotted a silver plate from a coffin of a civilian who died of a heart attack during the Battle of Nashville and …"

"No."

We seem to have this Vulcan Mind-Meld-like thing, just like Spock in the old *Star Trek* TV series, in which I don't even have to say a word before suffering instant rejection and humiliation. Minutes after arriving in Sharpsburg, my Civil War home away from home, I spotted a historic house for sale on the main drag, across the street from Nutter's Ice Cream, where you can get two huge scoops for a pittance. I called Mrs. B, who blurted:

"No, we're not moving to Sharpsburg."

I didn't even get to say hello.

Now sometimes I summon the courage to simply do my own thing. At the Rally Hill mansion—site of an epic Confederate wedding in 1863—the current owners' rescue dog dropped a deceased groundhog at the feet of a guest. I'm like that with battlefield "witness tree" hunks, which I plop in our garage or toss into the back of Murray. Two forgotten hunks of Champion Hill witness tree in Murray earned me a trip to the doghouse.

To close my Civil War deals with Mrs. B, I resort to my three-word strategy at the very beginning of conversations. But like George McClellan changing his base during his 1862 Peninsula Campaign, it often earns me ridicule, and, ultimately, rejection from my leader.

"I love you."

"What do you want to buy?"

Ugh.

Sometimes I simply lower my standards. At a flea market in Leiper's Fork, Tennessee, near where the Yankees burned a gristmill in 1863, I purchased a 100-year-old bottle of laxative, which had formed into a weird, black goo. It cost less than my allowed limit but still earned me an eyeroll from Mrs. B. Now it sits in my home office, nearly forgotten, near two bricks from a Civil War fort.

You'll find Mrs. B sprinkled throughout these pages—not because she made me do it, but because I can't tell this story without her. Besides, Mrs. B is my hero. And she is ultimately responsible for releasing me into the Civil War wild—from Vicksburg, Mississippi to Charleston, South Carolina, where my first adventure begins in a flat-bottom aluminum boat with an Englishman, who explored with me a smelly Confederate fort occupied almost solely by pelicans.

So let's go. Together, perhaps, we can laugh a little on our Civil War journey, too.

CHAPTER 3

Charleston, South Carolina

STORMING
A REBEL FORT
WITH AN ENGLISHMAN

Ominous, gray clouds gather on a late-summer afternoon, hardly prime time for a boat trip on choppy waters to a Civil War fort. No, my destination isn't Fort Sumter, whose bombardment by the Rebels marked the official beginning of the Civil War. Mrs. B is going there. I'm heading to Shutes Folly Island, a spit of land roughly a mile offshore in Charleston Harbor, for a visit to Castle Pinckney—the first Federal property seized by Southern forces.

My guide is Matthew Locke, a 47-year-old Englishman with a fascination for the fort and the Civil War and a keen sense of adventure and the ridiculous. He enjoys warm beer, but I like him anyway.

Before our departure, Locke hands me ointment to rub under my nose to blunt the horrid smells on the odoriferous, private island.

"Could be little bit ropy out there."

"No worries, I'm *totally* prepared," I say, lying.

At the dock of the tony Carolina Yacht Club, we are met by "Captain Doug," a longtime member of the Sons of Confederate Veterans. The Vietnam vet lives on nearby James Island with his nine chickens.

Before we shove off in his flat-bottom aluminum boat, the captain hands me a waiver to sign. I nervously scribble my name. Naturally, the wind picks up as Captain Doug launches his tiny vessel for our trip to Shutes Folly.

Near my feet rests a postage stamp-sized floatie.

"Damn, is that my life preserver?" I mumble to myself.

"Is this the appropriate time to tell my boatmates that I can't swim?"

Captain Doug navigates into the harbor, past the dock and a decoy of a fox. Then the wake of a large vessel helps launch us about a foot out of the wind-swept water, propelling my heart into my throat. Out in the harbor I spy the remains of Castle Pinckney, guarded now by a flock of pelicans and seagulls. On the horizon, about three miles away, stands Fort Sumter.

Constructed in 1809-10, the brick-and-mortar Castle Pinckney was named for South Carolina politician Charles Pinckney, a two-time loser as the Federalist Party's candidate for U.S. president. The once-foreboding place was called a castle because of its feudal appearance.

Castle Pinckney served as a bit player in the slave trade in Charleston, America's capital of the practice. In 1858, 50 years after the banning of slave trading in the U.S., it became a temporary home for slaves who had been illegally transported to America.

"Many were reduced to walking skeletons," a Charleston newspaper reported, "and some evidently in a dying condition."[1]

On December 27, 1860, a week after South Carolina became the first state to secede from the Union, 150 soldiers from three Southern militia units gathered on the green at The Citadel in Charleston. The soldiers boarded a steamer, which made a beeline for Castle Pinckney. Their mission: Take over the U.S. installation, manned by a commanding officer, an ordnance sergeant, four mechanics and 30 laborers.

The militia quickly forced the surrender of the garrison, whose commander and a party of others fled on a rowboat for Fort Sumter.

On April 12, 1861, the small Confederate garrison at Castle Pickney had almost a ringside seat to the awe-inspiring bombardment of Fort Sumter. But no witness accounts from anyone on Shutes Folly are known to exist.

---

1. *The Charleston Daily Courier*, Aug. 30, 1858

Within sight of Castle Pinckney, hundreds of Charlestonians flocked to The Battery, the city's promenade, to watch the spectacle. "The curling white smoke hung above the angry pieces of friend and foe," a Charleston newspaper reported, "and the jarring boom rolled at regular intervals on the anxious ear."[2]

In late 1861, Castle Pinckney served as a prison for roughly six weeks for more than 150 Union soldiers, mostly from the First Battle of Bull Run. "Chiefly from among those who had evidenced the most insolent and insubordinate dispositions," a Charleston newspaper reported of the U.S. Army prisoners.[3]

During the day, many of the POWs wandered freely about the place. At night, their captors confined them to cells in the fort. But even for the Rebels who had the freedom to roam the grounds anytime, Castle Pickney was no cushy assignment.

"We are treated worse than negroes here," a Confederate soldier wrote. "We don't get enough to eat, and what we do get is the coursest [sic] and most common description. If you hear of anyone getting the Southern Rights Fever as strongly as I had it, just show them this, and if it does not cure him, nothing will."[4]

Bonk!

After our treacherous harbor crossing, Captain Doug hits shore. Locke, wearing a golf hat and knee-high boots, plunges into three feet of water and scurries out of the boat. Wearing a newly purchased Indiana Jones-like explorer hat and cheap, ankle-high boots, I follow him, nervously. Then I bid goodbye to Captain Doug, who promises to return in an hour or three. An ugly storm is brewing, after all. We crawl over rocks to get to the muddy western side of Shutes Folly.

In 2018, I survived the visit to this uninhabited island and fort, which have *zero* ambience thanks to an accumulation of dead fish, dead birds, dead rats, pelican poo and who-knows-what else. Before we enter the fort this time, Locke shows me the spot where Confederate Zouave cadets had their picture taken outside the massive walls in the fall of 1861. I shoot an image for comparison.

---

2. Ibid, April 13, 1861

3. *The New York Times*, Sept. 15, 1861

4. Ibid, March 20, 1861

Matthew Locke stands where Confederate Zouave cadets had their picture taken outside the massive walls of Castle Pinckney in fall 1861.

Confederate Zouave cadets at Castle Pinckney. How many of these young men survived the war? Library of Congress

Then we limbo-dance under the brick entrance, past live and dead pelicans, and traipse through waist-high vegetation that covers most of the fort's interior. In the 20th century, Castle Pinckney was filled with tons of sand, probably from a nearby sandbar, so the interior looks nothing like it did during the war.

And, yes, this place still stinks.

Locke, who grew up outside London, moved in 2004 to Charleston, where he joined the local chapter of the Sons of Confederate Veterans. An ancestor of his served in the 13th Battalion North Carolina Light Artillery (CSA). His great-grandfather suffered a wound at the Battle of the Ypres, the horrendous World War I battle. Locke, an avid Civil War reenactor, relishes his Confederate connections. I relish returning to shore and not becoming fish food.

"There's a bloody, great hole here somewhere," Locke says. "I know because I dug it."

"*Ahhhh*!" he shouts as he stumbles into a shallow dip.

Seconds later, Locke returns among the living, unharmed physically from his descension into "The Pit of Death."

A huge lightning bolt shoots across the sky, above historic St. Michael's church in Charleston, where George Washington and Robert E. Lee worshipped. A boom of thunder follows.

Things are getting ugly.

"This is solid ground right here," Locke says, trying to guide me to safety. Then he lines up another Civil War "Then & Now" image, this one of the barracks that once stood at the fort.

In 1861, George S. Cook of Charleston shot images of the Union prisoners at the fort—the war's first photographs of POWs. Demonstrating a sense of humor, 21 soldiers in a Zouave regiment posed near an entranceway and below a hand-made sign that read "Hotel de Zouave."

In another image, Yankee prisoners gathered near the casemate by an entranceway and under a hand-painted sign that read "Music Hall, 444 Broadway." In that same photograph, more than two dozen of the Union soldiers' captors—including four by a massive cannon tube—relaxed above them on a parapet.

After we come down from our Civil War photography high, Locke offers words of encouragement:

"That's a huge drop there. Watch yourself."

"These plants are a pain in the ass."

"If you fall into a cistern here, there's a long way to go to the bottom."

Following the war, Castle Pinckney became a federal military prison, sort of an East Coast Alcatraz. Then it languished.

"Practically a wreck and useless for purposes of defense," an U.S. Army engineer said in 1878.[5]

Plans to make the place a retirement home for U.S Army veterans went nowhere in the 1890s.

"While a little over 100 years old, Castle Pinckney has been overshadowed by more historic and more effective forts in the harbor—Moultrie and Sumter—in the hearts of the people," a newspaper wrote.[6]

Early in the 20th century, the place nearly became a death trap for real. In the dead of a late-spring night in 1903, "violent barking" by watchdogs awakened the keeper of Castle Pinckney, then used as a Navy supply station. Wooden casks had somehow been set ablaze, threatening to ignite a nearby oil house that held 15,000 gallons of kerosene. The keeper and his family rolled the casks into the harbor, saving themselves.[7]

In the late 1960s, the Sons of Confederate Veterans maintained Castle Pinckney for a time, intending to open a museum. But upkeep proved daunting, and the island reverted to the state. Castle Pinckney has sat vacant for decades—well, except for hundreds of pelicans and other critters—and become a destination for vandals and, ahem, the occasional pleasure-seekers.

In 2011, South Carolina sold the fort and part of the island for $10 Confederate (seriously) to the Fort Sumter Camp No. 1269, Sons of Confederate Veterans, who are protective of their private property. "We didn't want to see something out there like a sports bar, with neon lights," the local SCV commander told me years ago.

---

5. *The New York Times*, Oct. 1, 1899

6. *Baltimore Sun*, Sept. 28, 1899

7. *Washington Evening Times*, June 7, 1902

Matthew Locke adjusts the web camera at Castle Pinckney.

I repeatedly look at my watch, wondering when Captain Doug plans to return.

I hope he's not feeding his chickens.

"There is a Coast Guard station over there." Locke says, pointing to the far distance. "But I'm not sure I can swim that far." Now I'm *really* nervous.

Then the Englishman launches into rapid-fire ornithology/safety/history lessons:

"*The pelicans lay their eggs from June to August, so I try not to bother them … We don't want people coming out here by themselves. They could get hurt.*" (No kidding.) … *There's a Brooke rifled cannon under this blue tarp.*"

Wait, what?!

Months earlier, another Sons of Confederate Veterans member discovered the behemoth—it weighs thousands of pounds—while using ground-penetrating radar to locate buried electrical lines. The tube may be the same one that appears in a wartime photograph. It will be years, if ever, before the ultimate relic hunting find can be unearthed.

At the close of the war, three 10-inch Columbiads remained at the fort, too. There's no record of the removal of those massive guns from Castle Pinckney, so who knows what might lie deep beneath the surface and pelican poo.

Castle Pinckney gunners fired few, if any, shots during the Civil War. But the Yankees targeted the fort during the siege of Charleston in 1863.

"[T]hree out of five shots smote the castle," wrote a Rhode Island artillerist. "We dropped our shells into Charleston whenever we pleased; but the size of the castle made it the smallest armed target that we had selected; and its occupants, feeling that they were exempt from our regards, and safe, were sitting and strolling about on the work. Our magnificent shots produced among them an indescribable excitement."[8]

Besides mammoth cannon tubes, Shutes Folly could hold other secrets—certainly more wartime artifacts. Civil War ordnance remains in the harbor. On a 2018 visit to Charleston Harbor, I spotted a hunk of cannonball washed ashore by a storm on the rocks outside Fort Sumter. Perhaps there's a rare miss from that nearly giddy Rhode Island artillerist somewhere in the muck near Shutes Folly.

Finally, Captain Doug joins us.

"I could have been surfboarding out there if I was not careful," he says about the hazardous return trip from Charleston.

Thunder grows louder. The wind kicks up. Beads of sweat form on my forehead.

Before we depart, Locke and Captain Doug must change out a 10-foot-by-7.5-foot flag atop a 35-foot flagpole. Down comes the Stainless Banner, a Confederate flag, and up goes the 1st National Confederate flag. The SCV also rotates other flags—Betsy Ross', the Irish flag and others—timed to historical events.

---

8. Denison, Frederic, *Shot and Shell: The Third Rhode Island Heavy Artillery in the Rebellion*, Providence, R.I.: Third Rhode Island Heavy Artillery Veterans Association, 1879, Page 252

Then Locke climbs an aluminum ladder to re-adjust the web camera for the flag.

"That thing ever been struck by lightning?" I ask about the flagpole.

"We don't want this to be the first time," Captain Doug says.

As the storm creeps closer, we admire the view of the historic Battery promenade and city skyline. Then my saviors discuss the greatness of Shutes Folly.

"Coolest real estate in Charleston," says Captain Doug.

"Most expensive, too," Locke chimes in.

I explore the rusty remnants of a post-Civil War railing, prompting a half-dozen unhappy pelicans to squeal. Then I spot bones on the ground: *Are they human?* My thoughts turn dark, like the sky.

"OK, time to close this shit down," says Captain Doug.

We gingerly step on dozens of large rocks to the rocking bass boat. But the Englishman is MIA. I wonder if he fell into the "Pit of Death."

Soon my guide reappears.

"Here," he says, handing me a gift.

It's a large brick from the other side of the fort, probably wartime. I'm touched.

The return trip is a blur of harbor spray, Hail Marys and hallelujahs. The next thing I know Locke and I are in the Blind Tiger Pub, throwing down beers near a woman wearing sunglasses and a pink-and-green yoga outfit.

It's raining like a pissing cow.

At the outdoor bar, a torrent of rain water rushes over rocks.

Moments later, I receive a flurry of texts from Mrs. B, who's on a tour boat to Fort Sumter in sideways rain:

"Hope I live. Storming."

"If I don't come back remember 29 years was a good run!!!!"

"Looking for life jackets."

"Lightning."

"Kind of cool actually."

You're telling me.

Days later, I'm mulling marriage, too. But it's not mine. It's the epic 1863 wedding of a Confederate cavalry commander at a mansion in Middle Tennessee.

CHAPTER 4

Columbia, Tennessee

MULES, 'MURDER'
AND MARRIAGE

A week after shooting a selfie with two mules at the annual Mule Day celebration in Columbia—the self-proclaimed "Mule Capital of the World"—I find myself back in town. This time I'm here to visit Rally Hill, the estate where Confederate glitterati attended an epic wedding of one of their own in the spring of 1863.

Rally Hill, whose guests have included a U.S. president, is the home of attorney Jason Whatley, a 50-year-old Texas native, Southern Baptist and bourbon aficionado; married father of five; descendant of a Civil War soldiers in the Georgia Militia; and surrogate daddy to Finn, a killer in cold blood of at least eight groundhogs that once roamed the property. The vigilant mutt has chased quarry into traffic and once plopped a kill at the feet of a houseguest.

Mrs. W loves Finn, whom she saved from a near-death experience, with all her heart.

"Women fawn over Finn," Whatley says.

I like him, too.

Since purchasing Rally Hill in 2017, the Whatleys have lovingly restored the circa-1840s house, which over the years has suffered the indignity of becoming apartments, a renovation into two separate residences and the nasty effects of abandonment.

In the 1980s, the community rallied to save the mansion from demolition and the ground from getting plowed over to become a parking lot.

Rally Hill vitals: Federal architectural style with Greek Revival touches; 6,000 square feet and 17 rooms (including a late-19th-century addition); the original staircase, doors, poplar floors and many of the original, wavy glass windowpanes; 14-foot ceilings; a detached brick kitchen; and a city park-like front yard featuring a massive, ancient catalpa tree.

James Walker, Rally Hill's original owner, touched almost every aspect of society in Columbia, a 50-minute drive south of Nashville. He became a newspaper publisher and editor, co-founded the county's first bank, helped run a stagecoach line, served as town mayor and co-owned an iron furnace, among many other endeavors.

Whatley heard Walker may have ridden a horse through the mansion's front door, but that story may simply be legend.

What's indisputable is this wealthy renaissance man was a slave owner (perhaps more than 12), a father of 11 and brother-in-law of James K. Polk, whom he advised during his successful run for U.S. president in 1844.

In April 1849, a month after the completion of his presidential term, Polk visited Rally Hill for dinner.

"In the afternoon, I walked into the lawn and remained a few minutes," the ex-president wrote in his diary.[1]

Three of Walker's sons served as Confederate Army officers.

During their extensive renovation, the Whatleys uncovered a rat's nest on the second floor. Inside the rodent relic they found an 1815 promissory note for $3,550 bearing the name "Polk," a piece of an 1850 newspaper and a 19th-century version of toilet paper (apparently used), which probably wouldn't command the minimum price if Christie's auctioned it.

"So, did you find any Confederate wedding invitations in that rat's nest?" I ask Whatley.

---

1. The Diary of James K. Polk during his Presidency, 1845 to 1849, edited and annotated by Milo Milton Quaife, Chicago: A.C. McClurg & Co., 1910, Page 419

Jason Whatley lives with his family and a dog named Finn in a mansion in Columbia, Tennessee where an epic Confederate wedding was held in 1863.

"No," he says, chuckling at my weak attempt at history humor.

On April 27, 1863, Rally Hill became site of the wedding of 27-year-old ladies' man Frank Crawford Armstrong, a brigadier general in the Confederate cavalry, to 19-year-old Maria Polk Walker, James Walker's granddaughter. The *Gone With The Wind*-like affair—one of many weddings held at Rally Hill over the years—included as guests generals Nathan Bedford Forrest (cavalry genius/notorious slave trader), Earl Van Dorn (womanizer and scoundrel), the staffs of Van Dorn and Armstrong, Rhett Butler/Clark Gable (kidding) and other Rebel brass.

Rally Hill was an "in-town residence," says county archives president Tom Price, who accompanies us on the grounds.

The place was not the fictional Tara plantation of *Gone With the Wind* fame, with fields planted with cotton. No farming for Rally Hill, which consisted of 12 acres—still more than ample space for a large military wedding and massive military egos. Almost every soldier present came attired in his full-dress uniform, with the fancy, yellow piping. You've probably seen photos of those uniforms in those old Time-Life Civil War books.

"It was by far the largest body of cavalry ever seen together at that time," a guest recalled, "and was a very impressive and imposing function."[2]

For Confederate sympathizers among the locals, the wedding was a rare bright spot amidst the gloom of war. In all, roughly 200 people attended.

Armstrong, the groom, was born in 1835 in the Choctaw Agency in Indian Territory (present-day Oklahoma), where his father served in the U.S. Army. In the 1850s, while in the army, Armstrong fought Native Americans in New Mexico and elsewhere. In the 1857-58 Utah War, he campaigned against the Mormons with Albert Sidney Johnston, the future Confederate general, who would suffer a mortal wound at Shiloh on April 6, 1862.

At the First Battle of Bull Run on July 21, 1861, Armstrong led a company of *Union* cavalry—the 2nd Dragoons. Less than three weeks later, Armstrong resigned his commission to join the Confederacy. Because his resignation did not go into effect until August 13, 1861, he technically served on both sides simultaneously—a rare, and perhaps unequaled, Civil War feat.

Armstrong served with distinction throughout the Western Theater—at Pea Ridge, Chickamauga, Atlanta, after the Rebels' defeat at Nashville in Forrest's rearguard and elsewhere. Following a skirmish at Middleburg, Tennessee in late August 1862, "J.P.P"—a letter writer to a Memphis news-paper—called him "the finest cavalry officer in our service."

"His men are devoted to him beyond anything I ever heard of," continued J.P.P. "On the field he is cool and collected, and moves his men about as Morphy moves his chessmen. Take my word for it, Frank Armstrong … is one of the greatest captains of this war, and with opportunity, will place himself *with* Stonewall Jackson, or in *front* of him."[3]

In 1863, Van Dorn pushed for Armstrong's promotion from colonel to brigadier general. "[T]he cavalry had no more active and daring, and at the same time careful, commander," a Confederate veteran recalled about Armstrong.[4]

---

2. White, Emma Siggins, *Genealogy of the descendants of John Walker of Wigton*, Scotland, Kansas City, Mo.: Tiernan-Dart Printing Co., 1902, Page 522

3. *Memphis Daily Appeal*, Sept. 3, 1862

4. Montgomery, Frank A., *Reminisces of a Mississippian in Peace and War*, Cincinnati: The Robert Clarke Company Press, 1901, Page 197

His bride Maria, also known as Mary, and her family endured tragedy during the war. Her father, Joseph, served as a 2nd Tennessee colonel (CSA). He also served as President Polk's private secretary and led a "life of delightful ease, indolence and gaiety" while he worked in Washington, but died in August 1863 after a lengthy illness.[5] His brother Lucius, a Confederate general, suffered a mortal wound in a duel at dawn in Arkansas with another Rebel general, who had accused him of cowardice.

Maria met Armstrong in the fall of 1862 while on a trip in the Deep South with her uncle, Colonel Sam Walker. After a brief courtship and engagement, she returned to Tennessee. But Maria "became greatly impaired from the shock" of reports of Armstrong's supposed wounding or demise. (He was fine.) So, Maria begged to be allowed to travel south to marry the former Yankee.

"This her father would not consent to," according to a Walker family genealogist, "but later when word came that General Armstrong's brigade would be camped near Columbia, where Colonel Walker's parents lived, [Joseph] gave his consent for Maria to go through the lines and be married at his mother's home. It was a long and hard trip made overland in any and all kind of conveyances, through Federal and Confederate lines."[6]

James Walker, who weeks earlier had celebrated his 50th wedding anniversary, gave away his granddaughter. Staff officers of Armstrong and Van Dorn served as wedding attendants. One guest described the striking contrast between the bride, a brunette, and "the blonde appearance of her handsome husband."[7]

Armstrong—or as I like to call him, "General Goldilocks"—lost nearly all his hair after the war. Immediately after the "I-do's," officiated by a reverend from the St. Peter's Episcopal Church, a brigade band played a "familiar air."[8]

News of the Armstrong nuptials traveled slowly throughout the Confederacy.

---

5. *Memphis Appeal*, May 12, 1888

6. *Genealogy of the descendants of John Walker of Wigton*, Page 521

7. Polk, Mary Branch, *Memoirs of a Southern Woman "Within the Lines,"* and a Genealogical Record. Chicago: The Joseph G. Branch Publishing Co., 1912, Page 23

8. *Genealogy of the descendants of John Walker of Wigton*, Page 522

A wartime image of Frank Armstrong, the groom. On right, Nathan Bedford Forrest, "The Wizard of the Saddle" and a wedding attendee. Wilson's Creek National Battlefield / Library of Congress

"The wedding was not an ostentatious or comprehensive one hence your correspondent did not attend," wrote grumpy "Pro Tanto Qui Tam," a pen name for a *Chattanooga Daily Rebel* reporter, in May 1863. "He however remained in his tent of wickedness, and drank to the happy couple from his camp cup a draught of limpid water, in it wishing them a long life and ineffible happiness."

Another wedding report called Armstrong the man who "has been playing the deuces with ladies' hearts" since the war started.[9]

The couple's marriage produced one child, a girl named Isabel. Maria died in 1872 of consumption. Like her father—who remarried in 1875 and died in 1909—Isabel had a connection with horses. In 1914, Holiday, the thoroughbred she owned, won the Preakness.

Now my own wedding prep with Mrs. B decades ago was minimal. ("I love the yellow napkins with the smiley faces and hearts, honey. Can I read my *Civil War Times* by the pool now?") But if I were the Armstrong-Polk wedding planner, Van Dorn would have been barred. He wasn't known as the "terror of ugly husbands and nervous papas" for nothing.

The married father of five (or maybe many more) had more affairs than dastardly Victor on *The Young and the Restless*. Van Dorn loved poetry

---

9. *Richmond Enquirer*, June 26, 1863

and painting—perhaps that's how he lured the ladies, who couldn't have been impressed with his height. He didn't stand taller than 5-foot-8.

The 42-year-old general paid for his life with his last dalliance. On May 7, 1863, at a mansion in Spring Hill—11 miles north of Columbia—a 51-year-old physician shot a pistol ball into Van Dorn's brain, killing him. Van Dorn was having an affair with the man's 25-year-old wife.

Inside the mansion, Whatley points out the original poplar sliding door to the dining room.

Scoundrel Earl Van Dorn, a Confederate general, attended Frank Armstrong's wedding.
The Photographic History of The Civil War in Ten Volumes: Volume Two

"I could be standing right where notorious womanizer Van Dorn was standing during that reception," I say to no one in particular.

"You probably are," says Whatley, giving me an instant history high.

Whatley gave a friend—a career military man—a history high, too, allowing him to keep the Minié he had unearthed at Rally Hill using a metal detector.

In the corner sits a display case that includes the rat's nest finds. We explore upstairs, including the rat's nest site, now a dressing room for the Whatleys' daughters. (The attorney swears me to secrecy. Whoops.)

In the two-story kitchen in the backyard, Walker's slaves toiled by the fireplace on the first floor and lived on the cramped second floor.

"You can barely dig anywhere here and not find animal bones," Whatley says of the backyard. Long-ago residents used it for garbage disposal.

Within shouting distance stands the old Galloway House, a private residence where Forrest recovered from a pistol bullet wound following his June 1863 confrontation with another Rebel officer. Days later, the man died in a room in the Nelson Hotel in Columbia from the knife wound inflicted by Forrest. (The hotel still stands.)

In the backyard, we speculate about the wedding reception site. Probably held out front, we all agree. Much more room. Whatley offers us a bourbon. It's still morning, so I pass. Incidentally, he faces exile if he and his wife sell Rally Hill before eldest daughter Mary Grace gets married. She wants to hold her wedding here.

I stand with Mary Grace. What a spectacular wedding venue—especially if Van Dorn's spirit stays away and Finn doesn't plop another dead groundhog at a guest's feet.

In the front yard—where a president walked eons ago—we admire Rally Hill while Finn probably contemplates another groundhog murder. Then Whatley points to the tall catalpa in the front yard. He says it could be more than 200 years old.

"Van Dorn may have taken a lady behind that tree," Whatley says.

"That's the 'Van Dorn Tree,'" I proclaim. Then I race to it for some hands-on history.

We all chuckle. Only true history nerds like us understand.

But it's time to leave the Rally Hill and Finn behind.

It's time to meet my Civil War poppa, one of my favorite people in the whole, wide world.

CHAPTER 5

Sharpsburg, Maryland

TALES FROM
MY CIVIL WAR POPPA

On a baby-blue sky afternoon, Richard Clem and I stand among remains of cornstalks in a rolling field on the old Otho J. Smith farm near the Antietam battleground. The South Mountain range stretches across the horizon; roughly 350 yards away stand large, modern farm buildings. A hint of cow manure wafts through the air.

Clem, a wiry 80-something with a soft, deep voice, quickly shifts into storytelling mode … and I love it.

"John, I remember coming out here relic hunting, and when the sunlight hit the field just right, you could see the glass glistening from the broken medicine bottles from that Union hospital."

"Mr. Smith's barn stood in the hollow out there. This hospital site was a mystery for many years."

"Right over here on this hill I found that soldier's ID disc of that VER-mont soldier."

More than a decade ago, I connected with Clem—a retired woodworker and lifelong Marylander—for a story about a Connecticut soldier who had been killed at the William Roulette farm at Antietam on September 17,

1862. Clem and I became fast friends, developing a sage-pupil-like relationship an ancient Greek philosopher might have appreciated. No visit to Sharpsburg is complete for me without exploring the battlefield with Clem or listening to him tell stories on the screened-in back porch at his house in nearby Hagerstown.

During our drives in my car on the Antietam battlefield, Clem talks of his relic hunting adventures and delivers mini religious sermons, usually peppered with tales about his eccentric brother. I call him the "Babe Ruth of Storytellers," a nickname he appreciates.

"John, I remember digging right there," he'd say while passing some farmer's field, crumbling stone wall or wood line. Then Clem might tell me how many bullets or belt buckles he had unearthed at the spot decades ago.

A relic hunt in a field near the Philip Pry house, a Union Army HQ at Antietam, proved especially productive.

"Brother and I dug 97 bullets there," Clem would often say about his bachelor sibling, Don.

I've never met this reclusive "Brother," but he seems like an old friend now.

"Brother says he's like a bear with a sore butt," Clem has told me. "He just wants to crawl in a cave and be by himself."

Don would have been a kindred soul of my dad, "Big Johnny," who toward the end of his life half-kiddingly yearned to live on his own planet, "Planet Me."

A half-century ago, a co-worker at the planing mill where Clem worked persuaded him to accept the Lord as his savior. This puts me on guard around Clem, a devout Christian, because I enjoy swearing, often at the slightest annoyance.

"My faith has gradually growed," he has often said on our battlefield sojourns. "Jesus is my closest friend. I feel like he's walking with me."

In the late 1940s, Clem's grandmother Betty—then in her 60s—fueled his interest in the Civil War. On Sunday afternoons, Clem's father pumped 50 cents' worth of gas into an ancient Ford for excursions with the family from Hagerstown to the Antietam battlefield. Grandma packed a container

Richard Clem, my Civil War poppa, stands near the site where he unearthed an ID disc of a Vermont soldier on the Otho Smith farm.

with sardines, crackers, cheese and water for the trips. Mom sat up front while Grandma sat in the back with Richard, whom she fondly called "Dickie."

While Dad drove over gravel battlefield roads or across the circa-1836 Burnside Bridge, then open to vehicular traffic, Grandma fed Clem a steady diet of local history. She knew people who had lived through the battle and even recalled Civil War veterans visiting Sharpsburg.

"Dickie," Grandma said during a battlefield trip, "that's the old Iney Swain home there, and she told me back when she was still alive that there were wounded soldiers in her barn from the state of Massachusetts."

At Bloody Lane, where the bodies of dozens of Rebels lay after the battle, the family ate picnic lunches. Then Grandma Betty would recount what locals had told her about the battle. "Even months after the battle, people would slip here on pools of dried blood," she told Dickie. Grandma could stretch the truth a bit.

On the return trip to Hagerstown on the Sharpsburg Pike, the Clems passed the site of Dunker Church, the battlefield landmark that had collapsed in a windstorm in April 1921. Only a pile of bricks from the original church remained then. Clem remembers when it was site of a gas station and a convenience store that sold ice cream, beer and sandwiches. In the early 1960s, in time for the Civil War centennial, the church was rebuilt on the site with many of the original bricks.

Although Grandma Betty didn't understand exactly what happened during the Civil War, it had a mystical pull on her. She would often tear up when talking about the war with Dickie.

Years later, Clem and Brother discovered the joys of hunting for Civil War relics. In those days, most of the Antietam battlefield was privately owned and few people had an interest in the hobby. So, on afternoons after work, Clem rode in Don's four-wheel drive jeep to Sharpsburg, where they would eyeball relics in the fields—with a farmer's permission, of course.

On the surface, just south of Bloody Lane, Clem found his first bullet—a fired Union three-ringer. He still has it. If Clem found four or five bullets back in those days, he considered it a good day. After a hard rain in the 1960s, Clem eyeballed 18 bullets behind the Dunker Church—a remarkable day that makes me yearn for time travel.

In September 1862, Alexander Gardner photographed this U.S. Army hospital site at the Otho Smith farm near the Antietam battlefield. Library of Congress

Later, the Clems discovered the joys of hunting for artifacts with metal detectors—a hobby that turned into an obsession for the brothers. Richard would often let others experience the thrill of holding a Civil War artifact.

One afternoon, while Clem and Brother swept their detectors across the Miller Cornfield, vortex of the 1862 battle, a visitor from New York approached them. Clem had already unearthed a pocketful of bullets— "little demons," I call them—including a dirt-encrusted .69-caliber Minié.

"May I look at it?" the excitable man asked.

Clem handed the one-ounce piece of lead to the man, who held it reverentially, as if it were a rare religious relic.

"You can have it," Clem told the man.

Then he pulled from his pocket a half-dozen more bullets and gave the "little demons" to the man, too. The New Yorker's knees almost buckled.

"John, I can still see the exhaust coming out of his car and his mouth running to his wife as he drove off into the sunset," Clem has told me a half-dozen times.

Over the years, the brothers unearthed roughly 30,000 bullets (and other artifacts) in Maryland, Virginia, West Virginia and Pennsylvania. Years later, they sold more than 12,000 of those bullets to artifact dealers for a buck apiece. Clem gave many away.

But these hunts were never business for Clem, who hung up his metal detector for good years ago. In a notebook, he documented where and when he recovered each artifact. For *Cracker Barrel* and *Gettysburg* magazines and the *Washington Times*, Clem authored deeply researched stories about his most remarkable finds. Most of Clem's relic hunts came a short distance from his house in Washington County, Maryland, where thousands of soldiers in both armies had fought and camped during the war.

Back at the Otho J. Smith farm, Clem and I walk steps from where Alexander Gardner—a photographer employed then by the famous Mathew Brady—set up his camera in September 1862 for a series of striking images. Here, at the division hospital for U.S. Army Gen. William French, doctors, volunteers and others cared for hundreds of Antietam wounded from both sides.

Two images Gardner shot on the farm intrigue me most. In a cropped enlargement of one, an unidentified man—undoubtedly a wounded soldier—rests in a makeshift, hay-covered tent. Another shows 14th Indiana regimental surgeon Anson Hurd standing among the wounded.

Clem and I often wonder about the heart-rending scenes that played out here.

"Almost every hour I witnessed the going out of some young life," recalled nurse Elizabeth Harris about her service on the farm.

On the brink of death, a blue-eyed soldier—a "mere youth" with a "full, round face"—captured Harris' heart. "Hold my hand till I die," the nurse recalled the soldier telling her. "I am trying to think of my Saviour; but think of my mother and father; their hearts will break."[1]

On another beautiful, fall day on the Smith farm in 1991, Clem unearthed a brass identification disc—roughly the size of a quarter—under five inches of earth on a cedar-covered hill. The rare find turned into another obsession for Clem, who has recovered three other soldier ID discs while relic hunting—a feat equivalent to Babe Ruth hitting four grand slams in a game.

1. Moore, Frank, *Women of The War, Their Heroism and Self-Sacrifice*, Hartford: S.S. Scranton & Co., 1866, Page 192

Dog tags weren't issued to Civil War soldiers; instead, they purchased their own "tags" in which they had their names and units stamped. No soldier wanted to be forgotten if he fell in battle or from disease. Letters, diaries, photographs and ID discs often aided burial crews in the identification of soldier remains.

A close-up of the Clem-unearthed ID disc of William Secor, a 2nd Vermont soldier who suffered a mortal wound at Antietam.

Clem's dogged research brought the owner of the Smith farm disc back to life. It belonged to a luckless 2nd Vermont color bearer named William Secor, a corporal, and the only soldier in his regiment to die at Antietam. Perhaps Nurse Harris aided the poor soldier.

Using a small hammer and lettered dies, a sutler probably hammered Secor's name and regiment into the gold-plated disc. It may have cost the soldier 25 cents for a pair—one for him, another to send home.

Secor stood 5-foot-6¼, with blue eyes and brown hair. From Halfmoon, New York, he had enlisted in neighboring Vermont. He was 21 and unmarried. At Antietam, Secor suffered a mortal wound at Bloody Lane—an old sunken, country lane during the battle and where the Clems picnicked decades later.

A condolence letter Clem discovered from Secor's commanding officer to his stepfather shed further light on his last day on Earth.

"I saw the Chaplain that was with him in his last hours, and he said that it might be of consolation to his friends to know that he lived with a hope in Christ and was resigned to his fate," Lt. Eugene O. Cole wrote. "As a soldier, there was none better."[2]

Clem believes U.S. Army comrades transported Secor to the Smith farm along with countless other casualties. Secor's ID disc may have fallen out when his remains were disinterred for a trip home to New York for reburial.

---

2. Copy of original in Clem collection

Before our visit to the farm ends, Clem pulls from his pocket the Secor disc—the relic's first trip back to the site of its discovery decades earlier.

"You know, John, I bet there are still bodies buried on that hill."

Weeks later, I visit the Clems at their house in Hagerstown, across the road from the farm where the Union Army's Sixth Corps camped in the aftermath of Gettysburg. Clem has unearthed thousands of relics from that rich Maryland earth—bullets, silver coins, knapsack hooks, buttons from almost every state in the Union and two soldier ID discs. In his own back-yard, Clem recovered his first U.S. box plate and 50-60 bullets.

Three miles south, on a chilly morning the day after Thanksgiving in 1986, fortune shined on Clem again. On the edge of a Union campsite, he recovered a bent, postage stamp-sized silver identification badge for 44th New York Sergeant Consider H. Willett. Later, Clem unraveled the story of Willett, a forgotten hero, whose quick thinking saved dozens of Rebels from friendly fire at Little Round Top on July 2, 1863.

On his back porch, Clem and I swap stories and laugh about another tale about "Brother."

Gregarious Gloria—Clem's delightful wife and Mrs. B's kindred spirit—jokes that Richard may get a big head because his picture made it into a recent issue of *Civil War Times* magazine.

"We may have to get a carpenter in here to make the door wider for Richard."

On leisurely walks with Gloria, Clem often stares at the ground, fixated on what Civil War-era metal might lie beneath the surface. They've been married for more than 60 years. Both remind me of my momma, Peggy, who always made everyone feel good.

Minutes before my departure, Clem hands me a gift: a pair of Union brass cavalry bridle rosettes he had unearthed in 1987 in Clarke County, Virginia. I'm humbled but not surprised. That's Richard Clem, my Civil War poppa.

We all hug in the driveway.

"I love you," I tell them.

"We love you, too."

In a snap, I'm back on the road, far too soon. I've heard about a great story in far-off Arkansas, near the banks of the mercurial Mississippi River.

CHAPTER **6**

Memphis, Tennessee and
Marion, Arkansas

AN OBSESSION
IN THE SHADOWS
OF HISTORY

On a levee at Mound City, Arkansas, 150 yards from Mound City Chute, a small lake formed when the Mississippi River changed course, Jerry Potter bares pieces of his soul.

"If I had not taken a shortcut through the National Bank of Commerce Building in Memphis and seen that painting out of the left corner of my eye, we would not be here," he tells me.

It was a summer afternoon in 1978, another sweltering day in West Tennessee. Potter was a 27-year-old trial lawyer seeking inspiration … a former college history major relishing historical research … a writer craving a great Civil War story of his own.

"I really didn't like practicing law at the time," he admits.

The painting that captivated Potter featured a burning side-wheel steamboat on the Mississippi River. Passengers hurled themselves from its decks into the dark, muddy waters on an inky-black night. Dozens of heads bobbed in the water like corks. Huge red flames leaped from the super-structure, partially obscuring the name on the steamboat.

39

Sultana.

"Why," Potter asked himself then, "have I not heard about this?"

The painting served as inspiration that morphed into passion that became an obsession.

"Why no one has made a movie of this …" the softspoken attorney tells me, slowly shaking his head.

I have traveled 3 ½ hours west from Nashville—to Memphis and eastern Arkansas—to learn more about America's worst maritime disaster. On my last visit to Arkansas two decades ago, I nearly ran out of gas in Little Rock. With a nearly full tank this time, I'm energized by the possibility of a visit to the *Sultana* wreck site. My guide is *the* expert on the disaster.

"The *second*-greatest *Sultana* expert," Potter says without a hint of braggadocio.

Gene Salecker, a retired cop and teacher from Illinois, is No. 1, Potter says of his friend.

Early on the chilly morning of April 27, 1865—18 days after Robert E. Lee had surrendered at Appomattox Court House—the *Sultana* sailed on the rain-swollen Mississippi River, seven miles north of Memphis. Its destination was Cairo, Illinois. The 260-foot, wooden steamboat carried about 2,000 paroled Union POWs, nearly all from the Cahaba camp in Alabama and Andersonville—the notorious Georgia camp. Many of the POWs remained weakened from the horrific treatment in Rebel camps.

In all, more than 2,200 passengers, crew and guards—as well as dozens of horses, 100 hogs and one pet alligator—crammed aboard. The legal capacity of the *Sultana* was 376 passengers. Corruption, incompetence and greed conspired to doom the steamboat. The captain received a fee per mile to transport the soldiers. A portion of that money he kicked back to a corrupt U.S. Army officer, who ignored the overcrowding.

As the *Sultana* sailed north, its decks creaked and sagged. Distant lightning bolts flashed across a pitch-black sky.

Disaster struck at 2 a.m. when the boilers exploded, reverberating throughout the vast woodlands north of Memphis.

"What a crash! My God!" recalled a soldier on the *Sultana*.[1]

---

1. Berry, Chester D., *Loss of the Sultana and Reminiscences of Survivors*, Lansing, Mich.: Darius D. Thorp, 1892, Pages 191-92

Nearly 1,200 passengers and crew either burned to death, drowned or died from exposure in river water made frigid by spring melts up north. The fiery glow of the doomed vessel could be seen from Memphis.

Another, more monumental event pushed the catastrophe into the shadows of history. The country, numbed by war and death on a massive scale, still mourned for President Lincoln, assassinated by John Wilkes Booth on April 14. The day before the *Sultana* disaster, the assassin had been cornered and killed in a Virginia barn.

"We have, as a people, become so accustomed to supping of horrors during the past few years," a Memphis newspaper wrote days later, "that they soon seem to lose their appalling features and are forgotten."[2]

Subsequent investigations pointed to a poorly repaired boiler patch as the culprit for the disaster.

After examining the painting in Memphis, Potter dived into everything he could find about the *Sultana*—from the *Official Records* and archived newspapers to a trove of rarely examined documents in the National Archives in Washington.

In 1982, Potter used old maps and Civil War records to pinpoint the location of a 19th-century steamboat under Sam Oliver's soybean field on the Arkansas side of the Mississippi. By then, the river had shifted course roughly two miles east since 1865. Potter and his wife, Janita, had often swept metal detectors across the site while their sons played in the dirt with a toy tractor. The Potters turned up riverboat relics roughly 50 yards from where Oliver's bulldozer uncovered large pieces of ancient metal—probably left by 19th-century salvagers who had discovered the wreck.

In Oliver's field that summer, Potter and Clive Cussler—the novelist and underwater adventurer who aided him in the search—turned up metal crates, piping, barrel rims, a cabin stove and other artifacts. It was confirmation, they believed, of the *Sultana* wreck.

But "[t]here's no way we can come out and say definitely unless we dig up a sign that says, 'Here lies the *Sultana*,'" Cussler told a reporter then.[3] He believed scores of other relics remained in the hull—legend has it that the *Sultana* carried gold in a safe. But time and Mother Nature had teamed

---

2. *Memphis Argus*, May 6, 1865

3. United Press International report, July 5, 1982

to cover the hull with 30 feet of black delta soil, making a complete excavation impractical.

In the late 1980s, Potter met with eight descendants whose fathers had survived the disaster—evidence memories of 1865 are fresher than you might think.

"Never been that close to the Civil War," he tells me.

The descendants' stories helped fuel Potter's 1992 book on the *Sultana* tragedy. One of them recalled how her father became depressed during an anniversary of the catastrophe.

"I can still hear the screams, but there wasn't anything I could do," the man told her of the deadly night on the Mississippi.

From the levee, about a mile south from the steamship wreck, Potter points to the near distance, where he once hunted for Native American artifacts near a general store on Oliver's 10,000-acre farm. Behind us, thousands of yellow wildflowers—"bitter weed," a local cattle farmer tells us—burst from green scrub on a levee slope. In this area, within sight of tree-covered Chicken Island across Mound City Chute, responders rescued *Sultana* survivors.

"Have you seen this?"

Potter shows the farmer a photograph of the overcrowded *Sultana*, taken from the bank by an enterprising photographer in Helena, Arkansas the morning of April 26, 1865.

"Yes, sir," the farmer says.

"Some of these guys had only 24 hours to live," Porter tells the man.

Riverboats lasted no more than three to five years on the lower Mississippi. Coated with flammable paints and shellack, they often caught fire.

"Organized piles of kindling," Potter says.

When they did catch fire, steamboat captains quickly steered their vessels to shore to unload passengers. The *Sultana,* though, never had the chance.

In addition to the lay of the land near the Mississippi, I get a bead on Potter and his family history. An ancestor of his—"a poor farmer with no slaves from Hickman County, Tennessee"—served under Nathan Bedford

Jerry Potter stands at the Mound City Chute, near where some Sultana *survivors were rescued on April 27, 1865.*

Forrest, whose troops captured many of the soldiers who died in the *Sultana* disaster. The man deserted in early November 1864 and missed the Army of Tennessee's bloody disaster at the Battle of Franklin.

"Probably a good thing," Potter says.

Frances and Elvis Potter—Jerry's mom and dad—raised a family in rural Only and Milan in Middle Tennessee.

"They were dirt-poor. We lived in a house with no indoor plumbing," Potter says. "Neither of them went to school past the ninth grade.

"But Mother loved education. Father was a farmer and worked as a cobbler in a shoe shop. Wisest man I ever met."

Their boys—Jerry and brother Larry—poured themselves into their own schooling. Larry became a judge—he's retired now. Jerry overcame a speech impediment and shyness to become one of the country's top trial lawyers.

"I'm a driven person. I *hate* to lose."

After the publication of his *Sultana* book, Potter missed historical research, a passion. So, he channeled his energy into what became another obsession: marathons. He ran two 50-mile ultra-marathons each in 11 hours and change. But the needle on Potter's inner compass always finds a way to swing to "S," for *Sultana*.

In Potter's pickup truck, we travel near the levee on a road as flat as the back of a clothes iron, leaving behind shanties on Lonely Street along Mound City Chute. The wreck site is inaccessible for us today. But that news doesn't stifle my history buzz.

"How sure are you that's the *Sultana* out there?"

"Ninety percent," Potter says.

"It rests below the water table, so it would probably take millions to recover."

He gestures toward to the backyard of Oliver's old place.

"Dumped large grates, hog chains, fire bricks right over there. All from Oliver's *Sultana* salvage pile."

"Do you think there are any bodies still on the wreck?"

"It's basically a tomb, just like the *Arizona* in Pearl Harbor," Potter tells me.

The *Sultana* dead and survivors have transformed from names on paper and microfilm into quasi-Potter family members.

The overloaded* Sultana *as it traveled on its fateful journey on the Mississippi River. Cowan's Auctions

"I feel like I know them all," he says.

English-born Ann Annis was traveling on the *Sultana* with her third husband Harvey and their eight-year-old daughter, Isabelle. He was a lieutenant in the 51st U.S. Colored Troops, heading home to Wisconsin after resigning his commission because of ill health. Annis' first two husbands, ship captains, had drowned at sea. From the lower deck of the *Sultana*, she watched, horrified, as Harvey and Isabelle drowned in the roiling, murky Mississippi.

"My husband and baby are gone!" she screamed.[4]

Eight members of DeWitt Clinton Spikes' family—his father, mother, three sisters, two brothers and a cousin—also died. An exhausted DeWitt saved more than two dozen other passengers before Confederate soldiers rescued him on the Arkansas shore. It was one of many acts of humanity on that bleak morning.

---

4. *Loss of the Sultana and Reminiscences of Survivors*, Page 215.

In Memphis, a saloonkeeper provided survivors with a suit of clothes and paid their hotel bills.[5] Stories like these pour from Potter like steam and embers once did from the *Sultana* smokestacks.

At Memphis National Cemetery, 15 miles from Mound City, Potter and I stand among rows of hundreds of gleaming white gravestones. A train rumbles in the distance while traffic drones on Jackson Avenue.

Dozens of unknowns from the *Sultana* rest here with 13,000 other Union soldiers. So do 28 known *Sultana* dead—including John Clark Ely of the 115th Ohio. From under thick limbs of a massive old oak, Potter and I stare at his tombstone.

"My hero," he says.

The 38-year-old married father of four hailed from northern Ohio. In the summer of 1862, he enlisted as a sergeant, serving mostly on guard duty in Tennessee the first two years of the war. On December 5, 1864, Confederate forces under "Fighting Joe" Wheeler captured Ely and about 200 of his 115th Ohio comrades at La Vergne, Tennessee, 20 miles southeast of Nashville. They ended up at Andersonville.

"Hungry, dirty, sleepy and lousy," he wrote in his diary from camp on December 25, 1864. "Will another Christmas find us again among friends and loved ones?"

On April 22, 1865, following his parole, he wrote a letter to his wife, Julia. Two days later, in Vicksburg, Mississippi, Ely boarded the *Sultana*.

"Very fine day. Still upward we go," he wrote on April 26.[6]

The next morning, Ely's body was floating in the Mississippi. The diary was found with him.

"Thank God it got saved," Potter says.

Back on the Arkansas side of the Mississippi, we have two more stops in Marion, the closest town to the disaster. At Tacker's Shake Shack, you can order a Sultana burger—two pounds of beef with cheese, chili, bacon, egg, hash brown, bun and gawd-knows-what-else. Cost: 30 bucks. Eat it in 30 minutes or less and get it gratis. Maybe I'll split one with Mrs. B the next time I come this way.

---

5. *The Memphis Argus*, April 30, 1865.

6. Transcript of John Clark Ely diary, Andersonville (Ga.) National Historic Site

At the small Sultana Museum nearby, manager Rosalind O'Neal sits on a bench outside, near a giant reproduction of a painting of the burning steamboat. It's like the painting that inspired Potter decades earlier.

"Sweet lady," Potter says of "Roz."

The Alabama native, nearly 80, is recovering from pneumonia. She grew up in Tuscaloosa and learned to fly a plane in Pottsville, Pennsylvania when she was 13. The illness hasn't dulled her sense of humor.

"My grandfather painted a mural in the house of a train going up a mountain and a moose in a bog," she says. "Grandmother made him paint it over. No one in Alabama has *even seen a moose.*"

On display in the main room of the museum is a 14-foot replica model of the *Sultana* inside a huge glass case. Nearby, a list of *Sultana* dead appears on a wall. On another wall hang huge elk antlers—the prize 19th-century riverboat captains received for winning a race on the Mississippi.

Besides the model, the museum has among its holdings the smoking pipe given to an Ohio soldier who bayoneted that pet alligator on the *Sultana*. He then used the animal's sturdy wooden crate to float to safety to Memphis.

Potter calls me into the museum entry room. Then he points to a long, dark streak in a huge enlargement of that *Sultana* image taken in Helena, Arkansas in 1865. It's an overflow of human excrement from the packed steamboat. Only true history devotees like us genuinely appreciate this bizarre detail.

But when it comes to the *Sultana*, no detail is too small for Potter, no dream is too big. He's donated thousands of dollars toward a new *Sultana* museum in the old Marion high school.

At the end of my *Sultana* immersion, Potter and I smile and hug.

"I'm glad someone else cares about this, too," he says.

Another trip complete, another friend made.

Now I have an adventure planned for rural Mississippi with a man whose ancestral land became the vortex of one of the war's most important battles.

CHAPTER 7

Hinds County, Mississippi

AN ADVENTURE WITH MY PSYCHOTIC CONNECTION

On the porch of a rickety cabin deep in the Mississippi woods, 63-year-old Sid Champion V—my folksy and eclectic Champion Hill battlefield tour guide—introduces me to his cats Inki and Thudd. Then he plops himself into a chair, invites me to sit down across from him and slides a fly swatter across the table. On this balmy morning in the Deep South, bugs already are selecting victims. Hanging from the cabin wall are signs reading "Psycho Parkway" and "Hunters, Fishermen, and Other Liars Gather Here."

We're at Midway Station, the home of Champions since 1865, starting with Sid's great-great-grandparents. Woozy from a lack of sleep, I hand Champion a crisp roll of five 20s—his standard fee for a tour of a battle-field intertwined with his family since the morning of May 16, 1863, when gunfire erupted near where we sit. This is the beginning of what Champion later calls our "psychotic connection." We're both Civil War crazy.

Champion, a widower, is a fan of botany, history, women, heavy metal and Frank Zappa; composers Bach, Brahms and Palestrina; funk and punk; deer hunting and fishing; James Cagney gangster movies; hanging out with

The signs at Sid Champion V's out-of-the-way cabin tell a story, too.

his "wooly-bully, good old boy" pals; and vaping ever since his doc told him he'd better give up cigs. His girlfriend lives in a house on the Federal siege line in Vicksburg, 20 miles west as a crow flies.

Champion considers himself the family Shinto, the keeper of stories. He's an epic storyteller, speaking in rapid-fire bursts punctuated with the occasional booming explosion of verbiage. He reminds me of that $25,000 Browning World War I "Potato Digger" machine gun I ogled at a military show in Franklin, Tennessee. The only thing ho-hum about Champion V may be his first name—the last in a long series of Sids. "Boringly dull," he says.

Minutes into our visit, I tell Champion about an adventure in moonshining and Civil War guerrilla fighting country in Middle Tennessee.

"Brother, you're in moonshining country *right here*. I've got some 'corn squeeze' in the kitchen in the deep freeze, 120 to 130 proof. Cleans coins as well as your arteries."

Now there may be a prohibition against the "squeeze" in the devout Champion's Southern Baptist church in Hinds County, Mississippi, where he sings in the choir and serves as pianist and organist. So, I consider keeping this secret. Besides, I'm not visiting for the 'shine. I'm here for the shrine—the hallowed ground that bears the Champion family name.

What a family history. What a battlefield. What a battle.

In 2019, the National Park Service incorporated 800 acres of the Champion Hill battlefield into the Vicksburg National Military Park. But core battlefield remains in private hands. In 2022, Champion, his California-based sister and two cousins sold 144 acres to the American Battlefield Trust, the national preservation organization. Champion initially was reluctant to sell. But he eventually came around because he retains hunting, fishing and access rights.

"Some of the finest white-tailed deer hunting right here," Champion says.

He plans to tear down the ramshackle remains of the house next to the cabin, build a new place to live in, and then move from Clinton, about 12 miles east. He might spend the rest of his life out here with his grumpy Italian honeybees and the spirits of kin buried in the family cemetery out back.

"This land was here before me, and it will be here after me. I'm just here to take care of it for a bit."

Champion *loves* it out here. There's no other place he'd rather be.

My visit falls on the 159th anniversary of the battle, which at least guarantees to raise the hair on the back of my neck. On that sweltering day at Champion Hill in May 1863, Ulysses Grant's 32,000-man army defeated roughly 22,000 Rebels under John Pemberton, a Pennsylvania-born lieutenant general many in the Confederacy gave the side-eye.

"One of the worst people," says the Vicksburg-born Champion of Pemberton, who was buried in Philadelphia, Pennsylvania, not far from where I came into the world.

The Battle of Champion Hill, known by some as the Battle of Baker's Creek, was a see-saw affair, with the U.S. Army turning the tide late in the fight. It lasted roughly four hours, "hard fighting," Grant wrote in his memoirs, "preceded by two or three hours of skirmishing, some of which almost rose to the dignity of battle."[1] Soldiers fired blindly in the woods as battle

---

1. Grant, Ulysses S., *Personal Memoirs of U.S. Grant, Vol. 1*, New York: Charles L. Webster & Co., 1885, Page 518

Sid Champion V relishes time spent at one of his favorite places, "The Hill of Death."

smoke made it almost impossible to see. "The dead men and wounded laid as thick on the field as sheep in a pasture," a U.S. Army soldier recalled of the carnage.[2]

Of his 29,000 soldiers engaged, Grant lost 410 killed, 1,844 wounded, and 187 missing. Pemberton's army suffered 381 killed, more than 1,000 wounded and more than 2,400 missing—mostly prisoners.[3] The Confederate Army of Mississippi fell back into the defenses of Vicksburg, never again a serious offensive threat. On July 4, nearly two months after their defeat at Champion Hill, the Rebels surrendered the strategic city— perhaps *the* turning point of war. The Yankees finally controlled the mighty Mississippi.

Of Pemberton's performance at Champion Hill, a prescient Georgia artillerist wrote the day of the battle: "He undoubtedly displayed bad generalship, and the day's work may cost us Vicksburg."[4]

Until his high school days in Jackson, Mississippi, Champion hadn't heard or read much about the battle on his family's land.

"Daddy didn't say much about it because he didn't see how you could glorify war."

Then a teacher brought Champion's battlefield connection to the attention of his classmates: "We have a *celebrity* in the house."

Champion's reaction: "*Say what?*"

"Then I started asking questions. And then I found out our family had dozens of letters between Sid and Matilda Champion."

In the early 1850s, Matilda Montgomery Cameron—a feisty, petite, redheaded divorcee with a young son—was living with her wealthy parents on a Madison County, Mississippi plantation when she met Sid Champion, a studious, literature-loving bachelor. During the Mexican War, Champion had fought under Jefferson Davis—the future president of the Confederacy.

---

2. John David Myers letter to Frances (Nickerson) Myers, May 15, 1863, published on Spared & Shared 18 web site, on March 22, 2019

3. Livermore, Thomas, *Number & Losses in the Civil War in America: 1861-65*, Boston and New York: Houghton, Mifflin & Co, 1900, Page 99

4. Diary of Wesley Olin Connor, CSA Cherokee Artillery, Battle of Champion Hill web site (battleofchampionhill.org), accessed Dec. 1, 2022. The original manuscript was donated to the Hargrett Special Collections Library at the University of Georgia by Margaret Wright Hollingsworth.

"Man, it was *chemical,*" Sid V says of the relationship between Sid and Matilda, his great-great-grandparents.

After Champion proposed, Matilda's father Eli was aghast: *No well-bred daughter of mine is going to marry the son of a dirt-poor farmer.* But Matilda and her mother persuaded Daddy to give the chemical connection his blessing. In 1853, the couple married. Champion was 30, Matilda 26. As a wedding gift, Eli Montgomery gave the couple 68 slaves, 1,200 acres and a two-story, white frame house near the Old Jackson Road. Later, the plantation expanded to 2,000 acres and more than 160 slaves. Champion Hill became one of the state's largest plantations.

In March 1862, nearly a year after the Rebels fired on Fort Sumter, Champion joined the Vicksburg-based 28th Mississippi Cavalry, serving as a third sergeant under Nathan Bedford Forrest, among others. Matilda bristled when Champion left her and their four young children behind with dozens of slaves and their overseer.

Back at Midway Station, Champion retrieves his 22-year-old ATV, our Champion Hill battlefield transportation.

"You ever hear of a man cave? Well, this is man land!" he hoots, stretching his arms wide.

Champion drives while I sit behind him atop a small, camouflaged pad thingy on a rack—no, not the medieval torture kind. But I consider sending Mrs. B a proof-of-life photo anyway.

Here's what you need to know about "man land": It ain't Antietam or Gettysburg, with paved park roads, granite statues of imposing soldiers toting muskets and an ice cream shop in town. Heck, the closest town is Bolton (population 900), four bumpy miles away. There's no ice cream shop there. No statues or huge monuments stand on the battlefield either.

Champion Hill itself consists of heavily wooded knobs, undergrowth and sharp ledges, with fields of wild rye occasionally breaking up the ground. Baker's Creek and its branches snake through this rugged, nearly pristine battlefield. On private and leased NPS land, farmers plant cotton, corn and soybeans.

The Old Jackson Road—once the main route between the state capital in Jackson and Vicksburg—winds through Champion Hill. Both armies used it. It's just a narrow, dirt road now. When they can, Sid and his pal Alvin clear it.

Now here's what you need to know about my ATV driver: Even at max cruising speed, Champion will not warn you about fallen tree limbs at head-high height across the Old Jackson Road. Duck or risk decapitation. In 2009, an accident on an ATV laid up Champion for six months. Our experience has all the thrills and terrors of riding a mechanical bull in a Texas bar, minus the beer and pretty women.

But my oh my, what an experience it is.

"What a special day it is to be here," Champion says while we rumble across the battlefield. We're both on a history high.

At our first stop, near the end of a long gravel lane to Champion's cabin, stands a large, overgrown graveyard, most of it in the woods. Only a modern marker for a Vietnam vet is visible to my eye.

"Shot six times by a drunk with a .38," says Champion, who helped bury the man in 1977.

Here, in the cemetery, Union Brig. Gen. Alvin Hovey placed more than 16 cannons to turn back the surging Rebels.

"My men were fighting stubbornly, but against almost overpowering odds," the future Indiana governor recalled of the action here. "If the centre had been broken our army would have been divided into two parts."[5]

Hovey's soldiers faced 4,500 veteran soldiers from Arkansas and Missouri under Gen. John Bowen, a West Pointer and an acquaintance of Grant's. The Missourians charged after their leader, Colonel Francis Cockrell, rode down the line holding a magnolia flower in one hand and a sword in the other.[6]

Champion steers the ATV down the Old Jackson Road, under a couple of those head-high fallen limbs. Then he navigates through the lot of the Champion Hill M.B. Church and parks.

"You ever hear *voices* out here?" I ask Champion, sounding almost conspiratorial.

"Oh, yeah."

---

5. *The Indianapolis Journal*, March 8, 1885

6. Smith, Timothy B., *Champion Hill, Decisive Battle For Vicksburg*, New York: Savas Beatie LLC, 2004

Now, I'm highly suspect of battlefield ghost stories, but open to the concept of spirit energy. During my first visit to Cold Harbor, the killing ground in Virginia, the hair on my arms and neck stood straight up on ground where the 2nd Connecticut Heavy Artillery suffered dozens of losses. The place felt spooky then and during subsequent visits. Champion Hill gives off that same spirit vibe.

Champion gestures to our left, where the ground undulates in the brush.

"Dead Confederates buried in the woods right over there.

"In one of these ravines beyond, they tossed amputated arms and legs."

To our right stands an ancient dead live oak—a battlefield "witness tree," planted by slaves at Matilda Champion's direction. Beyond it, in a patch of woods, stood the Champions' wartime home. Nothing of it remains, not even a foundation stone. When they departed in summer 1863, the Yankees burned it.

On the day of the battle, Matilda descended into the cellar with her children. As the fighting raged, she clutched her two-year-old son. Grant claimed her house as his HQ. The Union Army, meanwhile, parked its ammunition train in the yard. Matilda's husband, who was with his unit in Edwards, about six miles west, watched in anguish as battle smoke rose from his plantation.

The couple's house, of course, became a hospital—for Yankees and Rebels alike. "There they lay, the blue and the gray intermingled; the same rich, young American blood flowing out in little rivulets of crimson; each thinking he was in the right," a Union enlisted man recalled.[7]

An orderly cut a hole in the floor for the blood to be swept. The Yankees scattered straw to make the floor less slippery, and Union surgeons used Matilda's dinner table for surgeries. Champion V owns the bloodstained relic. A giant cast-iron kettle, used to cook food for the wounded at the house, survives, too. It sits behind Champion's cabin, next to the family cemetery where Sid the First and Matilda rest.

"You want some of that witness tree?"

Are you kidding me?

---

7. Crummer, Wilbur Fisk, *With Grant at Fort Donelson, Shiloh and Vicksburg*, Oak Park, Ill.: E.C. Crummer & Co., 1915, Page 104

Champion breaks off two hunks and checks them for fire ants. I toss them onto the ATV rack before we roll to our next destination—the most haunting stop of all. Yards into the woods, the ground dips along a ridge. It's a Union burial trench, the bodies having been removed shortly after the war for reburial in the national cemetery in Vicksburg.

"It was five feet deep, three feet wide, 78 yards long" Champion says. It may have held dozens of bodies.

"Right now," Champion says, "there was a lot of killing going on here 159 years ago."

Scores of soldiers recalled the intensity of the fighting in the Champions' woods.

"I never hugged Dixie's soil as close as I have to-day," an Ohioan wrote in his diary on the day of the battle.[8]

"I had my big toenail shot off and was struck with a spent grapeshot on the right knee and the left elbow, and a ball on the left ankle—which was a glancing shot—cut my pants and left quite a welt on my ankle," an Iowan wrote. "The other two shots did not penetrate the flesh but lamed me considerable."[9]

Burial parties tumbled Confederate dead into a ravine near where we stand. It's almost entirely obscured now by trees and brush.

"There are a bunch of Confederates in that hole, brother," Champion says. "The Yankees later said they saw bleached bones here."

Near the lip of the ravine, Champion brushes weeds and wildflowers from a modern marker for Elias Adams, an 18-year-old private in the 26th Mississippi. The U.S. government supplied the stone to a descendant of the fallen teen. Champion placed it near the ravine, where Adams' bones probably lay somewhere under the Mississippi earth.

At the Crossroads, where three strategic roads intersect below the crest of Champion Hill, Sid performs a spot-on imitation of Ed Bearss' booming voice near a marker for the legendary National Park Service historian. Bearss, who began working for the NPS in Vicksburg in the 1950s, loved this battlefield. When he was 92, Bearss—who died in 2020—even led a charge of a tour group up Champion Hill.

---

8. Diary of Osborn H. Oldroyd, 20th Ohio Infantry, Battle of Champion Hill web site (battleofchampionhill.org), accessed Dec. 12, 2022.

9. Myers letter, May 15, 1863

I ride precariously on the back of Sid Champion V's ATV on the Old Jackson Road through the Champion Hill battlefield.

"He and granddaddy used to sit on our porch, enjoying bourbon and running their mouths," Champion says.

Naturally, I steer our conversation to battle relics. In the Old Jackson Road, Champion once stubbed his toe on a large canister ball. He recalls a relic hunter lying on the ground on the battlefield, staring at the side of a rut.

"What are you doing?" Champion asked.

"Looking for stuff," he replied.

Sure enough, the man found battle artifacts. Oh, what I'd give to spot just one dirt-encrusted Minié.

"Most of the big stuff is gone," Champion says. "But bayonets, swords tips, still a lot of Miniés, buck and ball—it's still out here."

Bones, too. And maybe spirits—at least according to Champion.

"Friends of mine, relic hunters, have heard voices in these woods right here. Both are Baptist, too. And they don't drink 'shine."

In the woods, a friend of Champion's found a bullet lodged in bone. A Vietnam vet, a former surgeon on a battlefield tour with Sid V, discovered an upper leg bone sheered by artillery fire.

"This is what you call traumatic amputation," the man said as he showed the grim relic to Champion and put it in his hands.

At the next stop, Champion rushes ahead, into the deep bed of a tributary of Bakers Creek. Confederates disappeared into it like phantoms as they sought safety from Union gunfire and artillery.

"Did you bring your pistol?" Champion asks.

Then he whips out a Ruger.

"I carry this just in case a water moccasin shows up."

We eyeball a mosaic of pebbles and stones in the creek. "Man, I'd sure like to find you a bullet," Champion says. But nothing Civil War turns up.

"Last time my friend was here he was finding daggum Miniés."

We briefly get lost in a tangle of trees and undergrowth in the Western Theater's version of the Wilderness.

I point to a suspicious hole in the ground.

"Is that a digger hole?" Champion asks. "I hope they found a beer can."

Finally, we reach Champion's sanctuary, at the top of a hill deep in the woods. It's one of his favorite places on the battlefield—one of his favorite places *anywhere.* He often comes here and sits on a bench or in the chair overlooking the forest—to contemplate life and listen to the songbirds, to clear his head, or just because. Decades ago, Champion and his alcohol-fueled pals careened down this steep hill on cardboard boxes for what he calls their "Mississippi Downhill." Crazy.

We park ourselves on a bench, steps from "The Hill of Death" historical marker with a heartfelt quote from Hovey, the Union brigadier general:

"I cannot think of this bloody hill without sadness and pride. Sadness for the great loss of my true and gallant men; pride for the heroic bravery they displayed."

Champion, clutching a ballcap, becomes contemplative.

"I could come up here and it could be 98 degrees," Champion says, "but it's OK. It's my place… it's my place."

The family Shinto weighs in on his wartime ancestors. Sid the First endured dozens of battles, a short stint in a Union prison camp after his capture at Vicksburg and a battle wound in the neck. While fighting in Georgia, he railed to Matilda about the "ruthless vandals of the North."[10]

---

10. Matilda Champion: "A Sorrow's Crown of Sorrow" by Rebecca Blackwell Drake, Battle of Champion Hill web site (battleofchampionhill.org), accessed Dec. 3, 2022

In July 1864, he recalled the "grand solemnity" of John Bell Hood replacing Joseph Johnston as Army of Tennessee commander.[11] Champion also witnessed the burning of Atlanta.

After the war, Matilda and Sid built another house at Midway Station. An unrepentant Rebel to the end, Champion died in 1868. Matilda often welcomed Confederate and Union soldiers alike back to the Champion Hill battleground. At the dedication of the grand Illinois state monument at Vicksburg, she had a place of honor on the reviewing stand. After her death in 1907, Matilda left behind signed photo cards from Ulysses Grant and Alvin Hovey as well as letters from Union veterans. "For your many kindnesses to me when I came to remove my Brother's remains 12 years since, I am very grateful," one of them wrote.[12]

Back where we started, Al—Champion's friend, barber, and hummingbird caretaker—nurses a beer on the porch. He offers me a brew. Then Champion waves me inside.

"Look at this."

In the dark, among the clutter in the cramped cabin, he stares at a TV playing a six-year-old video from a Champion Hill trail camera. As a fridge on the back nine of life rattles, I inch closer. In the background on the screen appears a human-like figure, moving about chaotically. It reminds me of a ghostly version of Pac Man, the old video game.

Then I remember a quote from a Union vet about Champion Hill: "All around us lay the dead and dying, amid the groans and cries of the wounded."[13]

Perhaps the video is proof their spirits linger in the woods—Sid Champion's woods—near a ramshackle cabin with a "Psycho Parkway" sign.

But I don't have time to linger or drink a beer. Sorry, Al. It's time to tell you about a side trip to Vicksburg with Sid V and the surprise of this Mississippi leg of my road trip.

---

11. *My Dear Wife—Letters To Matilda, The Civil War Letters of Sid and Matilda Champion of Champion Hill*, edited by Rebecca Blackwell Drake and Margie Riddle Bearss, self-published, 2005

12. Matilda Champion: "I was in the Cellar During the Fight," Rebecca Blackwell Drake, Battle of Champion Hill web site (battleofchampionhill.org), accessed Dec. 3, 2022

13. *With Grant at Fort Donelson, Shiloh and Vicksburg*, Page 104

CHAPTER 8

Vicksburg, Mississippi

'WHOA, HE'S A BLACK GUY'

Sid Champion V briefly swerves his 2009 Toyota pickup into a rutted field to avoid another god-awful, bumpy stretch of Mississippi country road. Champion has a Wile E. Coyote sticker plastered on the left quarter panel and an odometer in the dashboard that brags of 258,000-plus miles from those six little cylinders under the hood.

"I'm not making you nervous, am I?" Sid asks as we bounce along, creating our own artery.

"Those are your tax dollars not at work, Sid," I reply, nodding toward the ragged road.

I wonder if Ulysses Grant's artillery used it for target practice and the Great State of Mississippi—the nation's poorest state—simply hasn't had the time or money to fix it.

"My grandma used to scare me half to death driving down these roads," Champion says.

We're taking the back roads to Vicksburg, roughly 25 miles away, for a visit to the Civil War museum run by Champion's friend, Charles Pendleton. Almost in passing, Champion had mentioned the man's collection before our Champion Hill battlefield ATV extravaganza.

Along Smith Station Road, Champion stops for me to take a picture of massive "witness tree" in someone's front yard. Then we park above the Big Black River, where Sid points out the foundation stones of a wartime bridge. Near the Big Black's muddy waters, the Union Army defeated John Pemberton's army again in the aftermath of Champion Hill, leading to the Siege of Vicksburg.

"I was giving a tour to a husband and wife and pointed out an alligator in the Big Black. Woman in the group runs to her car and locks herself in. No alligator is gonna chase her up here!" Champion scoffs.

In Vicksburg, where Champion burst into the world in 1958, he puts on (figuratively) his foodie hat, pointing out the best places to get a steak dinner, doughnuts and cake. Then he parks on a downhill slope on Washington Street in the historic district.

On my last trip to "The Gibraltar of the Confederacy," in the late 1990s, I lost a chunk of cash in 25 minutes playing blackjack aboard a steamboat/casino anchored in the Yazoo River Diversion Canal. Today, that money would have purchased an artillery shell or another Civil War relic for Mrs. B. to stash in our garage.

"Get your wallet ready. Charles charges $7 to get in," Champion says.

Then I open the museum door, followed by Sid, who introduces me to Charles, who grins and shakes my hand.

"Whoa," I think to myself, "he's a Black guy."

I've visited many Civil War museums over the years but never one owned, operated and curated by a Black person. In fact, Pendleton's probably a universe of one. So, don't be floored by my initial reaction.

Pendleton is a 53-year-old, Vicksburg-born former owner of a pallet company, current owner of three oil change stations and a married father of three. One of his daughters works as a registered nurse. The other is an attorney and the Vicksburg mayor's chief of staff. His son serves in the Marines. Pendleton is the museum's president. Champion, great-great-grandson of slaveholders, is quasi president of his fan club.

To Pendleton's left stands a freezer filled with Blue Bell ice cream. On the counter rests a photo of his son, the Marine, in his dress blues. The blues play on the sound system. To Pendleton's right hangs a framed copy of the museum's mission statement.

"Our goal is NOT to EDUCATE YOU," it reads, in part. "Our aim is to INSPIRE YOU to want TO BECOME MORE EDUCATED."

I'm already inspired by a nearby display of original Civil War-era photographs. But that's just the start of it.

Behind glass partitions, near display cases of dozens of muskets and pistols, sit more than 100 artillery shells—one of the finest such collections I've seen. In a case stands a pike used by a motley band led by John Brown, the madman abolitionist, during his Harper's Ferry, Virginia raid in October 1859. Displayed nearby are a Chattanooga battlefield war log with an embedded artillery shell, a drum canteen of a Rebel soldier killed in Vicksburg and a Klansman's robe.

Champion waves me into a small room.

"Down there is that canister ball I stubbed my toe on in the Old Jackson Road."

The Champion Hill relic rests on the bottom shelf of a display case of Champion family artifacts Sid V loaned to Pendleton.

"Sid, this is an amazing collection."

"Told you."

Back at the front of the museum, I lob questions at Pendleton. He wears a checkered shirt and tan slacks and sports a goatee with strands of gray. Pendleton has an engaging smile, often squinting when he does. My one word for him: "Contemplative." Champion's: "Unique." Pendleton clearly has thought deeply about the Civil War—especially its causes and how it echoes today.

"At the Civil War shows I've attended, people would come up to me and say, 'Well, you know the war's not about slavery,'" he tells me. "Then I started researching it, and *holy shit*, it was *all* about slavery." So, Pendleton's museum isn't just guns and cannonballs. He aims to tell the full story of the war and its aftermath, ugliness and all. That means confronting its root cause head-on. This isn't critical race theory, it's critical race fact.

As visitors enter the museum, they see a display of copies of the complete letters of secession for the Confederate states. Each prominently mentions slavery as the reason for the state's departure from the Union.

"Our position is thoroughly identified with the institution of slavery—the greatest material interest of the world," reads a line in the Mississippi document.

Charles Pendleton calls his impressive Civil War collection "just crap to look at." He hopes visitors discover a deeper message in his museum.

"[The Northern states] demand the abolition of negro slavery through-out the confederacy," the Texas document reads, in part.

"How can you debate facts?" Pendleton says.

In the back of the museum stands a replica slave cabin, one of several displays emphasizing the experience of Black people during and after the war. A video on slavery plays on a screen above an exhibit of a slave laboring in a cotton field. Framed on a wall in the back—near a set of slave shackles—are bills of sale for a young slave named Ella from 1848. She served as an inspiration for the museum.

Pendleton hopes the secession letters, along with placards of the words from Union and Confederates soldiers about slavery, pique the interest of visitors.

"The rest of this stuff," he says of the artifacts, "is just crap to look at."

Pendleton's Civil War collection began in 2018 not with slave relics but with guns. A local man coveted a 1965 Chevy Nova 2 Pendleton had parked in front of one of his oil change stations. Pendleton collected classic cars. Instead of selling it, he and the man agreed on a trade: the Chevy for a

1955 Thunderbird, a Model A Ford pickup and five or six guns—including two or three from the Civil War.

"The more Civil War guns I got," Pendleton says, "the more I wanted."

He even traded a 1966 Chevelle from his classic car collection for a rare, Civil War-era musket made by a Vicksburg gunsmith named Louis Hoffman. Then Pendleton sold the other 15 classic cars to focus on his Civil War collection, which mushroomed into artillery shells, chairs, images and everything in between.

Pendleton didn't plan to acquire thousands of Civil War relics. It just sort of happened, like kudzu growing overnight along Mississippi back roads. When Pendleton realized he didn't have any swords, he'd buy two or three. Before he knew it, he had 30. It's an addiction—a good one.

"Everyone thought I was nuts—wife, kids, everyone," Pendleton says.

He filled four safes with guns and swords. Even the pool table in the family game room became a landing spot for Civil War antiques. Pendleton's wife, Betty, didn't want the entire collection—"junk," she called it then—to remain in the house. So, Pendleton renovated a 3,000-square foot building at the corner of Washington and China Streets for a non-profit museum to house the burgeoning collection.

The structure previously housed a drugstore. In the front, the owner sold shampoo, gum, toothpaste, deodorant and the like. In the back, he sold "voodoo lotion," some worthless rub to make gullible folks feel better. He displayed Civil War relics, too. This is Vicksburg, after all, the town along the Mississippi River that the Union Army put under siege for 47 days in the spring and summer of 1863. Trip and fall here, and you're bound to stumble upon something connected to the Civil War.

Pendleton initially worried if he could fill the museum.

"Just a guy in my oil change shop and me put in stuff to see where it would fit," he says.

To my untrained eye, it looks like the work of a professional curator, though Pendleton isn't one.

"When you do something you love, I think it shows," he tells me. "People can come in here, eat some Blue Bell ice cream, take some pictures."

Dozens of visitors attended the museum opening in May 2021—including Sons of Confederate Veterans members and Bertram Davis, Confederate president Jefferson Davis' great-great-grandson. A year before the debut, Pendleton became so preoccupied with the museum that he turned over the day-to-day operation of the family's oil change stations to his wife. When he attends Civil War shows, Betty serves as his stand-in in the museum. Even Betty's on board with her husband's obsession: "She loves it now."

Champion wanders over to join the conversation.

"Where's my amputation table?" he asks.

He had loaned Pendleton a bloodstained dinner table from his great-great-grandparents' plantation house for display. At the Battle of Champion Hill on May 16, 1863, the Union Army requisitioned it for surgeries. But Pendleton has no room for it, so he stores it for future display. The omission fails to break the Champion-Pendleton bond.

"When I met him, I took to him," Champion says. "We're like kindred souls."

Nearly all the thousands of museum artifacts came from Civil War shows—the biggies at Franklin, Tennessee, Gettysburg and Dalton, Georgia, as well as smaller events. These Civil War carnivals skew overwhelmingly white, male and over 60, like me. The shows often have bizarre items for sale. At the annual Franklin event, I have spotted a real Civil War cigar ($15)—or *cee-gar*, as it was touted—as well as a Confederate general's silver suspender buckles ($2,750) and a man who had the prosthetic arm of his Union ancestor (not for sale, thank God).

Pendleton is a celebrity at the shows not just because he's Black, but because he's a buyer.

"People know that when I'm there, I'm spending money," he says.

While we chat, a tourist from London offers Pendleton a museum review.

"Well done," he says, shaking the curator's hand. "Amazing. Brilliant."

A steady stream of Mississippi River boat tourists—"100 to 150 a day," Pendleton says—visit the museum. Nearly all visitors are white. As I eye a tintype of a Confederate with a huge Bowie knife, Pendleton welcomes two young Black visitors. They make his day.

"I wish more Black people in the area had more appreciation for history," Pendleton says. At his all-Black Southern Baptist church, Pendleton read to the congregation parts of young slave Ella's bills of sale. But no one showed much interest. It's both sad and puzzling.

"Hey, we need to go," Champion says.

My ride with Wile E. Coyote beckons. So, I order a cone of chocolate Blue Bell to go for five bucks and arrange for another meeting with Pendleton in the morning. We have more to discuss.

While waiting for Pendleton to open the next morning, I watch the world go by from a chair in front of the museum. From the museum's speaker blares B.B. King's "The Thrill Is Gone."

As it turns out, Pendleton's views of the Civil War are much more nuanced than you might suspect. If your ancestor fought for the Confederacy, he's cool with that. Pendleton is good with monuments for the Confederate common soldier. He's even OK with monuments to leaders such as Robert E. Lee—if they are put into context. Lee fought to preserve slavery. Don't sugarcoat that, Pendleton says.

A few visitors have questioned Pendleton's exhibits.

"Some people come in and say, 'You have a nice museum, but you should take down that KKK stuff.' But you can't tell the whole story if you don't have that stuff."

I ask Pendleton what it's like to be a universe of one—a Black man who owns a museum whose visitors are almost exclusively white.

"Sometimes I get questions like, 'How long have you been working here?'"

"I tell them, 'Well, about a year.'"

He smiles.

"And some will ask, 'What do you do here?' and 'Did someone donate this to you?'"

Somehow our conversation ends up on Stevie Wonder, and I'm reminded of one his songs, "Superstition."

"When you believe in things that you don't understand ..."

And then I'm off. Northwestern Georgia is on my mind.

CHAPTER 9

Resaca, Georgia

CHARACTERS, COONSKIN CAPS AND COGNAC 'CEE-GARS'

On a soon-to-be-sweltering Sunday afternoon in Resaca, Georgia, reenactor Tony Patton waves from his Confederate camp amid tall pines.

"I'm up here eating a Civil War-period hot dog!" he kids as I make my way to his knoll.

Patton, who portrays a Georgia division adjutant, wears a long-sleeved checked shirt, blue officer's trousers and black brogans. His brown slouch hat looks like those worn by Confederate prisoners in that famous photo taken on Seminary Ridge in Gettysburg. I have no desire to walk in Patton's ugly shoes, mainly because his attire looks like it would turn me into a steaming puddle of goo.

Within an hour or so, Patton will be fighting at the 38th annual Resaca reenactment—one of the few reenactments held on the actual ground where the armies spilled blood.

"It's more special on the actual field," the 57-year-old Georgia native says.

For many reenactors, the fighting takes a back seat to the camping and other off-the-battlefield camaraderie. It's a chance for PhDs, doctors and lawyers to interact with plumbers, teachers and tree cutters. Hell, sometimes even journalists.

But reenacting isn't what it was in its heyday in the 1980s and 1990s. Participation has waned, and as reenactors age out of the hobby, fewer from the younger generations have filled the ranks.

Longtime reenactors talk in awe about the 125th anniversary Gettysburg battle reenactment in 1988. On an oppressively hot day, an estimated 60,000 to 75,000 spectators witnessed the recreation of Pickett's Charge by 10,000 reenactors. A local newspaper described the reenactment as a "beach party with cannons."[1]

Over two days at Resaca, roughly 800 reenactors battled before about 4,000 paying spectators.

As in the hobby's heyday, the Resaca reenactors—some prefer "living historians"—are almost exclusively white and male. Most are middle-aged or older and look like they'd fit right in in a church softball league I played in when we lived in Texas.

Few are "hardcore." In other words, they probably would never sleep in the woods overnight near a real Union burial trench, as Sid Champion V's smelly reenacting pals did in 2013 at the 150th Champion Hill battle anniversary. Or go sans underwear, as a hardcore reenactor did at the 1988 Gettysburg "beach party" because he could not secure a pair his Civil War brethren might have worn.

In the 1990s, a living historian named Robert Lee Hodge—the most hardcore of the hardcore—aimed to perfect the ghastly appearance of a fallen soldier. "Hands are a problem," he told author Tony Horwitz of *Confederates In The Attic* fame. "It's hard to give them that authentic, bloated look unless you've really been dead for a while."[2]

---

1. *The Gettysburg Times*, June 27, 1988
2. *Wall Street Journal*, June 2, 1994

Reenactor Tony Patton, a historian and preservationist, says it's a thrill every time he walks hallowed ground at Resaca.

BATTLE OF RESACA

May 14: Stewart's Div., Hood's Corps ▰ moved
from intrenchments near the John Green house
and attacked left of Federals then extending
toward the State R. R.
This attack fell upon the left of Stanley's (1st)
div. 4th A. C. and 5th Ind. Battery ▰ (on
ridge NW). The timely arrival of Williams' (1st)
div. 20th A. C. ▰, checked Stewart's ▰ advance
and stabalized the left flank of the Federal forces.
May 15: Stewart ▰ repeated attack of 14th-
the assault falling on Williams' div. ▰ astride
road here - and with like result.

I don't see anyone bloating at Resaca. And I don't have the guts to ask Patton about his underwear. No beach parties break out either. But I do spot a man selling coonskin hats, a food stand offering "beef-n-venison" meat-loaf and a reenactor in his 80s whom a comrade once called the "oldest living veteran of the Civil War."

Patton and most of his kin have lived on or near the Resaca battlefield all their lives. An ancestor of Patton's fought in the battle with the 5th Georgia. A distant uncle of his in the Confederate Army was killed at Chickamauga. Another ancestor served with the 10th Tennessee Cavalry in the U.S. Army.

While sitting on his grandparents' porch as a youngster, Patton watched people walk into the woods in Resaca with metal detectors.

"What are those folks doing?" he asked.

"Oh, they're just Minié ball hunting," his grandparents explained.

"My dad picked up Miniés and cannonballs from the battlefield and area camps when I was a kid," Patton says.

Then, in words that torture my soul, he tells me what Dad did with those relics: "He threw them all away. The relics were so common around here then."

At the Resaca reenactment, Patton often finds himself staring at the ground, searching for battle relics. His eyeballing has yet to yield a reward—join the club, brother—but reenacting pals of Patton's have kicked up a Minié ball or two on the battlefield.

From Patton's Confederate camp among the pines, we scan the battle-ground before us. Only one monument, to the 123rd New York, stands on this part of the field. The battlefield reminds me of a suburban Pittsburgh municipal golf course of my youth: rolling hills of green grass, a tree-lined ridge and stands of pine.

In the distance, the railroad track follows the wartime path of the Western & Atlantic Railroad, a strategic supply artery of the Confederacy.

At Resaca on May 15, 1864—the second and final day of the battle—Union Gen. Thomas Ruger's brigade swept from the woods behind us with bad intentions. Real Rebels and real Yankees lay dead on these hills. About 350 yards away, 27th Indiana Captain Thomas Box captured a 38th Alabama flag and earned a Medal of Honor.

"Poor men of the misguided South!" a 27th Indiana soldier recalled of the fighting among the dips and rises. "It was all over in one terrible minute of time, and the story is soon told. Thirty-three of those men who, a moment before, were advancing so confidently, lay dead at our feet! Fully as many more were too badly wounded to be able to move without assistance."[3]

Resaca was one of the early battles in Union Gen. William Sherman's Atlanta Campaign. It resulted in a draw, with roughly 5,600 casualties overall.[4]

For Patton, a historian and preservationist, it's a thrill every time he walks this hallowed ground. He sometimes searches the battlefield for bricks from wartime houses.

"You already got 20 bricks," his wife tells him. "What do you want with another one?"

In the early 1960s, the feds bisected the battlefield with the construction of Interstate 75. On the west side of I-75, the state has preserved 1,100 acres of hallowed ground as a historic site. It opened in 2016. But most of the battlefield is privately owned—including the reenactment site on the east side of the interstate.

With the landowners' permission, reenactors camp on hallowed ground for the annual reenactment.

The plan for this afternoon's showdown is for the Rebels to leave their earthworks for an attack.

"Controlled chaos," Patton calls the choreographed event.

Safety is paramount.

"You don't want to bust someone's ear cap with a musket," Patton says.

While Patton prepares for battle, I reconnoiter the rest of the field, a petri dish teeming with interesting characters.

On Sutler Row, I visit briefly with April, who's hawking replica 19th-century pipes ($10) and cigars flavored with French vanilla, watermelon, cognac and mango, among many other goods. At a reenactment near Shiloh, she claims to have sold 400 cigars—or "cee-gars," as the Virginian calls them. The cognac ceegars are popular.

---

3. Brown, Edmund Randolph, *The Twenty-seventh Indiana Volunteer Infantry in the War of the Rebellion, 1861 to 1865*, Monticello, Ind., 1899, Page 472
4. American Battlefield Trust web site

April calls everyone she likes "Sugar," "Darling," "Honey," and "Baby." Affixed on back of her cash register is an "Eat More Possum" sticker. A customer wears a T-shirt reading: "We Don't Need Permission to Honor Our Ancestors."

It's surreal to see vendors selling boiled peanuts, Fried Nutter Butter and sno-cones from stands set up on hallowed ground. But that's 'Merica.

A Resaca sutler pushes possum.

At the Sons of Confederate Veterans tent, Confederate-themed T-shirts are among the wares. One with a peach emblazoned with a Rebel flag reads: "If You Don't Like My Peaches, Don't Shake My Tree."

For a buck, I buy a "We Will No Longer Be Called Hillbilly Rednecks. We Will Henceforth Be Known As Appalachian Americans" bumper sticker. In a carefully worded text message, I ask Mrs. B about placing it on "Murray," her nickname for our SUV that I drove to Georgia.

Her response is brief and pointed, like the edge of sharpened bayonet. "No."

Before departing, I ask the late-60ish gent manning the SCV tent who's going to win the battle.

"The South always wins!" he bellows.

We both chuckle, but he seems serious.

In another tent, I visit with Gettysburg-based Dirty Billy, who makes replica Civil War-era headgear. A 4th Texas kepi goes for $225.

Near Old Doc Bell's soda stand, a mid-60ish sutler named Chuck sells books (*The Quotable Stonewall Jackson*), signs ("Keep Calm and Fix Bayonets"), General Grant "cee-gars" and other knickknacks. He almost spit out his beef-and-venison meatloaf upon hearing the news a group of Yankee reenactors had skedaddled early.

"*Pansies*," he scoffs.

While sweating profusely in the steamy tent, he recalls his own reenacting days in the 1980s and early 1990s. He reenacted with the 30th Georgia,

Company E, the "Clayton County Invincibles." A reenactment in Franklin, Tennessee decades ago chilled Chuck to the bone.

"Five degrees without the wind chill," he says. "We couldn't get water. It froze over."

Chuck suspects wives of the current crop of reenactors have turned them soft with conveniences such as A-frame tents.

Chuck lives in a small house in Jones County, Georgia, where Confederate Gen. Alfred Iverson was born. We compare notes on walking the ground where the Union Army ambushed Iverson's brigade at Gettysburg on July 1, 1863. Then a friendly Georgian interrupts us.

"Do you have any black powder in here?" she asks Chuck.

She needs it for her husband, who reenacts with the 5th Georgia and will protect the homeland in the afternoon's battle.

While tractors tow spectators on flatbeds to the battle site, I walk to the crest of a hill for an examination of the remains of Confederate embrasures in the woods. It almost looks as if you could roll the cannons behind them today. This historic ground isn't part of the pretend battle. In the distance traffic drones on the interstate. I stare into the woods, mesmerized.

Late on May 15, 1864, Colonel Benjamin Harrison of the 70th Indiana led an attack here against a Confederate battery commanded by Maximilian Van Den Corput, a Belgian-born captain. Two Union regiments overwhelmed the "Cherokee Battery," who abandoned their guns.

"I cheered the men forward, and with a wild yell they entered the embrasures, striking down and bayoneting the rebel gunners, many of whom defiantly stood by their guns till struck down," recalled the 30-year-old Harrison, who became 23rd president in 1889.[5]

Severe fire from a Confederate line 25 yards behind the battery, however, forced the Federals to retreat, leaving the artillery in no-man's land.

"When we first entered the embrasures of the outer works the enemy fled in considerable confusion from the inner one, and had there been a supporting line brought up in good order at this juncture the second line might have easily been carried and held," Harrison wrote in his after-action report.[6]

---

5. *Official Records*, Washington, 1894, Vol. 38, Part 2, Page 372
6. Ibid

Future U.S. president Benjamin Harrison led troops that captured Confederate cannon at these earthworks.

Under the cover of darkness, Union soldiers advanced to the earthworks and dragged the four Confederate cannon back to their lines.

Kaboom!

A cannon resounds in the far distance, startling me. The one-hour sham battle has begun. I hitch a ride to the battleground on one of the flatbeds. The temperature has soared into the low 90s.

Atop a knoll, partially covered by a stand of pines, hundreds of spectators watch the warring parties. A woman in a period dress fans herself. I sit on the ground atop a pine cone. An ambulance is parked near the crest of the hill just in case someone gets smacked with a musket in the ear cap or keels over from heat exhaustion.

At a distance, the muskets sound like popguns. The cannons sound like … real cannons. After each boom, a mesmerizing cloud of smoke forms a giant "O" ring and slowly drifts away.

"If God wants us to have it back, you will get it," Melea Medders Tennant told herself about the Resaca battlefield.

An older reenactor, with long, gray hair, gallops past on a horse. Trumpets blare. Then I hear a weak Rebel Yell.

The Johnnies are charging!

Brave Billy Yanks stand near a giant U.S. flag. Then the Rebs turn their backs to the Federals and briefly retreat.

"That one looks like he's dead over there," a teen spectator says. She points to a soldier lying on the ground in the far distance.

"No, he's literally sun-bathing," her friend says.

I'm not sure she grasps the concept.

The afternoon turns sublime when I spot retired grade-school teacher Melea Medders Tennant. In 2019, she showed me those Harrison-charged Rebel artillery embrasures. Her great-great-grandfather, Daniel Chitwood, served as a private in Company A of the 23rd Georgia, the "Bartow County Yankee Killers."

As a child growing up in nearby Whitfield County, Tennant played in the remains of wartime trenches.

The ground upon which the reenactment is held—the Chitwood place— had been in Melea's family for generations. Then it slipped away.

"If God wants us to have it back, you will get it," Tennant told herself on walks on her property adjacent to the old farmland.

At an auction in 2021, her family banded together to reacquire the ground, more than 400 acres in all. Her sister received the news of the deal closing on vacation as she spotted the "Where Dreams Come True" sign at Disney World.

Tennant says a group of Northerners came to the reenactment wanting to fight as Confederates. I wonder if they are the "pansies" that miffed Chuck, the beef-and-venison chomping sutler. Naturally, I ask the lifelong Georgian who will win the battle.

"Well, we have homefield advantage," she says.

At the end of the hostilities, all the soldiers remove their headgear. I'm not sure who won. A bugler plays *Taps*. It's moving.

"That's the biggest clump of Confederates I've ever seen out here," Tennant says of grouping of "dead" near the Union earthworks.

As I make my way to Murray, parked near the Possum Holler Express truck, Patton catches up. On weekends, Patton—a pressman in his real gig—serves as a jack-of-all trades/guide at the Resaca historic site across the interstate.

"Hey, how'd the battle go?"

"We didn't get our colors captured like we were supposed to because there was a lack of Federals," Patton says.

I wonder if the departure of the "pansies" ruined it.

You can't be a pansy if you intend to walk the Perryville battlefield in Kentucky. That's our next stop.

We're headed to Lincoln country.

CHAPTER 10

Perryville, Kentucky

'WHAT A PISSER'

O n a devilishly chilly morning, I travel east on windy, rural roads through Kentucky, the state of Abraham Lincoln's birth and the self-proclaimed "Bourbon Capital of World." In 1809, the future president was born in a cabin near Hodgenville. Two years later, the Lincolns moved to a remote farm nearby between steep, heavily wooded hills—"knobs," they call them in this part of the country.

Those Lincoln knobs are too far off the beaten path for a side trip, and it's too early for sipping bourbon on the Kentucky Bourbon Trail. But it's never too early for a visit to a battlefield. I'm heading to Perryville, population 800, where the armies clashed in one of the deadliest battles in the Western Theater.

In the battlefield parking lot, near the small visitors center, I meet my gravelly voiced guide, Chuck Lott. He's dressed in a camo jacket, white hoodie and light-brown khakis. Lott bears a passing resemblance to Shelby Foote, the writer made famous by Ken Burns in his epic 1990 Civil War documentary on TV.

We are joined by my battlefield tramping pal Jack Richards, a retired lawyer, full-time history enthusiast and part-time humorist. He traveled here from his home base in Middle Tennessee on his own.

When Lott examines a battlefield, he sees something much different than Richards and I do.

"Every stretch of ground is a chance to die," he tells us.

Then Lott gestures toward dips and rises at Perryville.

"I'm thinking, 'That's good for concealment, that's good for cover.'"

Lott's "battlefield vision," as I like to call it, is a product of experience and perhaps family genes.

Lott witnessed the carnage of war in Vietnam, where he served as a medic. His father served as a Marine during World War II, surviving the bloodbath at Okinawa in the war's waning weeks. An uncle stormed Anzio in Italy in 1944; another one fought in the Korean War. Six of his great-great-grandfathers served in Michigan regiments during the Civil War.

Soon after Lott and his wife moved to Kentucky in 2005, he immersed himself in the history of the Perryville battle, visiting the field on his days off from his job as a hospital technologist.

"Widowed the wife," our soft-spoken guide tells us.

Lott eventually became a Perryville battlefield interpretive specialist. Over the past decade, he has given hundreds of tours and U.S. Army staff rides on this hallowed ground in central Kentucky.

"There are about 58,000 stories out here," he says, "and we only know about 2,000 of them."

Nearly as it appeared in 1862, Perryville is a battlefield wanderer's paradise of heart-racing ridges and scenery an impressionist painter might appreciate: hills of deep green and rich, golden brown with occasional splashes of ruby red and orange.

"Lord there sure are a whole bunch of 'knobs' here," I think to myself.

But thank God, we're not walking.

Instead, we travel the battlefield in Lott's Gator, a golf cart-like utility vehicle. It's a lot more comfortable, and much safer, than my death-defying ride on the back of Sid Champion V's ATV at Champion Hill in Mississippi.

Only five monuments and markers and 47 modern interpretive tablets stand in the nearly 1,200-acre battlefield state park. Remove the power lines, and you're projected back to the 19th century. But the battle that largely snuffed out Confederate hopes in Kentucky is hardly top of mind with Civil War historians or travelers. On a virtually cloudless morning, only a handful of other visitors roam the battlefield.

Perryville was hardly top of mind with the public in 1862 either, coming three weeks after the much-bloodier Battle of Antietam in the Eastern Theater.

This battle was a strange but vicious five-hour brawl on October 8, 1862, resulting in an astonishing 7,600 casualties in five hours. A fresh breeze blew from the southwest that day. Temperature: An unseasonably hot 85 degrees. Terrain: "Boldly undulating," according to Confederate Gen. William Hardee.[1]

"Shaped like the inside of a giant egg crate," Lott says of the battle-field—a description that captures Perryville perfectly.

The weather and terrain conspired to cause a phenomenon called an "acoustic shadow." Army of the Ohio commander Don Carlos Buell didn't hear the roar of artillery and gunfire from his headquarters three miles from the battle's epicenter. That could be the reason he didn't deploy the full weight of his forces against the outmanned Army of Mississippi, commanded by ill-tempered Braxton Bragg. Meanwhile, a Confederate adjutant 45 miles away distinctly heard the cacophony of battle.

Perhaps Buell, whom many on his staff despised, simply should have stayed home. In a letter to his wife shortly before the battle, a Federal officer wrote of his disappointment that the general had not broken his neck in a recent fall from a horse.

And so roughly 13,000 U.S. Army soldiers squared off against about 16,000 Confederates, who soon after sweeping the Federals from one ridge found their enemy had a defensive position on another.

"Almost like playing a game of Whac-A-Mole," Lott says.

"What a pisser," Richards says of the Confederates' plight.

Atop Parsons Ridge, one of those "Whac-A-Mole" hills, we gaze toward a fence line, the Confederate position, about 100 yards away. To our left is battlefield land saved by the American Battlefield Trust. Nearly 400 yards behind us is another one of those challenging ridges; above us soars an eagle, one of two that Lott says nests somewhere on the battlefield.

Steps away, a historical marker tells us this was the place that Union Brig. Gen. James Jackson, "the highest type of Kentucky gentleman," suffered a mortal wound. The 39-year-old's *New York Times* obit wasn't as kind: "In manner he was brusque and overbearing, and as a consequence was a party to numerous quarrels, which sometimes resulted in duels."[2]

---

1. *Official Records*, Vol. 16, Part 1, Page 1120

2. *The New York Times*, Oct. 11, 1862

My guide Chuck Lott, a Vietnam vet, sees a battlefield differently than most of the rest of us.

But I'm more interested in what Lott says happened here to grunts in the 123rd Illinois.

"Fresh fish," he calls the regiment.

Only a month earlier the Illinois boys had been mustered into service.

As Confederates swept toward the crest of Parsons Ridge, the Illinoisans received orders to make a bayonet charge. Among them was Private Alfred Hall, the 24-year-old son of Lincoln's stepsister, Matilda. As an overwhelming enemy force advanced, Hall and his comrades did what most sensible soldiers would: They shifted into reverse, leaving dozens of their dead and wounded in their wake.

"He was a pretty good sprinter," Lott says of Hall, who retreated several hundred yards.

Near the bottom of the reverse slope of Parsons Ridge, we rumble on the Gator past a lengthy double-fence Lott constructed in about a week. "A hate fence," he calls the wartime original that separated the properties of two feuding farmers.

Yards away, we stand by the site of a cornfield where the rookie 21st Wisconsin lay awaiting their baptism of fire. Even today, I can sense the green regiment's fear in their perilous position.

As scores of Confederates streamed over Parsons Ridge, the Midwesterners' commander, Colonel Benjamin Sweet, still recovering from a bout with malaria, arrived on the field in an ambulance and mounted his horse. The 30-year-old officer had suffered a severe wound in the right arm, an injury that never healed, and later in the neck. (He later became commander of the notorious Camp Douglas POW camp in Chicago.)

Our Gator chugs up Starkweather Hill, named after 1st Wisconsin Colonel John S. Starkweather, whose troops courageously defended the ridge. Lott shows where Sam Watkins, who wrote the classic Civil War memoir *Company Aytch*, and his 1st Tennessee comrades aimed to outflank the Federals on a steep side of the hill, below Union batteries.

Then Lott drives us to one of the more beautiful spots on this special battlefield: *another* of those damn "Whac-A-Mole" hills.

At the high-water mark for Bragg's army, a small section of stone wall remains on ground behind which the Federals deployed. Below us, Georgians swept through the ravine; Lott says relic hunters found Georgia-manufactured bullets there before it became part of the state park. This area also was the site of heroic efforts only fully appreciated by examining the ground yourself.

Lott points to the steep incline where Union soldiers somehow dragged two cannons to safety while under fire. Nearby, John S. Durham, a 19-year-old 1st Wisconsin sergeant, grabbed the regimental colors from a dying color sergeant "amid a shower of shot, shell, and bullets" and advanced with the flag midway between the armies.[3] Durham, who ran away from home at age 7 and was adopted by a showman, received the Medal of Honor in 1896 for valor at Perryville.

"Your conduct in the battle," Starkweather wrote Durham decades after the fight, "was the most conspicuous act of bravery on the part of a soldier that I have ever witnessed."[4]

---

3. Congressional Medal of Honor Society citation
4. *The Kansas City Gazette*, Dec. 3, 1896

A magnificent Perryville battlefield "witness tree."

Heroism, of course, wasn't confined to soldiers in blue. In one of the most audacious acts of the largest battle ever fought in Kentucky, 900 Mississippians in Colonel Thomas Jones' brigade charged through a deep valley against 3,000 Federals supplemented with six cannons.

"Like storming a castle wall," says Lott.

When I had walked Jones' Ridge weeks earlier, my heart raced to 125 beat per minute.

More than a decade earlier, Lott and battlefield wanderers on hay wagons pulled by tractors examined this valley with Ed Bearss, the renowned Civil War historian, then in his early 80s.

"Get off your wagons, guys, you better start walking," said Bearss, mocking the laggards in his distinctive, booming voice.

Lott walked with Bearss, a World War II Marine who died in 2020, during a particularly steep stretch.

"I did not plan to shift into a lower gear," Bearss growled, "but I think I just did."

Every Civil War battlefield has a story about warfare ravaging luckless families. At Perryville, the war dealt poor Henry Pierce Bottom's family an especially cruel blow.

"Squire" raised cows, sheep, and pigs and grew corn on more than 600 rolling acres near Doctor's Creek. The battle decimated his crops, and Rebel artillery set his barn afire, destroying it, too. His farmhouse became a makeshift military hospital. The battle crushed Bottom's psyche, too.

Asked after the war if "Squire" recovered from his losses, a Perryville doctor replied, "No sir, he never did. He was broken in spirit from that time on until he died."[5]

Bottom sought more than $4,000 in compensation from the U.S. government. He never received a penny during his lifetime.

Lott unlocks the door to the privately owned Bottom house and escorts us through a marvelously restored Civil War time capsule. Covered by small pieces of Plexiglas, bullet holes pepper the interior.

On the second floor, Lott reaches under a bed and pulls out a remarkable relic: an original door used as an operating table during and after the battle. Luminol sprayed on it revealed the presence of blood.

On the opposite side of Doctor's Creek, we didn't need Lott's gift for spotting good cover and concealment to know a massive, almost 200-year-old oak would be excellent for a game of cat and mouse. The imposing monster—the last witness tree on the battlefield—also would have served as a fabulous extra in *The Blair Witch Project*, the 1990s horror movie classic.

It just another reason to appreciate Perryville.

As Lott likes to say, "This place *matters*."

In Middle Tennessee, meanwhile, another unheralded battlefield awaits exploration. On a late-winter day in 1863, a teenage girl there briefly commanded center stage.

---

5. John Bolling testimony before War Claims Commission, 1904, National Archives, Washington, D.C.

CHAPTER **11**

Thompson's Station, Tennessee

ALICE'S 15 SECONDS OF FAME

In the basement of the Homestead Manor mansion astride the old Columbia Pike, Aaron Sanders hoists a giant enlargement of a photograph of a beautiful young woman from a pile of odds and ends.

"Here she is," he says of the Battle of Thompson's Station heroine.

The woman, Alice Thompson, wears a checked dress, earrings, broach and a hint of a smile. I understand how she caught the eye of a Confederate surgeon she married.

In 1863, Homestead Manor was home for the family of Thomas Banks, a Rebel officer, and no relation to your present company. His nine-room mansion became a temporary battlefield hospital during the battle, and years later, it served as a post office, general store, farmers market and then a restaurant. Now the mansion is operated as a church, coffee shop, and community gathering spot. Sanders is Homestead Manor's operations manager.

On March 5, 1863, as the battle raged around her, Thompson found refuge in this cramped cellar. Not quite 17, Alice—daughter of a physician for whom the Tennessee town was named—peered from a window while cannons boomed and the muskets of grim-faced soldiers belched volleys of lead.

When a wounded 3rd Arkansas Cavalry color-bearer collapsed a few feet away, Thompson rushed from the room and grabbed the soldier's flag, waving it over her head.

"Boys," shouted a colonel, "a woman has your flag!"

An artillery shell landed near her, spraying Thompson with dirt, but it failed to explode. Then a Rebel soldier escorted the energized teen back into the basement, where she rejoined family members of the owner, his slaves and neighbors.

Her 15 seconds or so of battlefield glory were over.[1]

Thompson reminds me of John Burns, the civilian who lugged an ancient flintlock to fight alongside the Union Army's Iron Brigade at Gettysburg and became an unlikely hero. Of course, Alice was more than 50 years younger and much more attractive than the craggy faced War of 1812 vet.

Over the years, the Homestead Manor basement has transitioned from storage area to restaurant wine cellar and secluded dining space to a refuge for Christian music songwriters. We're only 40 minutes south of downtown Nashville, after all.

"So, which of these two windows did she look out?" I ask Sanders.

He doesn't know, but his answer fails to blunt my Civil War high.

Upstairs in the mansion, while patrons stare at their laptops or iPhones, Sanders reveals evidence of the battle.

From a display cabinet, he pulls a tray of battlefield relics, including a 12-pound solid shot that supposedly crashed through the roof of the house. Over the decades, Homestead Manor owners have used the artifact— roughly the size of a shot put—as a doorstop.[2]

On the second floor, Sanders points to small, dark splotches on steps leading to a third-floor room.

"That's blood."

A test on the stains commissioned by the previous owner revealed "110 different strands of DNA," he says, which seems to confirm the use of the mansion as a hospital. I wonder if a Civil War surgeon tossed amputated limbs from windows, forming a gruesome pile where today's customers sip $5 lattes in an outdoor courtyard.

---

1. *Confederate Veteran*, June 1900, Vol. 8, No. 6
2. National Register of Historic Places Inventory Nomination Form, April 29, 1977

Aaron Sanders holds a giant enlargement of Confederate heroine Alice Thompson in the basement where she watched the battle unfold.

For decades, Thompson's Station was a sleepy town along the Nashville & Decatur Railroad line, probably with more cows than humans. Now it's a booming suburb along an interstate corridor about nine miles south of downtown Franklin. Farms held by families for generations have become residential housing developments. A new home easily could set you back a cool million.

Alice, this ain't your father's Thompson's Station.

Like good manners in Congress, the battlefield where 6,000 Rebels fought 3,000 Yankees is largely forgotten. Only pockets of hallowed ground remain among rolling hills, ridges and remaining farm fields. A historical marker astride the pike denotes the battle's significance, but I've never noticed a soul reading it. For a battlefield fix, most civil warriors bypass Thompson's Station for Franklin.

Homestead Manor, where Alice Thompson served as a battle nurse, became the eye of the battle storm. But scores of other dramas played out nearby—at the seldom-visited railroad track behind Banks' mansion, on a hill near the train depot and elsewhere.

At Thompson's Station, Maj. Gen. Earl Van Dorn, a womanizer and scoundrel, commanded the Confederate forces against a U.S. Army brigade under Colonel John Coburn. You may remember Van Dorn as an attendee at the epic Confederate wedding in nearby Columbia, Tennessee. The heavy lifting for the Rebels at Thompson's Station, however, fell to Nathan Bedford Forrest, the third-most glorified commander in the Confederate Army behind Stonewall Jackson and Robert E. Lee.

Ruthless and ingenious on the battlefield, Forrest earned the nickname "The Wizard of the Saddle." He was equally ruthless off the battlefield. Two months before Thompson's Station, the former slave trader had brutally conscripted men and boys for service in the Rebel army. "The bloodhounds ... are pursuing their miserable victims, with fresh fury," wrote a Union-leaning Nashville newspaper.[3]

Midway through the fighting at Thompson's Station, Forrest's division of cavalry swept around the Union Army's left flank, cutting off its escape route on the pike. The abandonment of the fight by its ammunition train, artillery and cavalry contributed to a U.S. Army fiasco. Astride Roderick, his favorite horse, Forrest appeared on the flank of one of his regiments, urging soldiers to charge on the beleaguered Federals on a hill north of town.

Thump, thump, thump.

Three bullets plunged into Forrest's chestnut gelding. The general dismounted and ordered his son, a 16-year-old officer, to escort Roderick to the rear. Then "The Wizard" mounted his son's wounded but still rideable horse and continued the fight. Stripped of his bridle and saddle, Roderick briefly remained behind the lines before galloping off in search of his master.

Fearful of his father's wrath, Forrest's son, as well as several attendants, chased Roderick, who leaped over three stone walls to reach the general. But the restless horse suffered a fourth, and this time fatal, wound.

As Roderick's life ebbed away, badass Forrest—who had many other mounts shot out from under him during the war—is said to have wept beside the animal. "A fitting sacrifice to the God of War," a 19th-century historian wrote of the horse's demise.[4]

---

3. *Nashville Daily Union*, Jan. 23, 1863.

4. Drake, Edwin L., *The Annals of the Army of Tennessee, and Early Western history, Including a Chronological Summary of Battles and Engagements in the Western Armies of the Confederacy*, Nashville, Tennessee: A.D. Haynes, 1878, Page 430

An out-of-the-way monument to Roderick, Nathan Bedford Forrest's KIA horse.

After the battle, Forrest had Roderick buried in an unmarked grave. A local historian says the remains may rest near the circa-1820 Spencer Buford house gruesomely altered by a 21st-century developer. Or perhaps Roderick's remains lie nearby in the upscale Roderick Place subdivision, which could lead to some weird conversations:

"Dear, the workers were digging in our garden, and they found this huge skull."

To this day, Roderick lives on in the imaginations of a few historians, horse lovers and strange people like me. In 2008, the town dedicated a statue of Roderick on ground where Forrest's soldiers formed for their attack. Let's just say the sculptor took a few liberties—hey, that statue is not a gelding! The next year, Thompson's Station awarded the Roderick Award of Courage to a 10-year-old girl who performed the Heimlich maneuver to save her grandma from choking to death on a piece of chicken.[5] But the town discontinued the award after only one honoree.

5. *The Tennessean*, Nashville, March 11, 2009

The human toll at Thompson's Station was a fraction of what it was at Franklin, where roughly 8,500 soldiers became casualties on November 30, 1864, or dozens of other Civil War battles. This fight claimed roughly 350 Confederates and 300 U.S. Army soldiers—casualty figures that nonetheless would horrify the country today. Dozens more Union POWs died at Richmond's notorious Libby Prison.

Private Judson Austin's tragic Thompson's Station story rocks me most. In many ways, he was the typical Civil War soldier—27 years old, a farmer, loved his family and country. "I am fighting to save our homes … Children & Wives from the curse of slavery and butchery," he wrote to his wife, Sarah. Thompson's Station was his first battle of the war, and he expected to give the Rebels the *"best pill in the box."*[6]

But the private in the 19th Michigan—one of four regiments in Coburn's brigade—soon found himself in deep trouble. From a knoll south of town—an electrical substation stands there today—Confederate artillery pummeled the 22nd Wisconsin and 19th Michigan, positioned on a rise across from Homestead Manor.

"Our Boys hugged the ground for a short time when we wer ordered to fall in & march to the right," Austin wrote about being under fire.[7] Then Confederates shot at fleeing Federals from a thick stand of cedars. In the battle against the enemy "bloodhounds," Austin was joined by his younger brother, Pasqua, whom he called "Pack."

Somehow, I cross the traffic-clogged, two-lane pike—State Route 31 to you who live in the 21st century—for an examination of ground defended by the Austin brothers and the rest of the Midwesterners. Here, across from Homestead Manor, "the lead flew from our guns like hail," wrote Austin.

To my right, beyond two modern churches, rise two hills. That's where troops commanded by Van Dorn lurked before the battle. To my left, across

---

6.   Judson L. Austin Papers 1862-1865, Bentley Historical Library, University of Michigan

7.   Ibid

The combatants tried to kill each other here during the Battle of Thompson's Station on March 5, 1863.

from an open field, stands a modern house and a huge, tall oak, which naturally gets me to thinking:

Could that be a "witness" tree?

And, if so, how much "hail of lead" could still be in that thing?

(Weeks later, I hauled off a couple hunks with the permission of a tree-trimming crew. Mrs. B made sure I deposited the haul in our garage.)

Fearful of being flanked, the Midwesterners re-deployed across the road by the railroad track that still follows its wartime path. Then "Butternuts, like mountain demons … came swarming like bees from every hill and valley and bore down upon our brave men," recalled a Michigan soldier.[8]

Not every soldier displayed manly courage. A 19th Michigan captain hid behind a beech tree and then "deserted his company… in a most disgraceful and cowardly manner," a commanding officer later wrote.[9]

"He is mine," Judson Austin later wrote of the deserter, "where ever he be."[10]

At the railroad track, the 19th Michigan briefly silenced the advancing Rebels with a volley. Then a shot from a Confederate took off a "little bark" from Judson Austin's right hand, narrowly missing Pack.

"We both steped back a step or too whare we wer concealed behind the point of a projecting rock that hapened to stick out on the side of the grade & unloaded our muskets at the butternut," Judson wrote.[11] The "projecting rock" piqued my interest, so I walked along the railroad track to find it. Sure enough, a large boulder juts out along the west side of the line, but who knows if it's *the* rock?

With hundreds of Rebels on their heels, Judson and Pack hustled to a ridge to join the rest of his regiment. For Judson, the battle became a blur of charges, countercharges, yells, arcing artillery shells, bullets falling about his legs "like hail" and fighting like "bush whackers."[12]

When he reached the safety of another hill, Austin lay down with his comrades amid barrages of Confederate artillery.

But where was Pack?

---

8. *The Hillsdale Standard*, Hillsdale, Mich., March 17, 1863

9. *Official Records*, Vol. 23, Part 1, Page 105

10. Judson L. Austin Papers 1862-1865

11. Ibid

12. Ibid

The last time Austin saw him he was crawling behind a large oak.

Amid whistling and hissing bullets, Austin made his way toward the last sighting of his brother. Soon, he found him. In one of the most gut-wrenching soldier accounts I've ever read, Austin described the scene to his wife:

> *I stooped to his ear & called his name, but no answer. I turned from one side to the other calling name each time I turned him; but no reply. Taking my handkerchief from my pocket I wiped his broken forehead washing it with my tears. All this time I was unconcious of danger I was in. A shell buzzed close to my head from one of the rebble guns brought me to my sences. I curled myself down close to the ground & stayed some time with my Dying Brother.*
>
> *When I left him the last spark of life seemed to have gon. I was obliged to leave him amidst the rore of battle. Here was a trying time for me. To leave a Loved one with a most tender and brotherly affection. Leave him on the battle field in the cold embrace of death & in an enamyes land I bid farewell to him for this world. Hoping to meet him at the judgemant seat of Christ with his sins washed & made white by the blood of the lamb.*[13]

As gunfire petered out, Austin and the rest of Coburn's brigade—more than 1,000 soldiers in all—surrendered at a hill nearby. "Coburn's Hill," some call the site—scene of one of the largest U.S. Army surrenders of the war.

After the battle, burial crews interred Union dead. Pack probably was among them. His remains rest today under a tombstone in the national cemetery in Murfreesboro, about a 40-minute drive east. Judson Austin survived a brief imprisonment in Richmond and the war.

On the battle's anniversary, I stand on a ridge above Thompson's Station. What an awe-inspiring scene. Hills and ridges stand out on a deep-blue canvas. A hawk soars above me.

Across Columbia Pike, in a rarely visited family graveyard deep in the woods, Alice Thompson rests under a canopy of black walnut trees and

---

13. Ibid

cedars. The graveyard is overgrown, choked by weeds and brush. The battle heroine died in 1870. Alice was barely 23. Below me is the field where Pack and Roderick fell and where Judson watched his brother die.

"I hope I never shal be called to witness another such seen," he wrote.

Some say other "Packs" remain buried here, forgotten like this Middle Tennessee battlefield.

A 25-minute drive south, in a farmer's field with two giant, gnarly ginkgo trees, once stood a magnificent mansion owned by Confederate officers.

What might I find there beneath the deep-brown Tennessee earth?

CHAPTER 12

Ashwood, Tennessee

THE 'LOST' MANSION OF 'THE FIGHTING BISHOP'

"**B**ring your boots."

After a rainy stretch in Middle Tennessee, farmer Campbell Ridley suggests proper footwear the day before our visit to the site of Ashwood Hall, once the magnificent plantation home of Confederate Lt. Gen. Leonidas Polk and his brother Andrew, also a Rebel officer.

For two decades, Ridley—a widower in his early 80s—has farmed land where Ashwood Hall once stood. His farm shop stands a musket shot from the antebellum Clifton Place mansion of Confederate Brig. Gen. Gideon Pillow, his ancestor. Nearby, yards from a small, rickety bridge over the east fork of Greenlick Creek, stand four original slave cabins from Pillow's era.

Ridley family roots run deep in the rural area 40 miles south of Nashville.

"About seven generations of my family have lived out here," the U.S. Army vet says.

Campbell's grandfather—who relished eating hog brains—once owned Clifton Place, too. In nearby Columbia, the self-proclaimed "Mule Capital of the World," Ridley's aunt Sarah Ann became the first Mule Day queen, a high honor.

But I'm not here for mules. I'm here for the mansion—or what little remains of it—and to commune with the spirit of Leonidas Polk, whom Union artillery nearly sliced in two at Pine Mountain, Georgia on June 14, 1864.

On a fall day in 1874, a caretaker of the Ashwood Hall mansion tried to determine the origin of a roaring sound. Frantic, he grabbed an axe, climbed atop the mansion and slashed through the tin, resin and gravel roof.

Then "a terrible flame leapt out like a wild beast released from prison."[1]

A blaze raced through the mansion, once one of the handsomest country residences in Tennessee. Rebecca Polk—owner of the uninsured home and Andrew Polk's widow—reportedly was roaming Europe with her daughters. Except for a young man's "fine shotgun," responders rescued most valuables from the flames.[2] The cause of the fire, which reportedly smoldered for two weeks, apparently was a defective chimney flue.[3]

No one rebuilt glorious Ashwood Hall.

Joined by Maury County archivist Tom Price, we trudge through a field of corn cobs and broken stalks to the Ashwood Hall site—about five miles from downtown Columbia, the county seat. Behind us spring peepers make a racket in a marsh along Old Zion Road. From the rise about 200 yards from Mount Pleasant Pike—a wartime route used by both armies—we see in the distance the slave-constructed St. John's Episcopal Church. It's the plantation chapel completed in 1842 under the direction of Leonidas Polk and three of his other brothers, George, Lucius and Rufus.

Before the war, North Carolina-born Leonidas Polk held various roles in the Episcopal Church, including Bishop of Louisiana. "[H]is zeal, intelligence and devotion to his sacred calling give promise of extensive usefulness," a Philadelphia newspaper wrote of that appointment.[4] When the war broke out Polk—who hoped for a peaceful separation from the Union—offered his services to the Confederacy.

In June 1861, Confederate president Jefferson Davis, Polk's West Point roommate, commissioned him as a major general. A Northern

---

1. *The Herald and Mail*, Columbia, Tenn., Nov. 6, 1874

2. Ibid

3. *The Tennessean*, Nashville, Nov. 4, 1874

4. *Niles National Register*, St. Louis, Mo., Nov. 6, 1841

correspondent described Polk—who became known as "The Fighting Bishop"—as "a rigid disciplinarian" and a man who "sits up o' nights to perfect himself in military tactics."[5]

But Polk blundered early in the war by ordering the occupation of Columbus, Kentucky, violating the state's neutrality.

"Bandits and traitors," a Louisville newspaper called Polk's soldiers afterward.[6]

In November 1861, a massive "Lady Polk" cannon—named for the bishop's wife—exploded during a demonstration, killing at least seven soldiers and tearing off the general's clothes.[7]

Polk might be best remembered for quarreling with his superior, irascible Army of Tennessee commander Braxton Bragg, who called him "unfit for executing the plans of others."

My favorite Polk anecdote comes from off the battlefields. At a christening for a slave's child at St. John's Church, he asked the young mother, "Name this child."

"Lucy, sir."

"That's no fit name for a child!" bellowed the hard-of-hearing bishop, who thought the slave said "Lucifer."

Polk baptized the girl "John."[8]

Before the war, Maury County was the state's wealthiest county. The Polk brothers owned enormous, adjacent plantations—George, Rattle and Snap; Lucius, Hamilton Place; Rufus, West Brook; and Leonidas, Ashwood Hall. Only the Rattle and Snap and Hamilton Place mansions remain.

Of the four plantations, Ashwood Hall may have been the most impressive. "[S]urrounded by one of the most fertile and magnificent farms of which the new world can boast," a local newspaper wrote of it.[9] Leonidas and his wife, Frances Ann, furnished the mansion with pricey pieces shipped from such far-flung places as Philadelphia and New York.

---

5. *Cincinnati Daily Press*, Oct. 23, 1861

6. *The Courier-Journal*, Louisville, Ky., Sept. 14, 1861

7. *The Louisville Daily Journal*, Nov. 20. 1861

8. "Ashwood: The Polks and the Pillows," Richard Hilary Quin thesis, Middle Tennessee State University, 1992

9. *The Herald and Mail*, Columbia, Tenn., Nov. 6, 1874

Farmer Campbell Ridley, standing under the limbs of a massive gingko tree at the Ashwood Hall site, is a direct descendant of Confederate Brig. Gen. Gideon Pillow.

In 1845, Leonidas—a second cousin of President James K. Polk—sold Ashwood Hall to his younger brother, Andrew, who greatly expanded the two-story residence. It included one-story wings, full-length windows, Corinthian columns, iron railings, a picture gallery, library and a billiard room. Plop the place in Beverly Hills today and no one would blink.

Unfortunately, I did not bring boots for our muddy trip to the site of Polk's palace. But I did bring my imagination. I can picture Ashwood Hall's once-exquisite grounds—the well-manicured lawns, the greenhouses and the orchards filled with fruit trees. The Polks even employed an English gardener.

I can imagine the iron gates swinging from massive stone pillars sur-mounted by inverted carved stone acorns—the Polk family symbol. Rare animals roamed the grounds.

During the war, Andrew Polk—a captain in the 1st Tennessee Cavalry—instructed soldiers in his Maury County Braves on the plantation. Gen. Earl Van Dorn set foot in the mansion. So did Army of Tennessee commander John Bell Hood, who briefly used Ashwood Hall as a headquarters before the Battle of Franklin in late 1864.

In spring 1862, Union Gen. Don Carlos Buell's soldiers marched past Ashwood Hall en route to Shiloh. The manion's occupants may have heard the Yankees blowing on the organ pipes they had swiped from St. John's Church.

The only tangible evidence we find of Ashwood Hall are scattered pieces of brick and stone; a decrepit building that may have been the mansion's kitchen; a railroad spike-like rod perhaps used for construction; and two massive ginkgo trees imported eons ago by the Polks from Japan. They each measure about 15 feet around.

Ridley chuckles as I examine the gnarly monsters, Ashwood Hall relics that have survived for at least 170 years.

"You like them, don't you?" he says.

The trees might be as close as I'm ever going to get to communing with the bishop.

Although we find little evidence of the mansion, much may remain underground from the plantation era. With Ridley's permission to hunt the private property, local relic hunters have uncovered scores of artifacts—a water pump with an 1854 patent date; broken pieces of dishes; a bronze piano foot; a gorgeous, decorative female figurine; an ornate wind-up key for a clock; the top of a champagne or wine bottle inlaid with gold; and a metal tag inscribed with Andrew Polk's name. They have even unearthed a bucket full of burnt relics, undoubtedly from the mansion.

My favorite relic hunter find is a bronze tag with "Leonidas Polk" and "Raleigh, N.C." inscribed on it in cursive writing. The detectorist speculates it belonged to Polk at West Point, where he roomed with fellow cadet Albert Sidney Johnston, who later became Army of Tennessee commander. (At Shiloh on April 6, 1862, he bled to death from a bullet wound to his right knee.)

A fire destroyed magnificent Ashwood Hall in 1874. Tennessee Library and Archives

More treasure may rest underneath the farm field—perhaps even the communion set Leonidas used at St. John's Church.

Of course, the Yankees figure prominently in Ashwood Hall's story, too. A relic hunter discovered a mangled Federal box plate on the grounds. But he hasn't found Andrew Polk's silver—if any of it is still out here.

Eager to keep the treasure out of Federal hands, Polk and a family slave hid the silver somewhere on the Ashwood Hall grounds. When rampaging U.S. Army soldiers found out, they demanded a slave tell them where. When he refused, the Yankees held the man's son—"about four years old," according to an account—over a well. The slave's repeated refusal apparently almost led to tragedy.

Leonidas Polk, "The Fighting Bishop."
Collections of the Alabama Department of Archives and History

"[H]orrible to relate," according to a diary of one of Polk's relations, "they dropped it & in the agony of the moment the unfortunate father gratified their cupidity! One of the number caught the child, it is true, after it had fallen out of the father's sight in the well curb, but the effect on him was the same as tho they had killed it."[10]

Damn Yankees. No word if the Federals landed the loot.

During the war, Union soldiers stripped Ashwood Hall of livestock, horses, fences and crops. But Andrew Polk, who had been seriously wounded early in the war, got a measure of revenge thanks to his beautiful, quick-thinking daughter, Antoinette.

On July 13, 1863, 15-year-old Antoinette Polk—who had been visiting cousins in Columbia—dashed on the Mount Pleasant Pike astride her thoroughbred, Shiloh. (Apparently, she didn't pay the toll road fare.) The skilled rider's aim: Race to Ashwood Hall to warn Confederate soldiers of the Yankees' presence in Columbia. Three Union soldiers chased her on horseback.

The cavalrymen dug their spurs into their horses' sides, straining to catch up with Antoinette. But she reached the mansion ahead of the Federals, roused the Rebels and nearly fainted astride Shiloh, whose clenched bit turned his mouth into a bloody mass of foam.[11]

The soldiers at Ashwood Hall avoided capture—or worse.

Mission accomplished, Antoinette.

For her bravery, Confederate Gen. Nathan Bedford Forrest gave the teen a flag captured from Union Colonel Abel Streight's brigade in 1863.

After the war, the Confederate heroine traveled to Europe, where the "beauty and belle" became a "great favorite of the Italians." Her riding exploits remained renowned.

"[S]he is a beautiful rider, fearless," according to an 1872 letter.[12]

In 1877, Antoinette married a French nobleman, becoming Baroness De Charette. When she met a group of soldiers from Tennessee on leave in France during World War I, the baroness told the doughboys: "I am going to kiss every one of you." She often entertained soldiers at her chateau.[13]

---

10. "Ashwood: The Polks and the Pillows"

11. *The Fort Wayne (Ind.) Journal-Gazette*, June 3, 1917

12. *The (Nashville) Tennessean*, May 28, 1950

13. *The Herald and Mail*, Columbia, Tenn. Feb. 28, 1919

"She felt, no doubt," a Tennessee newspaper wrote after the baroness's death in 1919, "that in ministering to these men she was but performing another chapter in that romantic career that began more than half a century ago when she outrode a squad of Federal troops from Columbia to Ashwood and prevented the capture of Confederate soldiers billeted in the palatial home of her father, Ashwood Hall."[14]

Just imagine the splendor of the place.

But it's time for me to put the gnarly ginkgos and remnants of a wartime mansion in the rear-view mirror. Mrs. B and I are going to Philadelphia, where our vacation could easily get steered toward the Civil War.

---

14. Ibid

CHAPTER 13

Philadelphia, Pennsylvania

MY VERY OWN
'PHILLY SPECIAL'

One of my great joys is sneaking historical side trips into family vacations, often to Mrs. B's dismay. Over four vacation days in Philadelphia, where Meredith, the younger of our two adult daughters resides, I somehow sneak in several. Let's call it my very own "Philly Special."

Massed forces fired at each other on Philadelphia battlefields during the Revolutionary War, but none did from 1861-65. Gritty Philadelphia does, however, have close connections to the Civil War.

Thousands of soldiers encamped in Philadelphia or received care in hospitals in the city, whose factories churned out munitions for the U.S. war effort. For two of the Civil War's most famous generals, Philadelphia was the end of the line.

In 1872, former Army of the Potomac commander George Meade— "Old Snapping Turtle"—died in a house on Delancey Street, now one of the city's toniest neighborhoods. In Philadelphia's vast Laurel Hill Cemetery, the general rests in a modest family plot on a bluff overlooking the Schuylkill River, a quarter mile from the grave of native John Pemberton, the Confederate lieutenant general.

On July 4, 1863, Pemberton surrendered Vicksburg, thus earning
the contempt of thousands of white Southerners. Sid Champion V, my
Mississippi "psychotic connection," as you may remember, had nothing
good to say about Pemberton, who died in 1881 and supposedly loathed
reminiscing about the Civil War.

While Mrs. B and Meredith—Daughter 2B—remain in the car, I visit the
generals at Laurel Hill. It's an outdoor museum, really, and the final resting
place for 38 other Civil War generals and hundreds of their comrades.

I loathe idleness, especially while on vacation, so I also persuade
Mrs. B and 2B to join me on a sojourn to South Philly, where no sane
person should remove a chair placed by a local to save a parking spot. On
Passyunk Street stands Pat's King of Steaks, a tourist trap where you can
get a cheesesteak with sweet peppers for 14 bucks and indigestion on the
side gratis.

But I'm mostly interested, of course, in what happened in this neighborhood during the Civil War.

At the corner of Reed and 10th Streets, one of the war's forgotten tragedies played out. About 8:45 on the morning of March 29, 1862, gunpowder
and cartridges ignited in Professor Samuel Jackson's fireworks-turned-
munitions factory. Many of the 78 factory workers, mostly women and
girls, never had a chance to escape the explosion and subsequent conflagra-
tion. In the war's first munitions factory accident involving a major loss of
life, 18 employees died while dozens suffered from burns or other injuries.

The scene was as ghastly as any following a Civil War battle.

"Heads, legs and arms were hurled through the air, and in some
instances were picked up hundreds of feet from the scene," a witness
recalled. "Portions of flesh, brains, limbs, entrails, etc. were found in the
yards of houses, on roofs and in the adjacent streets."[1]

While Mrs. B and Meredith absorb South Philly ambience elsewhere, I
explore the neighborhood near where the factory once stood. It's a quint-
essential Philly 'hood of three-story brick rowhouses, first-floor flower
window boxes and narrow streets marred by potholes.

Outside a rowhouse, I approach a 50ish man with gray hair and a
broom. While he sweeps his walk, I pepper him with questions about the

---

1. *Philadelphia Inquirer*, March 31, 1862

neighborhood. Then he stops and turns aside and gestures with his head toward the second floor above a store across the street.

"They deal drugs up there," he says in a low voice.

He tells me this South Philly area is a working-class, diverse and unpretentious.

"Italians, recent Central America immigrants, hardcore liberals and Republicans," he says.

"Rugged elegance."

On 10th Street, a ballfield dedicated in memory of a local physician occupies ground once part of a massive cemetery. In the 1940s, workers disinterred most of the bodies—including those of Civil War veterans—for reburial elsewhere. But the contractor who did the grisly work botched the job, leaving remains behind. So, there's no telling what might be under the pitcher's mound.

In "Little Saigon" on 9th Street, a short walk from Pat's King of Steaks, chickens meet their maker at Shun Da Market. Online reviews of the live poultry market range from awful ("I can't stand to walk by that place") to horrendous ("smells like shit"). I'm not feeling a Civil War vibe.

At the corner of 10th and Reed, Jackson's factory site, stands a three-story building with a drab bar occupying the ground floor. A goofy, six-foot-tall painting of "Gritty," the Philadelphia Flyers' mascot, adorns an outside wall. Before I go inside, a historical marker directly across the street beckons.

At gloomy, castle-like Moyamensing prison on May 7, 1896, a hangman executed H.H. Holmes. "Considered America's first serial killer," the historical marker says. "Take your time about it," Holmes had told his executioner, "you know I'm in no hurry."[2] Decades earlier, Edgar Allan Poe, the famous horror writer, supposedly slept off a bender at Moyamensing. A supermarket and parking lot occupy the ground of the former prison today.

In 1862, the explosion at Jackson's factory sent its female superintendent of children hurtling across the street into Moyamensing's thick, outer wall. The woman survived, losing the $60 in gold she carried. As it turned out, she was among the lucky employees. Three of her children, all employed in the factory, suffered severe burns.[3]

2. *The Philadelphia Times*, May 8, 1896

3. *Philadelphia Inquirer*, March 31, 1862

No historical marker memorializes the tragedy, which was major news in 1862.

Seeking answers, I meet Mrs. B and Meredith at the corner bar. While they eat chicken wings, I ask anyone who will listen what they know about what happened on this very spot in 1862. For me, at least, it's surreal to see patrons nursing beers and cocktails at the site of the catastrophe.

On my iPhone, I show a newspaper illustration of the explosion to a waitress and a woman with orange-tinted hair and a nose ring. I get mostly confused looks, not unlike the ones Mrs. B gives me when she spots a hunk of battlefield "witness tree" in my car trunk. No one seems to know a thing about the explosion.

"You know, this place had a weird, vacant bar vibe before it became the tavern," the waitress tells me.

I'm depressed but not finished with Philadelphia. I've also set up a rendezvous with a docent at a museum in Northeast Philly that features the mounted head of Old Baldy, Meade's favorite horse.

Pardon the digression, but here's a confession: I have a "thing" about Civil War horses. Three million horses and mules toiled during the war—moving artillery and other equipment, carrying soldiers into battle and helping deliver messages, among many other duties. As many as half may have died. They're the war's unsung heroes.

One of my favorite horse stories involves Dixie Bill, a bay ridden by a U.S. Army brigade commander from Iowa named Sylvester Hill. At the Battle of Nashville on December 15, 1864, the 44-year-old colonel led an attack on Redoubt No. 3. Its meager, ivy-covered remains are behind a Methodist church in the heart of urban schlock south of downtown. I've visited the site a half-dozen times—once inadvertently pulling my car into an outdoor Sunday service in the church parking lot during the height of COVID.

During the morning assault, Hill suffered a mortal wound—the third soldier to die in battle while riding Dixie Bill. Soldiers thought the horse "became hoodoo"—jinxed, in other words.[4] The 35th Iowa chaplain acquired Dixie Bill, taking the outcast home to Iowa, where the horse was treated like a king until his death in 1881.

---

4. *Muscatine (Iowa) New-Tribune*, Oct. 12, 1906

In the backyard of his house in Des Moines, the chaplain gave his beloved horse a military funeral. Dozens of Civil War veterans attended. "[G]reater sorrow could not have been felt from a human being than was felt by a number of people over the death of the faithful old steed," an Iowa newspaper wrote.[5]

After narrowing the location of Dixie Bill's burial, I sent Russell, the Des Moines-based brother of my brother-in-law, on a bicycle scouting mission. But his exploration to confirm Dixie Bill's burial site proved fruitless.

"Sketchy house, sketchy neighbors, lots of pit bulls and a Rottweiler to make a cyclist uncomfortable," Russell reported. "Three tough-looking guys staring me down. Pretty sure they thought I was just a stray crazy guy."

Days later, a Hill descendant told me Dixie Bill was probably buried under an interstate instead of in that "sketchy" neighborhood. I didn't have the heart to break the news to Russell.

Am I about to join this "stray crazy guy" club in Philadelphia?

In one of the sketchiest parts of the city, Mrs. B and Meredith accompany me to the Grand Army of the Republic Civil War Museum on Griscom Street. It has Old Baldy's head in its vast collection. But my white-knuckle drive through the rough neighborhood is not going well. The museum is housed in a large, late 18th-century mansion once used by the Sons of Union Veterans of the Civil War.

"Settle down. No one is looking at you," says Mrs. B, my co-pilot. In the back seat, 2B taunts me with chuckles and silence.

The fictional severed horse-head-in-the-bed scene in *The Godfather* in 1972 haunted me throughout my childhood. But this decapitated horse story is 100 percent true. Someone *really* cut off the noggin of Old Baldy— while the animal was dead, of course. Then, as the story goes, his front hooves became inkstands.

Old Baldy took a beating during the war, suffering as many as a dozen wounds. In 1864, fearing the enfeebled, battle-scarred horse would become an embarrassment on future campaigns, Meade sent Old Baldy home from Virginia to Pennsylvania.[6]

---

5. *The Muscatine (Iowa) Journal*, Oct. 17, 1906

6. The George Meade Society of Philadelphia, Meade letter to Captain Sam Ringwalt, Sept. 24, 1864

After the war, the horse—beloved by veterans, too—marched in parades and in the November 1872 funeral procession for his Meade through Philadelphia. Before his death, the general gave the charger to a blacksmith named John Davis. Meade's conditions: Never sell Old Baldy into servitude, and when his quality of life deteriorated significantly, put him out of his misery humanely.

Old Baldy, believed to be about 30, was dispatched on December 16, 1882, with two ounces of cyanide of potash and a pint of vinegar poured down his throat.

"Not a word was spoken," wrote a local reporter, who witnessed Old Baldy's demise. "True, it was only a dumb animal that was about to stagger, fall and die beneath the deadly action of the potent drug. Yet the mind would conjure up a widely different scene in which Baldy, gay in the trappings of war, with proudly arched neck, heaving flanks and panting nostrils bore amid the clashing of sabers and the hot fire of musketry, the Hero of Gettysburg—Pennsylvania's noblest son!"[7]

Then things really turned weird.

With Davis' blessing, two Civil War veterans from a local Grand Army of the Republic chapter exhumed the horse's remains around Christmas Day 1882 on the blacksmith's farm, cutting off his head. For display at the post, they had the nag's noggin stuffed and "very tastefully" mounted on a large plaque, which included the name of each battle in which Old Baldy received his wounds.[8]

In 1958, decades after the last vet died, the post's vast Civil War collection found a home at the mansion on Griscom Street. Old Baldy's head and a section of the bloodstained pillow from Abraham's Lincoln's death bed were among the leading attractions.

In the early 1980s, the Grand Army of the Republic Civil War Museum loaned Old Baldy's remains to another museum in the city. The head remained popular.

---

7. *Public Spirit*, Jenkintown, Pa., Dec. 23, 1882

8. Meade Post #1, Grand Army of the Republic in Philadelphia minutes, Feb. 26, 1883

The display case for Old Baldy's mounted head is "filled with gasses," my Philadelphia-based daughter reports. That sounds ominous. Meredith Banks and Thomas Lantz

'S
E.
OUNDED –
ettysburg,
July 3rd. 1863.
– RIBS. –
Weldon R.R.
Aug. 25th. 1864.
Struck by 12 lb.
pent Shell.
Dec. 16th. 82.
30 YEARS.
A.R

"If my wife could take anything home in the museum, including me, it would be Old Baldy," the museum curator said in 1995.[9]

Old Baldy's stuffed head, however, was so heavy that it pulled plaster from the wall. So, the museum had the remains placed in a reinforced steel display case. Meade's descendants occasionally showed up to visit the ragged remains.[10]

When that museum closed in 2008, it wasn't eager to part with Old Baldy. After some behind-the-scenes wrangling, the Grand Army of the Republic

Old Baldy's preserved hoof. Was it used as an inkwell? Old York Road Historical Society, Jenkintown, Pa.

Civil War Museum on Griscom Street got the horse head back. But as crime increased in Northeast Philly, visitation at the museum plunged to a trickle.

"When you get here, park around the side," a museum docent texts me before my visit.

We drive slowly past the museum, the first one I've seen with bars on its windows. Parking in a narrow, fenced-in driveway seems problematic. Civil War adventuring requires boldness, but I surrender without a fight. I text the docent a lame excuse.

Good-bye, Old Baldy. See you someday at a new museum in a safer area of Northeast Philly.[11]

We're outta here.

Alas, word now will filter to the masses: *Civil War adventurer chickens out of opportunity to inspect head of Old Snapping Turtle's favorite horse.*

What a trip—even if ends in failure.

---

9. *Philadelphia Inquirer*, May 21, 1995

10. Ibid

11. In late 2021, the museum sold a rare U.S. Colored Troops flag for nearly $200,000 to help purchase a smaller museum building in nearby Holmesburg, a neighborhood in Northeast Philadelphia. The museum re-opened at the new site in Philadelphia in 2022.

I offer a silent toast:

Here's to you, Dixie Bill and Old Baldy. May no one ever rein in your earthly spirits.

Perhaps the only victory for me in this sordid tale is tracking down one of Old Baldy's hooves, which allegedly were turned into inkstands. One is in the collection of a historical society in Jenkintown, Pennsylvania.

"I'm a horse person, but I can't tell if it's a right or left hoof," a museum spokesperson later tells me. The other forehoof is lost in the mists of time.

For Mrs. B and Meredith, this is the end of their historical side trips for now. But not for me. I am heading to West Virginia to walk in the footsteps of one of my Civil War heroes.

CHAPTER 14

Shepherdstown, West Virginia

IN THE FOOTSTEPS OF
A CIVIL WAR BADASS

Achy and tired following a long drive from Philly, I slump into a metal chair outside the Sweet Shop Bakery in Shepherdstown, a quaint college town astride the Potomac River. As an old journalist pal of mine might say, I look like 40 miles of bad road. On an exterior brick wall of the bakery, a plaque says the late 18th-century building was used as a wartime hospital. Inside it's surreal to see eclairs, oatmeal cookies, pastries and other delights for sale where Rebel surgeons amputated limbs in September 1862.

Four miles northeast, across the Potomac River, is Sharpsburg, Maryland, site of the Antietam battlefield, where the armies clashed in the war's deadliest single-day battle on September 17, 1862. Less than a mile away, in Elmwood Cemetery, rest dozens of Confederate dead from Antietam and Shepherdstown—the final battles of Robert E. Lee's Maryland Campaign. Shepherdstown was part of Virginia in 1862 and part of my life in 1981, when I toiled as a rookie journalist for a small newspaper nearby.

Two sips into a hot cup of Colombian, a helmet-clad man on a whirring, humming Segway rolls up, looking like he means business.

Part-time parking enforcement officer Stephen Alemar operates his Segway near a building that served as a Confederate hospital in Shepherdstown.

CIVIL WAR HOSPITAL SITE
✚
MOULDER HALL

Was used as a hospital during
The Maryland Campaign 1862
PRIVATE PROPERTY
courtesy of S.H.A.F.

10

CIRCA
1791

"Are you John Banks?"

"Yes."

Visions of Paul Blart in *Mall Cop* swirl in my brain.

"I'm Steve Alemar."

He's just the man I want to see.

Alemar, the late 60ish, part-time parking enforcement officer in Shepherdstown (population about 1,800), is president of the Shepherdstown Battlefield Preservation Association. He has secured permission for me to visit privately owned battleground outside town, where Gen. A.P. Hill's soldiers routed a U.S. Army brigade on a bluff and fields above the Potomac. My goal is to walk in the footsteps of 118th Pennsylvania Lieutenant Lemuel Crocker, a badass whose heroics at the Battle of Shepherdstown on September 20-21, 1862, should be legendary and more widely known.

In his six years on the parking enforcement gig, Alemar has seen a little bit of everything—flashers, drunks, bottle throwers and other belligerents. A skin cancer survivor ("508 stitches in my face"), he uses the Segway because he has a heart condition and a right knee replacement. I am tempted to ask for a spin on the thing, but there's a battlefield for me to see. We agree to meet in 90 minutes on River Road, at historical markers near the ruins of wartime cement mill buildings along the Potomac River.

Before I depart, I order another cup of joe in the Sweet Shop Bakery. Of course I ask the woman behind the counter whether she knows about the bloody past of the bakery building. It's my silly attempt to give her the willies, an act for which I'd receive an instant reprimand from Mrs. B if she were here.

"My own house is haunted here, so it doesn't really bother me," she says.

And then I am off.

I have advanced on Shepherdstown from all directions over the decades—by car from my home in Martinsburg, West Virginia to cover football games at Shepherd University as a cub newspaperman long ago; by bike from the Antietam battlefield; and by wading the Potomac from the Maryland side of the river, an exhilarating experience if one knows how to swim and can keep an iPhone from plunging into the murky water.

In the early 1980s, a newspaper pal and I used my cheap metal detector to scour a Shepherdstown hillside for battle relics. We unearthed an impressive haul of pull tabs from beer and soda cans but no bullets, bayonets or belt buckles.

From the late 1990s to the 2010s, a local I know—let's call him "Relic Man"—recovered hundreds of artifacts from the battlefield and 50-some Federal artillery shells in the Potomac River. Those beasts were so heavy that it's no wonder they remained in place until Relic Man and his pals discovered them.

"There were days when I'd park along the river and just disappear into the woods and come out at dark with piles of stuff," he told me. With his buddies, Relic Man would eat pizza among the riverside ruins—"It was a big party area in those days," he said—and eyeball case shot and artillery shell fragments on the ground.

Like John Buford at Gettysburg, I scout the ground along River Road, not for battle relics, but to get the lay of the land. Oh my, what a treacherous place this was for Crocker and the rookie 118th Pennsylvania, the Philadelphia-raised "Corn Exchange" regiment. "A sad and purposeless affair, with a most disastrous and fatal termination," a 118th Pennsylvania regimental historian called the U.S. Army's defeat.[1]

To my front is the steep, craggy bluff over which a few 118th Pennsylvania soldiers plunged to their deaths as they hastily retreated. In the heat of battle, some Pennsylvanians discovered that they had been issued defective Enfield muskets, compounding the regiment's misery. Others huddled along the river by the Boteler's Cement Mill kilns, where friendly artillery fire from the Maryland side of the Potomac wreaked havoc among them.

In the distance behind me, about 15 yards away, flows the Potomac. Barely in view, between a stand of trees, stretch the remains of an old mill dam. As 46-year-old William Madison of the 118th Pennsylvania made his escape across it, Confederates peppered him with five shots, including one that shattered his jaw.

---

1. *History of the Corn Exchange Regiment, 118th Pennsylvania Volunteers, from their first engagement at Antietam to Appomattox*, Compiled by John L. Smith. Philadelphia: J.L. Smith Publishers, 1888, Page 71

"He vented his anger in a frightful howl," according to the regimental history, "and facing squarely about gave his enemies the last shot he ever fired in the army, for his wounds terminated his service, but not his life."[2]

Crocker, a burly 33-year-old with a big, bushy beard, had made his own hasty retreat across the slippery mill dam to the Maryland side of the Potomac. Two hours later, 20 Pennsylvanians—10 wounded and 10 "whose courage had given out"—remained on the Virginia side of the dam.[3]

No inducement from Crocker or any other Union soldier could lure them across. So the lieutenant borrowed a revolver, removed his field officer's jacket and under the cover of soldiers on the Maryland side, recrossed the river by himself. He brought every man to safety except for the wounded and dead men on the bluff.

The next morning, Crocker pleaded with his colonel, the brigade commander, for permission under a flag of truce to retrieve the remaining dead and wounded of the 118th Pennsylvania. The colonel sent the request up to the Fifth Corps commander, Maj. Gen. Fitz John Porter. His answer: *Forget it. No truce.* But the headstrong lieutenant had other ideas.

In one of the ballsiest moves of the war, Crocker—dressed in his full officer's uniform and carrying a sword and pistol—recrossed the river. Then he began his mercy mission.

"Bravery beyond my comprehension," another officer in the regiment recalled.[4]

One by one, Crocker carried bodies to the Virginia riverbank. He was in the process of carrying another man over his shoulder when an aide to Porter commanded his attention.

Stop and return at once, he said, *or a battery will open fire to persuade you.*

"Shell and be damned," shouted Crocker.

Crocker was returning for a seriously wounded comrade when a Confederate general, accompanied by his staff, approached the lieutenant.

---

2. Ibid

3. Crocker's account of battle in letter to parents, Sept. 22, 1862, published in *The Advocate*, Buffalo, N.Y., Oct. 2, 1862

4. Donaldson, Francis Adams, *Inside the Army of the Potomac: The Civil War Experience of Captain Francis Adams Donaldson*, ed. J. Gregory Acken, Mechanicsburg, Pa: Stackpole Books, 1998, Page 139

The general's aide asked Crocker what the hell he was doing. No truce had been called after all.

"I come in the cause of humanity," said Crocker, covered with dirt and blood. "If you are human, let my mission proceed."[5]

How long have you been in the army? the general asked.

"Twenty days," replied Crocker.

"I thought so," the general replied.

Sympathetic to Crocker, the general pointed to a boat on the shore that he could use, posted cavalry to protect him and let him go about his grim work.[6]

Lemuel Crocker, my hero. Ronn Palm collection

Two days after the battle, Crocker described his harrowing battle experience in a letter to his parents.

"As we got to the river-side we had to go near a half a mile to a dam over which our men were attempting to cross; and to make this dam many a man lost his life, as the rebels were stationed on the bluff taking deliberate aim during the whole fight," Crocker wrote.

"I was cool and collected during my travel by the riverside," he continued, "but when I reach[ed] this dam, I think my cheek blanched, for it seemed to me certain death to cross it, as the rebels had got into a large brick building below the dam, and the main body above on the bluff, picking off our poor fellows."[7]

Ravaged by time, nature and graffiti, that brick building used by Rebel soldiers as cover still stands.

In the end, Crocker received nothing more than a reprimand for disobeying a general's order. How could Fitz John Porter punish such a brave soldier?

---

5. *The Buffalo Advocate*, Oct. 2, 1862

6. *History of the Corn Exchange Regiment*, Page 77

7. *The Advocate*, Buffalo, N.Y., Oct. 2, 1862

The ruins of a wartime building along the banks of the Potomac River. Confederate soldiers used the building as cover while shooting at 118th Pennsylvania soldiers.

On this muggy afternoon, I'm eager to see what Crocker saw in 1862. I'm also eager to avoid the bears, coyotes and snakes that are said to lurk in the woods on my route to the top of the bluff.

Minutes after examining ground along the river saved by the Shepherdstown Battlefield Preservation Association, Alemar arrives on River Road in his black truck. Only a few cars pass by us on this relatively remote stretch of road. In the distance, near a trail toward the bluff, a deer bounds through the woods.

"I used to love to come here," he says. "It's so peaceful."

Alemar tells me about remains of Confederate artillery emplacements in the woods. We discuss non-Civil War topics, too—his mom worked as a secretary for FBI director J. Edgar Hoover; his dad served with the Office of Strategic Services, the precursor to the CIA. Alemar, a former U.S. Postal Service employee, also served as a ranger for two years in the 1980s at the Vietnam Veterans Memorial in Washington. It was an especially moving experience because he is a Vietnam vet himself.

Alemar also recounts his own life-altering war experience. This man can relate to the disastrous and deadly circumstances that Crocker and his comrades had faced.

On October 1, 1972, Alemar was an 18-year-old sailor aboard the USS *Newport News* off the coast of South Vietnam. About 1 a.m., the 21,000-ton heavy cruiser's guns were firing on enemy targets when an eight-inch shell in the center gun of Turret 2 exploded, killing 20 and injuring 36 aboard. The battleship became a horror show of fire, thick green smoke and burning flesh.

Alemar, who was above Turret 2 when the disaster occurred, suffered a crushed ankle and from smoke inhalation. The memory of that awful day still cuts deeply for Alemar.

"Those things never go away," he says.

Armed with a Tennessee walking stick purchased at Fort Pillow, a new iPhone and curiosity, I eye my route through the woods to the bluff above the Potomac. Alemar offers instructions and insect repellent. There are ticks up there, too.

While Alemar returns to town in his truck, I make my way to the top, past the ruins of another giant kiln. Years ago, Relic Man discovered artillery shell fragments throughout this area. Near the top of the bluff, a snapped-off bayonet from the battle is said to remain in some nook or cranny.

After a few minutes, I reach the bluff, my heart pumping at 125-plus beats a minute. No other soul is in sight. Thankfully, no coyotes, bears or snakes lurk either—at least as far as I can tell. The panicked Pennsylvanians fled from this ground, now woods and tall grass. In the distance, across an open, rolling farm field, came A.P. Hill's boys in hot pursuit.

This may seem odd, but when I'm alone in a cemetery or on a battlefield, I try to commune with the spirits of long ago. If a bird circles overhead, that's a sign they know of my presence.

"Lemuel Crocker, where are you?"

A breeze rustles leaves in the trees. But no birds appear overhead. I don't hear a soft echo of long-ago musket fire, a rumble of cannon or the moans of wounded either. But I can imagine that hell.

"Crocker, where are you?"

After his death in Buffalo in 1885, apparently from a stroke, no mention appeared in a local newspaper of Lemuel Crocker's long-ago heroism. A respected businessman, "he was noted for his liberality, public spirit and kind-heartedness," an obituary noted. "He had many warm friends by whom his sudden taking off will be greatly deplored."[8]

As I lean against a post of a barbed-wire fence, I ponder one question: *How did Lemuel Crocker not receive a Medal of Honor?*

No soldier deserved one more.

And then I'm back on the road, rambling south. For me, the Civil War is about to become "Civil Weird."

8. *The Buffalo Commercial*, March 28, 1885

CHAPTER 15

Franklin, Tennessee

'HYPNO-HISTORY' AT A U.S. ARMY FORT

In the pre-dawn darkness, before I leave our Nashville home for a hypnosis session at a fort in Franklin, Tennessee, groggy Mrs. B delivers a warning and advice from underneath bed covers.

"Don't come back clucking like a chicken."

Then my very own Civil War Mission Control pauses for comedic effect.

"And wear pants."

The instigator of the hypnosis session is my friend Jack Richards, a 71-year-old retired attorney, part-time humorist/amateur poet and serious collector of rare Major League Baseball cards. He lives in Franklin, a short walk from the battlefield where John Bell Hood's Army of Tennessee made its doomed charge late in the afternoon of November 30, 1864.

Richards, a fellow Western Pennsylvanian, broached his mind-numbing idea via text one afternoon:

"We get to Fort Granger early in the day before any crowds. I bring folding chairs. We find a quiet place. We take 20-30 minutes and do a hypnotic session with an emphasis on what happened there in 1864. Want to meet there around 6:30 a.m. P.S.: I was a psych major at Penn State with an interest in hypnosis."

"Hell yes," I replied. "Let's do it."

A millisecond after sending the reply, I harbored doubts.

Firstly, "psych major" and "Penn State"? Seems sketchy.

Secondly, what if under deep hypnosis I babble about some transgressions from decades ago? At West Virginia University, I had helped friends of mine dangle a small person by his belt from an uppermost floor of a freshmen dorm. Will Mrs. B seek an annulment if she reads this?

Thirdly, what "crowds"? I've never spotted more than five people at a time at Fort Granger.

Throwing caution (and potentially 30 years of a rock-solid marriage) into the wind, I head to Franklin at 5:55 a.m. anyway.

This adventure, of course, doesn't fit the *modus operandi* of most of my Civil War road trips. Because it's not a journey of hundreds of miles, I don't pack a large cooler with a half-dozen peanut butter-and-jelly sandwiches, a half-dozen bottles of iced tea and a giant bag of red licorice. Nor do I toss hiking boots, three battlefield guides, a dozen pairs of underwear, two phone charging cords and a selfie stick into an overnight bag.

But I am armed with a reporter's notebook and pen, an iPhone and an open mind. I've seen hypnotism work on *Forensic Files* on TV, but will it work on me? I am a hypnosis rookie after all.

If Sid Champion V of Champion Hill battlefield renown is my psychotic connection, Richards is my ultimate Civil War connection. Every historically minded adventurer needs a friend like Jack, whose inner compass, like mine, usually points to "CW," for Civil War.

As we traveled toward Pulaski, Tennessee early one morning, destined for the obscure Anthony's Hill battlefield, Richards even incorporated Civil War and fast food into the same sentence.

"Do you think Hardee's has any connection to Confederate Lt. Gen. William Hardee?" he asked. At the time, we were passing one of those burger chain franchises in Spring Hill, Tennessee.

In Franklin alone, Richards and I have walked together into woods in a vain effort to find a spring used by the Union Army, climbed to the top of Roper's Knob in search of evidence of a wartime signal station, raised our cups of joe in salute to a "hidden" antebellum battlefield wall, visited a museum to peer into an iron casket of a Confederate officer and wondered where the Federals parked their mule teams along Franklin Pike.

Retired attorney Jack Richards, a part-time humorist, put me under hypnosis at Fort Granger.

Like my childhood pals in Western Pennsylvania, Richards has a rapier wit that he deploys liberally. But he often taps into his serious side by writing poetry. I'd never tell him this to his face, but he's pretty good. The Missing Soldiers Office in Washington, where famed Civil War nurse Clara Barton compiled information for loved ones about the fate of Union soldiers, served as his inspiration for this stanza:

> *Clara's stairs are long and steep*
> *They creak at every step*
> *They talk to me in voices past*
> *With tears that haunt me yet*

At 6:21 a.m., as I pull my car into the gravel parking lot at Fort Granger Park, poetry is the farthest thing from my mind. And the only voice I hear is inside my head: *Am I really at an earthen-walled Civil War fort at this ungodly hour?*

Fort Granger Park is a mini oasis of oaks, tall grass and mounds of earthworks amid suburban clutter in Franklin, 20 miles south of downtown Nashville. Franklin, population 80,000 with a bullet, is the seat of Williamson County, one of the country's wealthiest areas. Country music stars live here.

In 1860, 2,000 souls lived in Franklin, which included several churches and the Tennessee Female College—one of the country's few all-girls schools at the time. Three years later, after the U.S. Army had occupied Middle Tennessee, Yankee soldiers marveled at its beauty.

"As nice a little town as I have seen since I crossed the Ohio River," an Iowa soldier wrote, "and the most beautiful country surrounding I ever saw."[1]

In early 1863, Union engineers made plans for a fort on a ridge called Figeurs Bluff, 75 feet above the serpentine Harpeth River. The U.S. Army wanted to protect the vital Nashville & Decatur Railroad and prevent Confederates from roaming the area. No place offered a more commanding view of Franklin. To build it, the army had a vast source of labor besides soldiers: escaped slaves.

"It is astonishing to see the contraband coming in—drove after drove," a physician with the 98th Ohio wrote. "There are not less than five hundred runaway slaves in Gen. [Gordon] Granger's Corps. They, at an average of $500, would amount to a quarter of a million dollars. Our mess has one that sold for $1,700 a few years since."[2]

It was hardly surprising: Franklin served as the seat of Williamson County, where slaves outnumbered whites.[3]

Under guidance of engineers, hundreds of Black men and white soldiers worked 16-hour shifts at the fort. They constructed massive earthen walls perhaps as high as 14 feet, dug rifle pits and moats and felled trees and sharpened branches for defenses outside the walls, among scores of other tasks. Some Black laborers got stiffed on their pay by a white army officer.[4]

---

1. *Burlington (Iowa) Weekly Hawk-eye*, Oct. 22, 1864

2. *Belmont (Ohio) Chronicle*, April 9, 1863

3. In 1860, the county's population was 12,367 slaves and 11,415 whites ("Population of the United States in 1860: Tennessee," census.gov.)

4. Impressment of Black Laborers by Union Forces in Franklin; Senate Report Condition and Treatment of Colored Refugees, 38th Cong., 2d sess., S. Ex. Doc. 28 serial 1,209, Dec. 28, 1864

Sparing no effort, the U.S. Army outfitted the fort with powerful siege guns, field artillery, a powder magazine for 1,200 artillery rounds and a storehouse for 70,000 rations.[5]

"The strongest and finest fortifications in the department of the Cumberland," an observer wrote.[6]

Union bigwigs named the fort for Maj. Gen. Gordon Granger, a career U.S. Army officer, who, in 1863, delighted visitors by firing two shots from its monster Parrott gun into a tree more than a mile away.[7]

In April 1863, Confederate cavalry under Earl Van Dorn, the scoundrel, tested Fort Granger with no success. The following June, Nathan Bedford Forrest's cavalry got within several hundred yards before being pounded into submission by Fort Granger's guns. After his horsemen skedaddled away, "The Wizard of the Saddle" left behind more than a dozen of his dead.

"The citizens of Franklin ran up their rebel flags while the battle was on," a Union veteran recalled, "but when we marched through, chasing the Confederates, they took them in and ran up the stars and stripes."[8]

During the Battle of Franklin, U.S. Army artillery from Fort Granger crashed into brigades in William Loring's division on the Confederates' right flank, a little more than a mile away. Soldiers stationed at Fort Granger had the best, and one of the safest, vantage points of the nighttime fireworks on the plain below them.

"After sundown, the sparks of rifle fire and the lightning, thunder and groaning of the heavy cannons was splendid and awe-inspiring for the eye and ear," wrote a soldier in an Indiana battery.[9]

Lt. Gen. John Schofield himself—the U.S. Army commander at the Battle of Franklin—peered through field glasses to watch the awful spectacle from the fort. When the carnage had ended about 9 p.m., hundreds of dead, mostly Confederates, lay on the field.

5. Zimmerman, Mark, *Fortress Nashville: Pioneers, Engineers, Mechanics, Contrabands & Colored Troops*, Nashville: Zimco Publications LLC, 2022, Page 154

6. Ibid

7. *The Nashville Daily Union*, Aug. 23, 1863

8. *Alton (Ill.) Evening Telegraph*, Aug. 7, 1909

9. Fout, Frederick, *The Darkest Days of the Civil War, 1864 and 1865*, English translation of Fout's 1902 *Die Schwersten Tage des Bürgerkriegs*, 1864-1865

Jack Richards walks between the massive earthen walls of the fort.

Beyond Fort Granger Park today are a patchwork of neighborhoods composed of 21st-century apartments, 1960s ranch-style houses, newer two-story homes and retail. A railroad line that follows the wartime route slices through the area. It's impossible to imagine today, but a tent city for as many as 10,000 men—infantry, cavalry, sutlers, and more—dominated the surrounding landscape during the war.

Decades afterward, time, nature and neglect conspired against Fort Granger, which became a haven for campers and hobos. In the late 20th century, Franklin made what remained of the fort a 14.5-acre park. A boardwalk cuts across the grounds, leading to stairs and a stony ridge and boulder-laden path that points visitors toward the Harpeth River, another city park, and flourishing downtown Franklin beyond. A Union soldier is said to have carved an eagle into the limestone cliff along the river, but I've never found it.

No hobos or any other humans are in sight when Richards and I drop our lawn chairs in a field near the middle of the fort. I plop into a flimsy seat, my back facing the remains of the sally port—the old entrance to the fort. Undulating ground to my left is the only hint that a powder magazine once occupied the grounds. Behind Richards towering oaks sprout from earthworks and their thick carpeting of grass and scrub. Sunlight bursts through the morning haze, revealing blue sky and birds.

"Relax," Richards tells me in a soothing voice. "Put this on."

He sounds like a DJ on a classical music station.

Then Richards offers his guinea pig/hypnotic subject a green-and-white checkered bandana for a blindfold.

I envision an early rising fort walker thinking, "Why is the man in a lawn chair holding that other man hostage at 6:35 a.m.?"

The next 25 minutes are a haze of hypnotic suggestions and historical tidbits.

"Tune out everything," Richards says.

"Concentrate on my voice."

"Focus on your feet."

"Focus on your knees."

And then come words that make me feel especially queasy: "Focus on your thighs. They are the biggest part of our bodies, and we rarely think about them."

Oh, Lord.

I nod off into some strange netherworld. You'd probably feel the same if you drank several cheap beers, burned lots of incense and watched *The Twilight Zone* on Netflix in a darkened room.

"Union troops hanged two Confederate spies here on June 9, 1863," Richards says.

"Fort Granger guns, commanded by Captain Giles Cockerill, tore at the Confederates with vicious enfilade fire."

"Fort Granger fired 163 rounds during the battle, or about 40 per gun."

"Think about the passage of time."

Now I'm not saying I was transported to November 30, 1864, but I did hear while under hypnosis church bells playing "My Country, Tis Of Thee" / "God Save The Queen" and roosters crowing. Who knows if those sounds were real? I also heard cannon fire, but that probably was my hypnotist playing a YouTube clip practically inside my eardrum.

Afterward, Richards and I compare notes and listen to "La Wally," an excellent operatic song, from his robust Spotify collection. It's an otherworldly experience, for sure. Then a dog walker finally shows up, no doubt wondering what the weirdos in the lawn chairs are doing.

Richards and I smile and wave, content with the knowledge that we just did something really strange and wonderful.

"So what do we call this?" I ask him after our mesmerizing morning hypnosis session.

"Hypno-history," he says with a sly smirk.

"Is that a thing?"

"It is now."

We chuckle as only two Civil War nerds can.

Weeks later, Richards and I return to the fort, but not for more "hypno-history." We're planning to find the execution site of those Fort Granger Rebel spies with a descendant of the man who had them hanged.

CHAPTER **16**

Middle Tennessee

SPIES, GAPS AND GRAVES

While Jack Richards, Taylor Agan and I trudge along a hidden stretch of railroad track near Fort Granger in Franklin, Tennessee, a text pings Agan's phone.

"Check this out," the 28-year-old Nashville songwriter says.

He holds up his phone to show me an image of a large, gold-framed painting of a bearded, sad-eyed man. It hangs in the Beverly Hills bungalow of his cousin Dennis, a producer of cult horror movie thrillers.

"Meet John Pierson Baird," Agan says of his distant uncle. "But this isn't coming back to Tennessee anytime soon. Too many bad memories here."

In the summer of 1863, Baird ordered the hangings of two Confederate spies—the dramatic conclusion to one of the war's more bizarre episodes. Our objective is to find the hanging site, which we believe is behind a neighborhood of modern houses near the railroad track and the Harpeth River.

Before Agan turns 30, he wants to follow in the footsteps of his many Civil War ancestors. He has more than a dozen on both sides, so that could mean road trips to the three main theaters of the war. For now, Richards and I are only committed to a Middle Tennessee leg of his journey to the hanging site and obscure Liberty Gap and Dug Hill battlefields.

It's doubtful any of Agan's other Civil War ancestors have a life story as eventful as Baird's.

Besides the Rebels, another enemy apparently dogged the 85th Indiana lieutenant colonel: alcohol. A government official claimed Baird was "consistently and habitually intoxicated."[1]

By the spring of 1863, he had already seen the inside of a Confederate prison after his capture at the Battle of Thompson's Station in Tennessee. Upon his return from a short stay at Libby Prison in Richmond, Baird received an appointment as commander at Fort Granger. He was only 33.

Confederate spies William Orton Williams (seated) and Walter Gibson Peter. Unknown photographer

At Fort Granger about dusk in early June 1863, Baird was talking with another officer when two uniformed strangers approached on horseback. One introduced himself as "Col. Lawrence W. Auton, acting inspector general," Army of the Potomac. The other said he was "Maj. George Dunlop, assistant inspector of the Western troops."[2]

The men told a convoluted tale of being ambushed while under a special War Department order to inspect all armies stationed in Tennessee. They produced authentic-looking documents from Union Major Gen. William Rosecrans, countersigned by his chief of staff, Brig. Gen. James Garfield, the future U.S. president. Then they toured the fort.

Soon after their departure early that evening, Union officers questioned the men's inspection story. Baird dispatched two soldiers in pursuit of the men. The Federals brought them back to camp, where they were placed under heavy guard.[3]

---

1. Letter from Horace Maynard, Attorney General for State of Tennessee, to Major General William Rosecrans, June 12, 1863, from John Baird's Military File, National Archives

2. *Harper's Weekly*, July 4, 1863

3. Ibid

Taylor Agan holds a wartime illustration of the hanging of the spies on the ground where we believe their execution took place.

Baird, meanwhile, telegraphed Garfield about the identities of the "inspectors." After midnight, the general replied: "There are no such men … in this army, nor in any army, so far as we know."

After interrogations, each man admitted to service in the Confederate Army. "Dunlop" was 20-year-old Lt. Walter Peter. "Auton" was Lt. Col. William Orton Williams, Peter's 23-year-old cousin.

"Gentlemen," Baird told them, "you have played this damned well."

"Yes," one of the men said, "and it came near being a perfect success."

Baird provided Garfield with his findings, adding, apparently with enthusiasm: "My bile is stirred, and some hanging would do me good." Wired the general: "Call a drum-head court-martial tonight, and if they are found to be spies, hang them in the morning without fail."[4]

At 3 a.m. on June 9, 1863, a court-martial convened. After a one-hour trial, the U.S. Army found Peter and Williams guilty and condemned them to death.

As it turned out, Williams wasn't just any Rebel officer. Like Lee, he had resigned his commission in the U.S. Army in 1861. He and Peter also were directly related to Martha Washington.

4. *Official Records*, Vol. 23, Part 2, Pages 397-398

In 1861, Williams had even proposed to Agnes Lee, the Marble Man's prettiest daughter. (She turned him down.) By then, war had morphed the once-gentlemanly Williams into a "drinker and an unpredictably violent man."[5]

Hours before the executions, Baird had second thoughts about putting such a well-connected man to death.

"Must I hang him?" he wired Garfield.

At 4:40 a.m., Rosecrans responded: Guilty men shall hang.[6]

Hours later, the corpses of Williams and Peter lay in poplar coffins. What mission they were on—and for whom—remains a mystery. Years later, General Lee still seethed over the executions. "An atrocious outrage," he called the deed.[7]

A wartime witness described the execution site as "about 40 yards up [from] the little branch from the [Harpeth] river, and about 15 or 20 yards southeast from the branch on the side toward the fort and railroad bridge." It was open ground in 1863.[8]

We three history amigos leave the tracks and walk behind a circa-1960s house in a neighborhood near the river. It's a secluded, mostly tree-covered ground in the middle of suburbia. Nearby, traffic rumbles across a bridge over the Harpeth. Along the river stands a homeless person's ragged tent. A Federal pontoon bridge crossed near here during the war.

The hanging tree—a wild cherry—is long gone. But all the witness' other landmarks check out. We're confident this is the site, although others have long thought the tree stood in another residential neighborhood nearby.

From his jacket, Agan pulls a copy of an illustration of the executions that appeared in *Harper's Weekly*, a wartime newspaper. In it, hundreds of U.S. soldiers—summoned to watch the hangings—eye the dangling corpses of Williams and Peter.

To stand on the same ground, one so important yet largely forgotten, is a history high for all of us.

---

5. Flood, Charles Bracelen, *Lee: The Last Years*, New York: Houghton Mifflin, 1981, Page 6

6. *Official Records*, Vol. 23, Part 2, Pages 416-417

7. Robert E. Lee to Martha Custis Williams Carter, Dec. 1, 1866, Lee Family Digital Archive (https://leefamilyarchive.org/)

8. "Confederate Spies Hung Near Ft. Granger," by Park Marshall (1855-1946), unpublished, Williamson County (Tenn.) Archives. As an 8-year-old, Marshall witnessed the aftermath of the execution. He became Franklin mayor and historian.

"This," says Agan, "is as close as we're probably getting to June 9, 1863."

In 1869, an event occurred that revealed the depth of Baird's torment over the hangings. He had resumed practicing law and was the defense attorney for a Civil War vet, who had been sentenced to death for murder —by hanging. As Baird watched his client die, the painful memory of the wartime hangings filled him with pain and regret. He sank into a deep depression.[9]

On April 1, 1876, weeks after the death of his only child, Baird voluntarily entered a hospital for the insane. "High sense of honor, truthful, scrupulously honest," a physician there wrote about him. Under cause of his "disease," someone wrote: "Excessive use of alcoholic drink."[10]

Once raven black, his hair and beard had turned white. His memory had faded, too. "He could not call up the past at the bidding of his will," said a wartime comrade.[11]

Perhaps that was a blessing. On March 7, 1881, Baird died in the foreboding asylum. He was only 51.

"A weird, haunting legacy," Agan says of his distant uncle.

* * *

Taylor Agan lives with his wife, Ashley, in Columbia, Tennessee, near Finn the groundhog killer. He's a devout Christian, but he has a little devil in him, too.

Years ago, Agan surprised evangelist Billy Graham in the kitchen at his North Carolina mansion. Our battlefield tramping pal, who makes friends easily, ended up befriending the head of the preacher's security detail.

Richards and I consider Agan an old soul because he enjoys hanging out with us gray-haired history geeks. Where he caught the history bug is

---

9. McCormick, Mike, *Terre Haute: Queen City of the Wabash*, Charleston, S.C.: Arcadia Publishing, 2005

10. Indiana State Archives, John Peter Baird file, Indianapolis

11. Brant, Jefferson, *History of the Eighty-Fifth Indiana Volunteer Infantry, Bloomington, Ind.: Cravens Bros. Printers and Binders*, 1902, Page 63

a bit of a mystery. Neither of his parents share their only child's interest. His dad is an air-traffic controller who loves to fix Volkswagens. Mom is a professor.

For our trip to the Liberty Gap battlefield, about an hour's drive southeast of Nashville, Agan packs heat. No, he isn't taking advantage of his Second Amendment right or wary of heading into a danger zone. The unloaded wartime revolver belonged to his great-great-great-great-grandfather Jonathan Rapp, a 49th Ohio sergeant who fought at Liberty Gap. He was only 23 then, five years younger than Agan, who's making his first trip to the battlefield.

Our first stop is a ramshackle barn, across the road from an abandoned farm and a small, overgrown family cemetery. The unmarked site is where August Willich, the Prussian-born U.S. Army brigadier general, made his headquarters.

After a brief visit, we hang a left on a country road and park near a large field of corn stalks on their last legs. No historical signs mark the battlefield, largely unchanged by time.

If you've never heard of the Battle of Liberty Gap, you're probably not alone. In a series of sharp fights here and at Hoover's Gap from June 24-26, 1863, Army of the Cumberland commander William Rosecrans deftly outmaneuvered Braxton Bragg, leading to the ejection of the Rebels from Middle Tennessee.

Over three rainy days, Rapp and his comrades pressed the Confederates at gaps in the hills southeast of Murfreesboro. The attack at Liberty Gap— along both sides of Liberty Pike—served as a feint, with Rosecrans' main thrust coming four miles away at Hoover's Gap.

"The affair at Liberty Gap will always be considered a skirmish," Union Brig. Gen. Richard Johnson wrote, "but few skirmishes ever equaled it in severity."[12] The casualties were low—"about 75" Confederate dead, Johnson reported, and about 60 prisoners. The Union Army suffered fewer.

One well-aimed bullet in this obscure battle, though, could have dramatically altered Agan family history.

"If Jonathan were killed here," says his great-great-great-great-grandson, "this moment would not be happening." Agan is moved. Jack and I are, too.

---

12. *Official Records*, Vol. 23, Part 1, Page 485

My favorite Liberty Gap anecdote comes from the first day of the fight. A mud-splashed, rain-soaked courier alerted St. John Liddell, commander of the Arkansas Brigade, that the Yankees had driven the 5th Arkansas from Liberty Gap.

Sound the alarm! the general ordered a bugler.

The enemy's untimely arrival spoiled the afternoon for those Rebels in the ranks who were enjoying a barbecue dinner.[13]

At the Liberty Gap battlefield, Agan holds an image of his great-great-great-great-grandfather Jonathan Rapp, who fought here with the 49th Ohio.

"We charged their camp, which they left in haste leaving everything," Rapp wrote of his regiment's attack that day.[14]

The Arkansans took a position on a ridge, but the Yankees compelled them to fall back. A handful of Confederate carried British-made Whitworths, long-range sharpshooter rifles that had eluded the blockade of Southern ports. It was the first time the Rebels had used the high-tech weapon in the Western Theater.

The next day, across Liberty Pike from where we stand, Rapp advanced in one of four battle lines, using a tactical innovation by August Willich, the Prussian-born general, called "advance firing." The first row fired a volley while the fourth row moved forward between the men to fire another one and so on. The tactic allowed the Ohioans to keep up a continuous line of fire and move forward at the same time. A shower of lead drove the Rebels from the field.

We walk along a country road bordering the field near where Rapp fought. To our right, about 700 yards away, appears the ridge the Arkansas Brigade defended. Then we scour the woods near a creek for battle evidence, perhaps a rare Whitworth round—oh, heck, for *anything*—from 1863.

---

13. *Arkansas Democrat*, June 27, 1903

14. Jonathan Rapp diary, Agan collection

"How's it feel to be out here?" I ask Agan.

"I don't think that 158 years later Jonathan expected his 4th great-grandson to be walking on this road with a plastic cup of coffee and wearing red sunglasses."

Then he surveys the raggedy cornfield.

"It's just crazy to see how providence works."

On our return down the country road, we meet a husband and wife on a Kubota with their lab. They're lawyers who live in a large, modern house on the battlefield. Over the years, Confederate and U.S. belt plates, a sword and Minié balls have surfaced in their fields. According to local lore, the Rebels hid weapons in a nearby cave.

"See over there," one of the lawyers says. She points toward a distant hillside.

"My relative was buried there with a bottle of whiskey in one hand and stones in the other. Supposedly so he could offer the devil a drink and then throw stones at him with the other."

Before departing this nearly pristine battlefield, we experience yet another Civil War high. From his SUV Agan retrieves Rapp's wartime diary—the first time it has returned to the battlefield since the war. Then the soldier's fourth great-grandson examines the entry from June 26, 1863.

> *5 a.m. In the valleys of Liberty Gap, the great mountains all covered with green trees. They lift their proud head so near to the sky. The rich valleys just ready for harvest; the wheat which is in abundance just ready to reap; the cornfields so green and so fine, just ready to shoot forth into blossom, but now are all trodden down by the soldiers of liberty.*

* * *

As Agan navigates his SUV on a serpentine mountain road 90 miles east of Nashville, Richards and I stare into the deep canyon to our right. We don't like what we see. There's no guardrail.

Taylor Agan stands on the site where we believe the combatants clashed at the obscure Battle of Dug Hill.

We're exploring the rugged countryside near Sparta, Tennessee, where guerrillas under the notorious Samuel "Champ" Ferguson wreaked havoc. John Parker—Agan's great-great-great-great-grandfather—joined a U.S. Army unit whose aim was to stop him.

Home for Parker was nearby DeKalb County, where a sizeable minority opposed Tennessee's secession in late-spring 1861. On April 25, 1863, Parker enlisted in Company K of the 5th Tennessee Cavalry. The blue-eyed 23-year-old was among roughly 31,000 Tennesseans who served in the U.S. Army—the most soldiers from any Confederate state who served the Union.

Dark-skinned with curly black hair, the Kentucky-born Ferguson weighed roughly 180 pounds, "without any surplus flesh." He had a "tremendous voice" that could be "heard a long distance when in a rage"—which apparently was often.[15] A "thief, robber, counterfeiter, and murderer," a 19th-century critic called him."[16]

Ferguson had a white-hot hatred for Yankees. Some say it was fueled by the rape of his wife and daughter and murder of his son by Union soldiers, which Champ himself denied.[17] In all, Ferguson may have killed as many as 120 men—all self-defense or acts of war, he claimed. But in actuality, he murdered dozens.

In late February 1864, 5th Tennessee Cavalry commander William Stokes was preparing for a speech at a celebration in Sparta. Fearing a surprise attack, the colonel sent 80-110 men to rid the nearby woods of guerrillas. The cavalrymen traveled up the Old Kentucky Road and then returned through the Dry Valley, on a narrow pass in the road near the Dug Hill community.

When Confederates realized Union soldiers were traveling through the area, two Rebel officers and Ferguson assembled a force of roughly 40 men and headed to Dug Hill.

Late on the afternoon of February 22, 1864, a Union scout advanced up the Dug Hill road with two comrades while the rest of the force lagged

---

15. Brents, John A., *The Patriots and Guerrillas of East Tennessee and Kentucky*, New York: Henry Dexter Publisher's Agent, 1863, Page 8

16. Ibid, Page 37

17. McKnight, Brian D, *Confederate Outlaw: Champ Ferguson and the Civil War in Appalachia*, LSU Press, 2011

behind. Then, about 100 yards away, one of them spotted two guerrillas astride horses.

"We were in the Dug Hill road, which ranged around the mountain about 600 yards from where we entered it," a scout recalled. "At the loose end of a thin hill was another line of battle. By this time another line had formed behind us, and the johnnies were cross-firing on us three ways."[18]

On a chilly afternoon, almost 160 years later, we explore the area, barely altered since the war. To our right are large boulders and a steep, thickly wooded ridge. Below us, from the middle of the lightly trafficked Dug Hill road (modern State Route 84), we see the swift-moving Calfkiller River, which flows past Yankeetown (really) and on toward Sparta.

Unlike Gettysburg, there's no first-shot marker here. In fact, no historical plaque anywhere marks this battlefield. Even for locals, the exact spot of the fighting remains murky.

Did Private Parker—present on the muster roll in February 1864—witness this bloodletting?

Agan tries to imagine his ancestor brawling with Ferguson's men.

"Like shooting fish in a barrel," he says, and the Federals were the fish.

As the firing intensified, battle smoke became so dense that the combatants couldn't tell friend from foe. A guerrilla called the battle one of the "most ridiculous … ever fought."[19]

One U.S. cavalryman hid in a hollow log until all was clear. Several Union survivors staggered back into Sparta, arriving as Stokes was about to deliver his speech.[20] Others surrendered to a regular Rebel officer, who passed them to the rear to Ferguson, "who shot them in cold blood," according to Union soldier. Some had their throats slit.[21]

Later, in a vacant storehouse, a local claimed to have examined the bodies of 41 U.S. Army dead—38 with bullet wounds in the head, three with crushed skulls.[22] But the exact death toll is unknown. The Rebels suffered

18. *The National Tribune*, Jan. 19, 1911

19. Dromgoole, Will Allen, *The Sunny Side of the Cumberland*, Philadelphia: J.B. Lippincott Company, 1886, Page 31

20. Ibid

21. *The National Tribune*, Jan. 19, 1911

22. *Nashville Banner*, Nov. 30, 1912

far fewer casualties, if any. Months afterward, skeletons are said to have turned up by the road and in the woods.

Farther down the Dug Hill road, we examine the scene of this war crime from a different perspective, near the Calfkiller. In the surrounding hills, locals hunt for ginseng. Others hunt for relics. A local man told us his wife had unearthed a Confederate coat button near where we initially tramped.

In nearby France Cemetery, at the top of a ridge, we find the grave of Ferguson, hanged after the war in Nashville for war crimes following a military trial. Two cans of cheap beer rest near Ferguson's marker. Coins lay atop it, including pennies, Lincoln side up.

"Karma," I tell my friends.

A 40-minute drive away, in DeKalb County, we explore another cemetery. We trudge on a muddy farm to a grove of trees on a slight rise. Dozens of toppled markers appear among brush and weeds. The place looks forgotten.

Years ago, Agan came here for the first time on a quest to find his ancestors' graves. Moments before leaving, his search apparently at a dead end, he consulted a higher power.

"Lord, where are those graves?"

Then he brushed aside a pile of leaves on the ground, and there he was: *John Parker, born July 27, 1840, died Oct. 20, 1883*

Next to him rests his wife, Elizabeth—Agan's great-great-great-great-grandmother.

Our adventures in the footsteps of Agan's ancestors are over. But my time in this remote part of Middle Tennessee is just beginning. In unincorporated Roberts Switch, a moonshiner's son has some interesting tales of his own to tell.

CHAPTER **17**

Roberts Switch, Tennessee

EXPLORING
GRAVEYARDS WITH A
MOONSHINER'S SON

While 75-year-old Tommy Roberts drives his pickup down a narrow and steep gravel road, I consider my options. Lean slightly to the left and it feels as if the vehicle might become the first to topple into the holler since a U.S. Army tank during a World War II training exercise. Slip out the front passenger door and Roberts and his daughter Angela, the backseat passenger, might consider me short on courage and common sense. So, I stay put until we reach our destination, a remote cemetery where my guides' Civil War ancestor rests.

Above us, two buzzards circle in a deep-blue sky. Let's hope it's not a bad omen. In the woods, Miller's Trace snakes its way to a 350-foot ridge. To our left, Mine Lick Creek winds through the holler, flowing into Center Hill Lake. Up the gravel road a way, Tommy carved his initials into the ancient "Initial Tree" in 1952, joining dozens of others who had done the same.

Out here in sparsely populated Middle Tennessee another kind of civil war was fought. A family's allegiance on one side of a ridge could be to the Union, on the other side to the Confederacy. This war wasn't just brother versus brother. It was neighbor versus neighbor. Sometimes it was guerrilla warfare, vicious and ugly.

Champ Ferguson, the notorious Yankee killer, roamed in the Cumberland Mountain plateau with his band of irregular fighters. So did his Yankee nemesis, "Tinker Dave" Beatty, an uncouth, uneducated mountain man.[1] They wouldn't hesitate to slit an enemy's throat or bash his skull in with a boulder. Neither would their followers.

Tommy Roberts is a retired Air Force command chief who lives in the house where he was born in Roberts Switch. It's a place so small it doesn't even have its own Wikipedia page. The unincorporated Putnam County town, 75 miles east of Nashville, was named after his kin.

Roberts and his wife, Gracie, married for 57 years, raised a daughter and son. Both attended the U.S. Air Force Academy and are retired intercontinental nuclear missile launch officers. Tommy has an affinity for family history and storytelling. Several Roberts ancestors fought in the obscure Battle of Dug Hill. Their descendant is going to school me on Civil War in the hollers.

In 1912, Francis Marion Roberts—a Civil War veteran and Tommy's great-great-grandfather—was buried in the clearing where we stand below the ridge. From the time of his death until she died in 1914, his wife, Sarah, collected her husband's $20-a-month military pension. Her remains rest next to his. Tommy and Gracie will be buried in this family graveyard, too. Their inscribed, gray-granite tombstone already stands on a patch of turf.

Francis Marion farmed in the Mine Lick Creek bottoms and near the railroad, corn mostly. A tall, blue-eyed, dark-haired private, Roberts served in the Union Army's 5th Tennessee Cavalry, an outfit apparently lacking in military deportment.

"They are under no control or discipline, as far as I can learn," a U.S. Army officer wrote. "Several instances have come to my hearing of their insulting unprotected females."[2]

Soldiers in the unit—many of whom hailed from the area—are said to have often wandered off—to tend crops, to visit with family, to sneak a little whiskey … or just because.

---

1. Beatty's testimony at Champ Ferguson's postwar murder trial helped convict the Confederate guerrilla and send him to the gallows.

2. *Official Records*, Vol. 52, Part 1, Page 428

Tommy Roberts crouches inside the entrance to a cave where his ancestor hid from Confederate soldiers.

In February 1863, near Murfreesboro, Tennessee, Roberts deserted from a forage train with his government-issued pistol. A year later, he sat out the fight at Dug Hill in a mountainous area north of Yankeetown and the White County seat of Sparta.

"There's danger out there. Don't go," the 28-year-old told his pals that day in February 1864, according to Roberts family lore.

Ferguson's guerillas ambushed companies I and K of the 5th Tennessee Cavalry, killing at least 21 Yankees in a three-hour, no-quarters fight on the treacherous terrain. "The brutal murder of some of our men who fell into rebel hands in that unfortunate affair on the Calfkiller river will never be forgotten," the *Nashville Union* wrote.[3]

"Wanna see the cave?" Tommy Roberts says. He points toward where, according to family lore, Francis Marion hid out from the Rebs, who often scoured the area for recruits and enemies.

"Heck, yes. I'm a nook-and-crannies guy," I tell Roberts.

---

3. *Nashville Union*, Nov. 27, 1864

Roberts seems unfazed by a steep and narrow, muddy path leading to the cave. I am fazed by a warning sign—"Danger Watch Your Step"—but proceed anyway. Angela, the first woman to serve as a Peacekeeper nuclear missile launch officer, stays behind. She's a cave veteran, after all. Wise, too.

"You must be more used to walking on cement," her dad tells me.

I gingerly walk along the slippery path along the holler, frequently grabbing metal stakes to stay grounded. One slip and my two girls could lose their papa.

Roberts points to where a fallen tree stopped his descent into the bottoms below us.

"Lay there for a few minutes to make sure I didn't have any broken bones," he says.

In the far distance, down in the bottoms, stood the old Roberts homestead, Francis Marion's place. In walks on Miller's Trace, Tommy Roberts has discovered scores of buttercups in the woods and clearings—a sure sign of other, long-gone homestead sites, he says.

We finally reach the cave, big enough for a large man to slip into and remain hidden for God knows how long. It may extend 150 feet, but I'm not especially interested in a first-person experience.

Francis Marion Roberts was no battle-hardened warrior like Sam Watkins of *Co. Aytch* fame. He mustered in in 1862, mustered out in the summer of '65. Roberts saw the elephant—a Civil War soldier's term for combat—but it was only a baby.

At the brutal Battle of Stones River in later December 1862, he missed the fighting while hospitalized. Roberts didn't earn a medal but survived the war, satisfaction enough. Three of his brothers served in the Union Army—two with the 5th Tennessee Cavalry, another with the 1st Tennessee Mounted Infantry. Five brothers-in-law wore Yankee blue. Another brother-in-law mustered in at gunpoint into the Confederate Army and later switched sides.

On February 22, 1864, at Dug Hill—roughly a 30-minute drive away—a Roberts family ancestor and two of his comrades suffered mortal wounds. We hop back into the Tommy's pickup for a ride to the remote cemeteries where they rest. The trip takes us over a railroad track that slices through Roberts Switch, population roughly 150 souls.

We descend a steep path deep into the woods, thankfully by foot this time. Roberts rushes far ahead. Here, on the old Herman Lee farm, Tommy sometimes ate bologna sandwiches, a rare treat. He walked out here with his dad, a moonshiner, and worked his granddad's adjacent cornfields, soaking up knowledge and sunshine.

Off to our right, in the bottoms along Mine Lick Creek, Lee farmed corn that he fed to his hogs. It also served as the main fuel for making moonshine—an activity that long pre-dates the Civil War. Farmers used the extra cash they made from selling moonshine to provide for their families and pay the bills. It's illegal to make the potent stuff, which can top 150 proof.

Back in Daddy Roberts' days, danger sometimes lurked in the woods where moonshiners plied their craft.

"Anytime you see a still," he told Tommy, "just keep on walking."

One family wouldn't hesitate to resort to violence if you stumbled upon their still. But Roberts insists his clan never would have shot a man who stumbled upon theirs. Tommy's pop once took the fall for another moonshiner, earning the standard sentence of 11 months, 29 days in the federal pen. A judge, however, gave him probation instead.

"My dad won't tell you," Angela says, as Roberts briefly walks out of view, "but he's responsible for saving this cemetery."

And then we discover "it."

No, not the off-the-beaten path graveyard.

"That," says Tommy, pointing to a blue contraption abandoned near Mine Lick Creek, "is the Elmore Town Casino & Spa." It looks like a decrepit bus to me.

Back in the day, the locals gambled and got liquored up in it. It's baffling how the thing ended up this deep in the woods.

"Are there snakes back here?" I ask.

"Oh, yes," comes a reply.

In a small clearing in the woods stands an old farm cemetery with about a dozen tombstones. Years ago, Roberts cleared the graveyard of undergrowth. Now he has a guy spray it with weed killer to keep it tidy.

In the plot surrounded by a barbed wire fence sit the side-by-side graves of Riley M. Richardson and John Goslin Richardson, Francis Marion's brother-in-law. Both served in the 5th Tennessee Cavalry. Each died at Dug Hill.

Tommy Roberts and his daughter, Angela, visit a remote graveyard where two Battle of Dug Hill soldiers rest.

On January 30, 1863, Riley—about 26 and no relation to John—deserted a forage train near Murfreesboro with *his* government-issued pistol. Shortly before his death, he went AWOL from the 1st Tennessee Mounted Infantry. He returned to the cavalry to finish his service. A bullet got him at Dug Hill, a cruel twist of fate. Riley's wife was three months pregnant with their first child. About 29, John Goslin left neither a wife nor children.

I wonder if dastardly John Gatewood, one of Ferguson's men, could be the reason the remains of these soldiers rest deep in the woods.

Barely 18, Gatewood shared Champ Ferguson's hatred of Yankees. A daredevil, he stood 6 feet tall, weighed 200 pounds, with a muscular, athletic build. With flowing red hair that dangled below his shoulders, he resembled a fearsome Viking. Gatewood preferred wide-brimmed hats, tilted back from his forehead. No Yankee wanted to fall into his hands alive.

"If pursued by no more than half a dozen Federals, [he] thought nothing of rushing back upon them, a pistol in either hand, and killing or capturing them before they recovered from their astonishment," according to an account.[4]

In the smoke-filled haze at Dug Hill, six 5th Tennessee cavalrymen became lost in the woods. Holding pistols in both hands, Gatewood confronted them. Erroneously assuming the guerrilla had reinforcements nearby, the U.S. Army soldiers immediately surrendered to the intimidating teen. Two Union soldiers escaped. Then Gatewood started shooting the others.

"Hold on, John!" one of Gatewood's comrades yelled after riding up to the scene. "Don't waste your ammunition, as we have to fight for what we get!"

Then he and Gatewood bashed in the heads of the remaining soldiers with heavy stones, killing them.[5]

Perhaps Private Lindsey P. Vickers became a victim of Gatewood's bloodlust, too. The 44-year-old was the married father of seven children. The Dug Hill victim's remains rest in a family cemetery beyond Miller's Trace and the ridge where our journey began. On his replacement grave, his great-granddaughter had inscribed C.S.A., a mistake rectified with a new bronze marker.

Minutes after we return to Tommy's house, I ask for a favor.

"How about some moonshine?"

Remote cemeteries and backwoods hiking can take a toll on anyone. Besides, I haven't sampled anything that mind-numbing since my college days. Roberts dials up a friend for a fresh batch. But my time runs out before the delivery.

An hour later a text from Roberts, accompanied by a photo of four filled canning jars, pings my iPhone.

"I am resupplied."

I shall return.

But first there's a trip to America's saddest place.

4. *The Commercial Appeal*, Memphis, Aug. 22, 1897
5. *Nashville American*, Feb. 21, 1904

CHAPTER 18

Andersonville, Georgia

VOICES FROM AMERICA'S SADDEST PLACE

With no customers in sight, Nancy Garrison feels comfortable swapping stories with me at Nancy's Treasure Chest, her small collectibles store in Andersonville, Georgia, site of the notorious prison camp. She's a 67-year-old three-quarter Cherokee, grandmother, whirlwind and former candidate for mayor in Andersonville, population 230.

"Make that 229 since we just lost one," Garrison says.

In between tales, she waves to passersby from a wooden chair in front of her shop, housed in the circa-1850s town hall. Across the road in 1864 and 1865, thousands of disheveled Yankee prisoners disembarked from crammed freight cars at the train depot. It's long gone, but a modern railroad track line follows the wartime path at the edge of the village.

In front of Garrison's shop, her husband painted a path of white footsteps on Prison Walk Street, simulating the route POWs took to the camp, about a quarter mile away.

"Eight hundred paces to hell," Garrison says.

Garrison talks about evolution, her grandchildren, some local dude named Jimmy Carter (the former president lives 22 miles southwest in Plains), the backwoods town where she has lived for more than a decade … and the ghosts and spirits of Andersonville.

"800 paces to hell," Nancy Garrison calls these painted footsteps that lead to the POW camp.

"You know, you ought to come back here in August, when the ghosts come around," she says.

"Ghosts?"

"I used to see shadows outside the window of my house here. I'd never invite the spirits in. They would just walk in themselves. I'd say, 'Guys, whoever you are, carry on your conversations outside.'"

I lean back on my flimsy chair while Garrison rambles on.

"Well, one of the spirits blew in my face," she says. "I just said, 'What the heck,' and went to get my coffee."

Before I depart, Garrison hands me a pair of Andersonville magnets. Then I back out my SUV onto Prison Walk Street, over those painted footsteps.

"If you see any of the black shadows passing ya by," Garrison says, "that's one I left ya."

Now this is just crazy talk anywhere else. But here, in America's saddest place, near the Civil War's deadliest ground, who knows?

I've walked Bloody Lane at Antietam alone at dawn, stood where Alexander Gardner photographed Confederate dead at Gettysburg and traipsed through woods looking for mass graves at Shiloh. But Andersonville is different than all of them—more deadly, more heartbreaking, more soulful. I almost expect the ground here to heave, sigh and groan.

This is not my first visit. But I aim to experience Andersonville differently this time—through the eyes of locals, with a park guide and through all my senses during a nighttime walk on prison grounds.

At Easterlin's Country Store, opposite an antiques store and catty-corner from the monument to Andersonville commandant Henry Wirz, manager Audra Warren preps a morning breakfast. On a wall hangs a large poster of the Andersonville camp flanked by American and Confederate flags. Below them are framed copies of the famous photographs of the prison grounds taken in August 1864 by Andrew J. Riddle. *Itsy Bitsy Spider,* the nursery rhyme, plays on the TV. A sign near the counter reads: "Many have eaten here. Few have died."

"People come here from all four corners—New York, California, Florida, Washington," Warren tells me. "We get locals, too."

The Swiss descendants of notorious camp commandant Henry Wirz ate at Easterlin's.

"They loved our cooking," says Warren. "One the people from Switzerland said we have the best green beans in America."

She calls her place "kind of a knock-off Cracker Barrel." The section of the building where antiques and collectibles are sold dates to the 1850s. Nineteenth- and early 20th-century proprietors sold caskets out back.

There's a sense of pride living in Andersonville, and Warren is eager to pass along its history to her young children.

"Every single headstone in the national cemetery had a wreath on it this year for Christmas."

But Andersonville, she says, can be "sombering."

"The air just feels sad. You can feel it."

As we chat in the antiques/collectibles area, I spot through a window the monument to Captain Wirz in the center of the village.

"A lot of people scapegoated him," Warren says.

On an oppressively hot, late-spring day in 1909, nearly 3,000 people gathered in Andersonville for the dedication of the 35-foot obelisk—the brainchild of the United Daughters of the Confederacy. It's hard to imagine that many people in this village. It's hard to believe the monument—a giant middle finger to the nearly 13,000 Union soldiers who died in the camp and the 32,000 who survived the hellhole—made it from someone's dream to reality.

A Union veteran called the monument a "disgrace to the nation."[1]

Another U.S. Army vet hoped a lightning strike would destroy it.[2] One suggested dynamiting it.[3]

An Ohio newspaper likened memorializing Wirz to "honoring Nero for burning Christians at the stake."[4]

"In Memory of Captain Henry Wirz," read the words inscribed in the Georgia granite on the east side, and below it: "To rescue his name from the stigma attached to it by embittered prejudice."

Statues to Robert E. Lee and Stonewall Jackson have found new homes far from the public eye. Communities have placed historical placards that provide context for Confederates monuments in Franklin, Tennessee and elsewhere. But somehow the monument to Wirz—scapegoat or not—has mostly eluded scrutiny. Maybe it's because Andersonville—in rural Georgia 125 miles south of Atlanta—is so far off almost everyone's radar.

Let it be, says Cynthia StormCaller of the monument.

She serves as the town's quasi tourism director for the Civil War Village of Andersonville and curator at The Drummer Boy Civil War Museum, next door to the Easterlin's. The former singer is part Comanche, part Cajun and a *full-blooded character*. I love her spirit. Mrs. B would, too.

"I've had a wild life. Trust me," StormCaller says from her chair behind the museum counter. "I didn't know who I was for years. Grew up in New Orleans. Ran away at age 10. Raised horses even though I didn't know how to do it. I'm a strange person."

StormCaller, who has degrees in linguistics, business and cultural anthropology, moved to Andersonville in 1995.

"Fell in love with a blue-eyed, blond-haired man," she says.

StormCaller lives on Rebel Road in town, which also has a street named for Wirz.

---

1. *The Akron (Ohio) Beacon Journal*, May 13, 1909

2. Ibid

3. Ibid, May 9, 1909

4. *The Salem (Ohio) News*, May 13, 1909

"I believe in this: 'Take your damn shoes off. Put your feet on the ground. And just listen,'" she tells me shortly after I introduce myself.

So, I lean against the counter and listen while StormCaller holds court. My feet remain planted, but the shoes stay on. In the glass case below me sits a bumper sticker that reads: "Save the Monuments. Get Rid of the Politicians." The last sentiment seems reasonable.

"Just don't play with the weapons or try on the uniforms," StormCaller tells visitors in between hot history takes.

"This," she tells me about Andersonville, "is about everyone's story. You can't just pick one side."

StormCaller complains of political correctness getting in the way of the park—the Andersonville National Historic Site—and the town, which is not part of it. She says the victors write history and slides a book about Black Confederates toward me while chatting with another visitor. Then StormCaller hands me her smartphone. I stare at a photo of a dozen reenactors taken on the pioneer farm next to the museum.

"What do you see to their far left?"

I spot a woman in a long-sleeve top and long, period dress. She looks mysterious. But a ghost? My sleep-deprived brain can't decide. StormCaller glances at me with her eyebrows raised.

"Are there spirits around here?" I ask.

"Oh, honey, there are spirits here everywhere."

StormCaller says she tossed a ghost hunter from the property, though, for mooning a security camera.

"I don't like ghost hunters. Ninety percent of them are fake."

I plop a $5 donation on the counter for entrance into the small museum. As I push through its doors to examine Union and Confederate artifacts, some of StormCaller's final words from our chat linger in my cluttered mind.

"We know spirits walk around us here *every* day."

I drive from the village, passing underneath the giant welcome sign flanked by rusty figures of Confederate and Union soldiers, to rendezvous at the prison camp with park guide Teri Surber. The historic site closes to the public at 5 p.m. We're going to walk the ground until after nightfall.

There's no other Civil War ground like Andersonville. No Civil War POW camp was more deadly. None is as well preserved or well interpreted.

The camp, which opened in late February 1864, was enclosed by a 15-foot stockade wall and initially covered about 16½ acres. By July 1, 1864, as the prisoner population swelled, Confederates had expanded Andersonville to 26½ acres.

At its peak occupancy on August 9, 1864, more than 33,000 POWs jammed the camp. Confederate authorities forbade prisoners from stepping beyond a "deadline," an area 19 feet inside the stockade wall, making the actual camp living space even less. Prisoners who crossed the deadline risked receiving a bullet in the head from a guard.

Two hills slope down toward ironically named Sweetwater Creek tributary, which cuts the camp roughly in two. Prisoners used the creek water for drinking, washing and as a giant toilet. It became a huge cesspool when the tributary backed up. Some POWs sank into the muck up to their waists.

"Literally alive with vermin and filth of all kinds," a Pennsylvania POW recalled about the stream.[5]

"[E]xcrement covered the ground, the scent arising from which was suffocating," wrote a Connecticut POW about the area called "The Sinks," the downstream end of the tributary.[6]

"They say you could smell this place in Americus, 10 miles away," Surber says of the camp.

The 42-year-old Georgia native and I bond over our passion for the camp, especially the personal stories of Andersonville POWs. A park guide for two years, Surber reveres this hallowed ground, often walking the site alone after closing. She's a married mother of three with a psychology degree. One of her ancestors was among the nearly 4,000 Confederate soldiers who died at Camp Douglas, the notorious Union POW camp in Chicago.

In one month alone at Andersonville, 3,000 prisoners died—about 100 per day. Dysentery, diarrhea and scurvy topped the causes of death. POWs buried the dead in a graveyard about a quarter mile from the camp. It's a national cemetery and our first stop in Surber's government pickup truck.

"There are 13,000 stories here," I tell Surber, who knows that better than almost anyone.

5. *Prison diary, of Michael Dougherty, late Co. B, 13th., Pa., Cavalry*, Bristol, Pa.: C.A. Dougherty Printer, 1908, Page 39

6. Kellogg, Robert H., *Life and Death in Rebel Prisons*, Hartford, Conn.: L. Stebbins, 1865, Page 58

On the well-manicured grounds, nearly 13,000 white tombstones for Andersonville's dead stand roughly six inches apart. Surber takes me to one of hers, Grave No. 5851 for Leander Farnham, a 45-year-old private in the 1st Vermont Heavy Artillery.

On June 23, 1864, Farnham and his brother Lorenzo, a 34-year-old sergeant in the same regiment, were captured at Weldon Railroad, near Petersburg, Virginia. Leander died on August 16, 1864—five days after the birth of his daughter, Rhoda Belle. Lorenzo died four days later. The day Leander died, Andrew J. Riddle—the Confederate photographer—shot his famous image of a burial party at the prisoners' graveyard. Leander's body may be the one in the foreground.

I take Surber to one of my gravestones nearby, No. 5044 for Emerson Nichols, a 16-year-old private in the 16th Connecticut. On August 8, 1864, comrades carried the grievously ill teen from the stockade to the camp hospital. He died the next day.

Nichols' death rocked his mother, who in the previous few years had lost a husband, another son, two grandchildren and a son-in-law—a Union soldier who had suffered a mortal wound on picket duty in Louisiana.

"I feel that the hand of God has been laid heavily upon me," she wrote of her plight.[7]

For the next three hours, we walk about the camp—the only two humans on the Civil War's deadliest ground.

We spot clumps of upturned earth and holes in the ground, perhaps the work of wild hogs. The few, scattered monuments look lonelier than usual.

"I think we're going to have a great sunset," Surber says.

In the distance, smoke rises from a kaolin plant. A palpable sadness hangs in the air, too. Andersonville feels like someone should cloak it in mourning crepe.

"I've never found a good word to describe this place," Surber confesses.

---

7. Emerson Nichols pension file, National Archives and Records Administration, Washington, D.C.

At Andersonville National Cemetery, park guide Teri Surber holds a famous image of the burial of Union dead where the photo was taken in 1864. Leander Farnham's body may be the one in the foreground.

"I've never found a good word to describe this place," park guide Teri Surber says of the Andersonville prison camp.

She's in good company: "There is no tounge or Pen that can discribe the situation of the sick Wounded & Rotten men in hear," a Vermont POW wrote in his diary while at Andersonville.[8]

We can walk from one side of the camp to the other in five minutes or less—a journey that would have taken a POW a half-hour or more.

"No one got a Medal of Honor for being here," Surber says.

We explore "The Sinks," the saddest place of all at Andersonville.

---

8. Danker, Donald F., "Imprisoned at Andersonville: The Diary of Albert Harry Shatzel, May 5, 1864—September 12, 1864," *Nebraska History* 38 (1957), Page 81-126

A wartime image shows "The Sinks," where U.S. prisoners languished—and many died. Library of Congress

"Is this hell?" newcomers who saw the spot for the first time wondered. I imagine the skeletal forms, sunburned and nearly naked, as they lay near the horrific morass.

"Under the summer sun this place early became corruption too vile for description," a New York soldier remembered.[9]

Of the ground where we stand, a Pennsylvania soldier wrote: "I saw to-day-a man lying on the bank of the stream being eaten to death by maggots."[10] A small sign near "The Sinks" warns today's park visitors of venomous snakes.

"Guys tried to build a house right here inside the hill. But it didn't work well," Surber says. She gestures toward area beyond "The Sinks," an ugly sight even today.

As the curtain falls on another visit, I imagine another one of my guys, William Nott, a private in the 16th Connecticut. I have a copy of his post-war diary. He survived the hell of Antietam, Andersonville and a deadly accident on the Potomac River shortly after Lee's surrender. Nott wrote

9. *Narrative of Privations and Sufferings of United States Officers and Soldiers While Prisoners of War in the Hands of the Rebel Authorities*, U.S. Sanitary Commission, Philadelphia: King & Baird Press, 1864, Page 263

10. *The Sentinel*, Carlisle, Pa., Feb. 26, 1927

Dusk at Andersonville. Unforgettable.

of prisoners sleeping in the mud at Andersonville, "just looking up to the skies and breathing the rains." At his parole, he weighed 85 pounds, down from his enlistment weight of 165.[11]

We make a final loop around the camp. The cool spring air invigorates. The sun dips below the horizon. Then I imagine 1864 and 1865 again—the stench, the smoke, the coughing, the groans, the agony, the chatter and the terror of the night.

I *feel* the spirits, too.

"Do you think the prisoners admired the sunset?" Surber asks.

In Andersonville, America's saddest place, I wonder if they ever noticed it.

But my time here is complete. I'm eager to visit Virginia, where an ancient plantation house writhes in its death throes.

What secrets does it hold?

---

11. Nott postwar diary, copy in author's collection

CHAPTER 19

Deatonville, Virginia

'THE HOUSE WITH NOBODY IN IT'

Outside an abandoned plantation house in rural, south-central Virginia, five miles northeast of the Sailor's Creek battlefield, the weather becomes a chameleon—brilliant sunshine one moment, gloomy and gray the next. A temperamental wind moans and howls. Rain and flecks of snow spit from the sky as the temperature dips into the high 30s. The circa-1790s house gives me the chills, too, but I'm going in anyway. There's Civil War treasure inside, graffiti left by Union soldiers in the war's waning days.

As if scooped out by a giant hand, nearly the entire back wall of the house is gone, exposing a time capsule inside. A pair of dresses sways from hangers. A rusty bedframe leans against a wall. Out front, several decent shoves could topple the wreckage of a porch, ending the entryway's misery. Twenty paces away stands a decrepit, tin-roofed smokehouse, a hint of the plantation's better days. "Private Property. No Trespassing," reads a sign near the basement entrance.

This place—unoccupied since the 1970s—reminds me of a stanza from Joyce Kilmer's mournful poem, *The House With Nobody In It*.

I never have seen a haunted house, but I hear there are such things;
That they hold the talk of spirits, their mirth and sorrowings.
I know this house isn't haunted, and I wish it were, I do;
For it wouldn't be so lonely if it had a ghost or two.

159

Truly Vaughan, a bachelor in his 50s, farmed more than 1,000 acres here during the Civil War. Fifteen to 20 slaves toiled for him, planting tobacco and other crops each spring. Truly's place became known to locals as "Bachelor's Rest," a nod to its owner. Besides the enslaved, he lived on the plantation with an overseer named Yelverton Craddock, who served with the 23rd Virginia and suffered a mortal wound at the Battle of McDowell in Virginia in May 1862.

In early April 1865, with Ulysses Grant on its heels, the Army of Northern Virginia retreated along the St. James Road past Vaughan's place. Meanwhile, roughly 10,000 soldiers in John B. Gordon's Second Corps, Lee's rearguard, played cat-and-mouse on the farm and nearby with the Union Army's 15,000-man Second Corps under Andrew Humphreys. But overwhelming Yankee firepower, dwindling resources and declining morale doomed Robert E. Lee's army, which would surrender on April 9, 1865, at Appomattox Court House, roughly 45 miles west.

As the curtain fell in the Eastern Theater, Bachelor's Rest became a makeshift U.S. Army division hospital for about 175 soldiers, including a few Confederates. In Vaughan's eight-room house, surgeons amputated limbs, bandaged wounds and consoled the unfortunates. "Helped amputate a reb lt. leg," a Union chaplain wrote in his diary. Some patients at the plantation wrote on the walls of Vaughan's bedroom.

"I already scared the turkey vulture," says Joshua Lindamood, our advance man. "He got me last time." The bearded bird chaser has cleared the way for my entry into the unknown. But who knows what else lurks inside?

Lindamood is a 35-year-old Sailor's Creek Battlefield State Park ranger. He and Michael Meehan, a 39-year-old federal employee, serve as my guides. In 2021, the out-of-state owner of the farm gave a local preservation group led by Meehan permission to remove the graffiti walls for display elsewhere. The owner isn't interested in tossing this ancient house a lifeline.

Civil War passion first heated up for Lindamood and Meehan in their single-digit years. Lindamood's ancestors fought on both sides of the war. One served in the 51st Virginia as a color-bearer, notably fighting under John Breckinridge at New Market in the Shenandoah Valley in mid-May 1864. Another fought for the 92nd Ohio in the major battles in the Western Theater. But I suspect Lindamood leans toward his Rebel side.

The discoveries inside this decrepit plantation house stunned Michael Meehan.

Meehan, a Virginia transplant from Pennsylvania, is a former 5th New York reenactor. He scored a bit part in the 1993 movie *Gettysburg* when he was nine. The back of his head appeared on the screen for several seconds.

"My mom said it was the best back-of-the-head scene of all time," he says. "Said I should have won an Oscar."

Two of Meehan's Union ancestors in the Army of the Potomac served through Lee's surrender.

Sparked by the treasure at Truly's place, the men founded the Appomattox-Petersburg Preservation Society and raised nearly $3,600 to remove the walls with the graffiti.

I elude a strand of barbed wire and descend into a basement *Twilight Zone* with my guides. A mid-20th-century Singer sewing machine stands in the corner. On a shelf rest large, sealed glass jars filled with peaches, eggs and more—bizarre relics from decades ago. Along a wall stands a squat, woebegone sofa. The Union Army supposedly stabled horses in the basement during the war. But the ceilings are barely six feet high, so that doesn't seem plausible.[1]

---

1. *Old Homes And Buildings in Amelia County, Virginia, Volume 1*, compiled and published by Mary Armstrong Jefferson, Amelia, Va., 1964

Eeeeeeek.

As we make our way to the main floor, wooden stairs groan, creak and whine. A gaping opening to the outside reveals a huge, empty field—that's where Vaughan's enslaved labored. Thick woods appear in the far distance. The plantation house is small—80 x 40 feet—but standard for the area. Its brick chimneys and a stone foundation hold out against time. Wood paneling inside may date to the late 18th century.

Must and melancholy linger in the air.

Original, wrought iron "H" and "L" hinges cling to the front door. Wooden pegs, shop-made nails and hand-hewn beams speak of long-ago craftmanship. On a stand in one room sits a postcard with a 1950 postmark: "*Dear folks. Wish you could see this great natural wonder ...*" Under a rug next to brick fireplace rests a 1946 newspaper. Harry Truman beams from its front page. A bird-less nest rests precariously atop a ceiling light fixture. From a windowsill hangs a dust-covered suit coat. Vines outside obscure the view from a window.

Lindamood stares at a fireplace and small rubble pile under the mantle.

"If this could only talk," he says of this wreck of a home.

Bachelor's Rest, how could you fall so far?

In the other first-floor room, a 1957 IRS income tax form lies on the original heart pine floor. In the corner sits a forlorn wooden chair, warmed by afternoon sunlight. A get-well card from July 1962 lies nearby: "*We trust you are improving and will soon be home.*" On a floor rests a wedding invitation: "*Mr. and Mrs. Leslie Tabor Figg request the honour of your presence…*" Scattered envelopes lie unopened.

We ascend a narrow, groaning staircase to the attic over splotches Lindamood suspects are blood from April 1865.

"Anyone want to pay $1,500 for a DNA blood test?" I ask.

I get no takers.

The cramped attic, stuffed with refuse and memories, has two rooms—one 7 by 10 foot, the other 7 by 18.

"All these floors are weight-bearing, right?"

"So far," the vulture vanquisher tells me.

I chuckle, nervously.

Joshua Lindamood inspects writing inside the plantation house.

Meehan speculates Vaughan's bedroom—the present-day attic—served as an area for walking wounded while the first floor became the emergency room and the basement served for other surgery. Other wounded soldiers lay outside. Cracks snake through the whitewashed walls, where the soldier signatures and graffiti appear.

"Isn't this cool?" Meehan says. He first explored the forgotten field hospital in 2021.

"Floored—never seen anything like it," Lindamood says of his reaction when he initially saw the inscriptions in early 2022.

Blown away, I call Mrs. B: "This is amazing."

"Look, it's a Civil War 'Kilroy,'" Meehan says.

He points to a cartoon-like, pencil drawing with tufts of hair. It reminds us of the World War II graffiti drawn by American GIs: *"Kilroy Was Here."*

Meehan and others have identified three soldiers who inscribed their names or initials on the attic walls and researched their stories. Perhaps the men did it for posterity, maybe simply out of boredom while recovering from wounds. Meehan spotlights his guy, John Shivler, whose name appears in large, flowing script. Below the signature he wrote his place of birth—"Mount Pleasant, Pa."—and regiment "105th P.V.," the 105th Pennsylvania Infantry.

In October 1861, Private Shivler mustered into Company K of the 105th Pennsylvania, recruited mainly from Jefferson County, northeast of Pittsburgh. Three years later, he became a corporal. A 24-piece regimental brass band entertained the Pennsylvanians, whose colonel and other officers chipped in more than $1,000 to purchase the instruments.[2] By late in the war, the 105th Pennsylvania had already experienced major combat in Virginia—at Second Manassas, Chancellorsville, the Wilderness, Spotsylvania Courthouse and elsewhere.

In the Virginia countryside in early April 1865, the Army of Northern Virginia suffered almost-incessant blows from the Army of the Potomac. "The country was broken, and consisted of open fields alternating with forests and dense undergrowth and swamps, over and through which the lines of battle followed closely on the skirmish line, with a rapidity and nearness

---

2.   Scott, Kate M., *History of the One Hundred and Fifth Regiment of Pennsylvania Volunteers*, Philadelphia: New-World Publishing Co., 1877, Page 262

of connection that I believe to be unexampled, and which I confess aston-
ished me," a Union officer recalled.[3]

In dizzying, near-continuous battles, thousands of Rebels became
prisoners as their bedraggled army lost a railroad supply train, dozens of
ambulances and wagons, 11 battle flags and artillery. "It was a running
fight all day," a U.S. Army officer remembered of the fighting on April
6, 1865.[4] But these unheralded fights earned only brief mentions in the
Official Records, the bible of the war for historians and researchers.

In Deatonville, near Bachelor's Rest on April 6, 1865, a bullet slammed
into Shivler's face, near his nose—a grievous, ugly wound. A 105th
Pennsylvania comrade feared he was dead. Shivler—who was serving in
the unit's color guard—staggered to his feet. As the corporal lurched from
the battlefield, an aide's horse trampled him.[5] Shivler—who was about
30 or 31—is believed to have walked about a mile to Bachelor's Rest for
treatment. For an unknown time, he occupied Vaughan's attic. Meehan
believes Shivler may have scrawled a depiction of his wound on Vaughan's
bedroom wall.

After the war, Shivler lived in central Pennsylvania, married a widow
named Maria and became a tailor. No photo of him is known to exist.
Imagine his torment in an era long before plastic surgery could make a
face—and a soul—nearly whole again. By 1902, Shivler resided in an
insane asylum in Mahoning Township, Pennsylvania. Nine years later, he
died at age 77, outliving Maria by 11 years. The veteran was buried in a
cemetery in South Philipsburg, Pennsylvania.

Steps from Shivler's inscription, we see a large, circular stain on the
floor—perhaps more evidence from the long-ago hospital.

"Could that be for a chamber pot?" Lindamood wonders.

He shines a light onto the mark in the corner. Dozens of penciled hash-
marks appear on the wall nearby.

Besides Shivler, Privates Luther Calkins of Company K of the 105th
Pennsylvania and 1st Maine Heavy Artillery Corporal George McKechnie
of Company I also signed their names on the attic walls.

---

3. Ibid, Page 133

4. Ibid, Page 132

5. John Shivler pension file, National Archives and Records Administration, Washington,
   D.C.

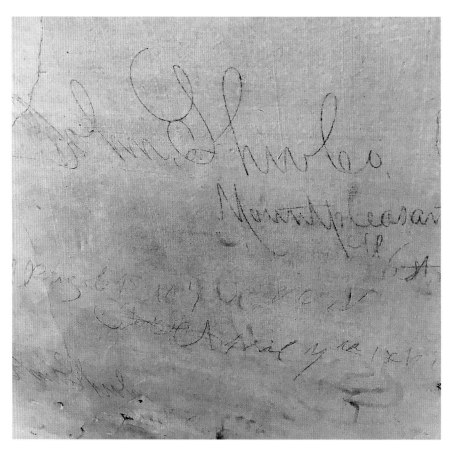

Private John Shivler's signature appears in flowing script on a second-floor wall in the plantation house. Courtesy Michael Meehan

On April 6, 1865, Calkins suffered a wound in his left foot, between his second and third toe, with the bullet coming to rest near his ankle. Less than a year earlier, he had suffered a wound in the right arm in brutal fighting at the Wilderness. After the war, Calkins married, raised a family and moved throughout the country.[6]

McKechnie, who battled dysentery in 1864, suffered a wound from a stray bullet in his left hand in support of a battery at nearby Amelia Springs in early April. The round tore through his index finger and middle finger, exiting below the thumb. Following the war, McKechnie—who was probably in his late teens when he enlisted—returned to Maine.[7] Meehan

---

6.   Luther Calkins pension file

7.   George McKechnie pension file

floored a McKechnie descendant when he contacted her about the soldier's plantation house graffiti.

At the bottom of the attic landing, Lindamood discovers another inscription. From the grave, a Civil War soldier sticks it to Confederate president Jefferson Davis.

"Old Jeff be damned. Old rascal."

"Look here," Lindamood says

He shifts his light on an inscription on the wall leading to the attack.

"Here's another signature, Pettit B."

Near the top of the stairwell more graffiti appears. Some of it may be postwar. Who wrote it and what it means may never be known. A professional photographer shoots closeups of all the writing.

"We're trying to save everything we possibly can," Meehan tells me.

The wind sneaks through attic crevices, producing a whiny pitch. Little light streams through a tiny attic window, the chief reason, perhaps, the graffiti survived.

In a downstairs room exposed to the elements, a framed sign behind cracked glass proclaims: "May happiness be in your heart."

But profound sadness cloaks this old plantation. Its floors creak and groan. Its walls buckle. Through a gaping hole out back, tattered clothing sways in the wind.

"The House With Nobody In It" writhes in its death throes. It can crush a soul.

A week after my visit, Meehan's twin brother and uncle—construction experts—successfully remove the walls from Bachelor's Rest. Donations funded their work—Meehan likened it to "surgery," the first since the last battlefield operation here 157 years ago.

But I was already well on my way to my next destination—a Virginia battlefield owned by a man who vows to be buried there.

CHAPTER 20

Farmville, Virginia

'THIS PLACE IS SO HUMBLING'

While returning to my hotel after a brief visit at dusk to Dirk Warner's farm, I break news to Mrs. B back in Tennessee.

An hour earlier, as Warner was explaining military movements on his farm, the heart of the Cumberland Church battlefield, I stepped into a mound of cattle "leftovers." Remnants ended up in Murray, Mrs. B's SUV.

"You better get all of that cow crap out of Murray!" Mission Control says.

Early the next morning, I return to the farm for a lengthier visit, chagrined and vowing to be more careful.

As I drive down a long gravel road to Warner's place, a mist curls over the fields. Frost clings to grass and clumps of upturned earth. A few cows graze in a field astride Jamestown Road. Richmond, an hour's drive east, seems a world away.

On his 127-acre farm, Warner often envisions April 7, 1865. Cannons boom, musketry rattles, battle smoke lingers, soldiers shout, blood flows. Then a spade plunges into the rich Virginia earth. A soldier rolls a friend into a grave. The cycle of war and death. How benumbing. How timeless.

Warner plans to be buried on his battlefield, too.

"Over there by those redbuds," he tells me as we walk his hallowed ground.

Until then, Warner has a battlefield to nurture, protect and interpret. Artifacts to uncover. A battle book to write. Dreams to turn into reality. A mystery to solve. I have one, too:

Why did it take me so long to hear about the Battle of Cumberland Church?

Before my journey to rural, south-central Virginia, I knew nothing about this battle fought in the war's waning days. The five-hour brawl five miles north of Farmville became the last bullet point on Robert E. Lee's military resume, his final victory. It resulted in 900 casualties—650 Union and 250 Confederate—but earned only a brief mention in the *Official Records*. Two days later, Lee surrendered at Appomattox Court House.

"History makes but little mention of the battle … as events of greater importance followed so closely," a Union veteran recalled, "but the participants know that troops never fought more valiantly than did Lee's soldiers in their last effort when they repulsed the assault of the veterans of the 2d Corps."[1]

Warner is a cattle farmer and a longtime producer and director for a Richmond TV station. Decades ago, he played guitar and wrote songs for amateur rock bands Captain Jack and Radio Silence. We bond over a mutual enthusiasm for Civil War history. He's a descendant of a soldier in the 118th Pennsylvania—the regiment of my hero, Lemuel Crocker.

Warner introduces me to his Siberian husky and American Eskimo mix named Izzy, who wants to kiss me. I shoot a selfie with his pet black Angus steer named Nibbles. "I don't have the heart to take him to market," Warner says. "Reminds me of my mom. She passed shortly after Nibbles' birth."

Until his death in 2010, Warner's father-in-law Dr. Wilson Taylor, a veterinarian and World War II vet, owned the farm and lived in the post-battle house on the property. He went by "Doc," same as my father-in-law, also a vet and WWII veteran. Warner lives in Doc's place now with his wife, Jane.

"He made two requests of me when I married his daughter," Warner says. "'Look after her and look after my place.'"

1. Miller, Delavan S., *Drum Taps in Dixie; Memories of a Drummer Boy, 1861-1865*, Watertown, N.Y.: Hungerford-Holbrook Co., 1905, Page 172

No problem. Married since 1992, Warner still cherishes Doc's farm 30 years later.

"Sacred ground," he calls the battlefield. "Incredible."

As we walk his farm on this frosty morning, Warner shows me where Union troops formed. Andrew Humphreys, the Second Corps commander, made his headquarters on the farm. The 54-year-old general may have trod on the original yellow pine floors incorporated into the postwar residence, built on the foundation of the wartime house. U.S. Army cannons belched iron and death from Warner's farm.

Confederate Gen. William Mahone—all 5-foot-6 and 100 pounds of him—made his headquarters a mile away at Cumberland Presbyterian Church. The commander of Lee's rearguard may have sought aid from a higher power. The Yankees outnumbered "Little Billy" and the rest of Lee's army at Cumberland Church by nearly 2-to-1. Almost immediately, Mahone's soldiers entrenched, as they had scores of times during the war, and fortified the ground near the church.

Cumberland Church, a brilliant, white beacon in morning sunlight, still holds services. But don't bring your metal detector. "No Relic Hunting," warns a sign out front.

"See that high ground," Warner says. "The Confederates commanded all that."

As we stand in a field in front of his house, Warner points into the distance, to a ridge beyond Bad Luck Creek and the Jamestown Road. That's where Rebel soldiers manned a strong line. Warner's sister-in-law sold land that encompasses part of the Confederates' position to the American Battlefield Trust, protecting it forever. The previous morning, I had explored well-preserved Rebel earthworks snaking through those woods with local preservationist Michael Meehan—my abandoned plantation house guide—and his three-year-old daughter, Jolene.

Across Jamestown Road, at the apex of a Confederate line shaped roughly like a horseshoe, Colonel William Poague placed an artillery battery. Rebel gunners gave the Yankees "hell with grape and cannister trimmings thrown in," a Union veteran recalled. Remains of earthworks stand in a front yard of a modern house there.

Dirk Warner wants to be buried on the Cumberland Church battlefield— his battlefield.

Near the corner of Jamestown and Cumberland roads, 200 yards from Warner's farm, hand-to-hand fighting broke out at the Huddleston place. The owner hid in the hearth of a fireplace with a slave during the battle, according to local lore. "Death stalked over field and dale," the owner's daughter recalled decades later. "The moans of the dying could be heard for hours after the battle."[2]

To bring this obscure battle into focus, Warner mines regimental histories, manuscripts and soldier letters—anything he can find—for a book he wants to write. He mines his battlefield, too. In 1989, Warner began finding Miniés while digging post holes on the farm for "Doc." He has since unearthed between 2,000 and 3,000 bullets—15 different varieties in all, including a rare Confederate Whitworth round.

"See where those cows are?"

Warner points to ground near a tree line.

"I found the Whitworth, a medical phalange, and a picture frame right there. Confederate shelling got so bad here, the Union soldiers had to vacate."

Fifty feet from his front door, Warner uncovered a Union spur. Near it, he found a beat-up U.S. belt buckle. Rings, trigger guards, lock plates, Spencer cartridges, artillery shell fragments and scabbard tips have turned up. Warner recovered two mangled brass mats for photographs. Perhaps they framed an image of a soldier's wife or sweetheart.

"See that humpy area." Warner gestures toward the middle of a field.

"A Confederate cavalry guy got killed out there. Found a whole bunch of Richmond Lab carbine bullets in the same spot. Someone lost an ammo pouch."

Warner suspects the remains of a dog—a regimental mascot for a Confederate unit—may lie out here somewhere, too.

"I found a blown-out Gardner right there near the hay," Warner says while Nibbles and his friends eye us.

Warner bags most artifacts he finds for storage in bins in his house. He displays dozens of the relics in his home office. Only one other person may relic hunt on his battlefield—a friend who hunts the fields with Warner and shares his passion for the battlefield.

---

2. *Farmville (Va.) Herald*, Jan. 19, 1940

Warner's beloved Nibbles gives me the evil eye at Cumberland Church battlefield.

"Everything he finds here, stays here."

Warner points out the "S" curve of an ancient stretch of the Old Jamestown Road that snakes through his battlefield. To our right stood a thick growth of pines in 1865. Shortly before advancing, officers in the 2nd New York Heavy Artillery peeked from the edge of those woods.

"Boys," a New York captain said, "there's another wagon train for us over behind the rebel lines."[3]

The Federals advanced over an open, rolling field on Warner's farm— "no man's land," he says. The soldiers halted briefly in a dip and charged as they closed to within 250 yards of their well-entrenched enemy.

Confederates answered Yankee cheers with the Rebel yell and sheets of lead and iron. Some Union soldiers reached the entrenchments and "fought to the death." The entire 5th New Hampshire color guard fell. The Yankees fell back. Amid a shower of bullets, a sergeant in the "Heavies" dragged and carried a wounded friend back to his lines.

_____

3. *Drum Taps in Dixie*, Page 171

Billy Cook, a first sergeant in the 2nd New York Heavy Artillery, had survived the war without a scratch. "The jig was about up with the Johnnies," he said the day before Cumberland Church. A Rebel bullet killed him on April 7.[4]

John Davis of the Heavies—a married father of six—fell here, too.[5] So did Edward Lindsey, the married father of two young girls.[6] The Heavies' Michael Connell, the married father of three, suffered a gunshot wound in the right thigh. Two months later, he died of exhaustion in a Washington hospital.[7]

Sergeant John C. Moorehead of the 148th Pennsylvania and his friend, 24-year-old bugler Joseph Harrison Law, surveyed the battle next to each other from astride their horses—probably on the very ground where Warner and I stand near the Old Jamestown Road.

Law, a blue-eyed, light-haired farmer, had enlisted in the 148th Pennsylvania in Punxsutawney, Pennsylvania. He served in Company E with his younger brothers, Charles and Daniel. He also went by "Harrison" or "Harry." Jovial and organized, Law seemed a natural for the army. "Always on the alert for frolic or adventure," a comrade recalled.[8]

The Law boys were close. At the Battle of Deep Bottom in 1864, near Richmond, Charles collapsed in the intense heat. Daniel and Harry carried their brother to a field hospital tent. A surgeon told them Charles neared death. But before he rushed off to care for wounded soldiers, the surgeon offered brief advice: *Give him whiskey.* Dan pried his brother's jaw open with a spoon handle and poured whiskey down his throat from a tin cup. For hours, he alternately massaged his brother vigorously and gave him the drink. About 4 a.m., Charles, woozy and boozy, regained consciousness and recognized his brother.

Later, Daniel carried Charles, who was 50 pounds heavier, toward a hospital boat. An ambulance completed the mercy mission. Harry, meanwhile, had returned to the regiment and written a letter to his parents: *Charles is*

4. Ibid, Page 166

5. John Davis widow's pension file, National Archives, Washington

6. Edward Lindsey widow's pension file

7. Michael Connell widow's pension file

8. Muffly, Joseph Wendel, *The Story of Our Regiment: A History of the 148th Pennsylvania Vol,* Des Moines, Iowa: The Kenyon Printing and Manufacturing Co., 1904, Page 667

dead. Daniel's letter detailing his brother's survival arrived in Pennsylvania the same day as Harry's. What a day for Mr. and Mrs. Law.

Shortly before he rode into battle at Cumberland Church, Harry Law said he was eager to return to his 20-year-old wife, Mary, and four-year-old son, Carl. He had not seen them since his enlistment in August 1862. "Lee is on his last legs," he told the regimental chaplain. "He will surrender in a day or two and then we shall soon get home."

Shortly after Law finished his bugle call to rally the Fourth Brigade, a Confederate artillery shell or solid shot carried away the top of his head. Moorehead leaped from his horse, plunged the brigade flag into the ground and pulled his friend from his saddle. The bugler became the 210th—and last— soldier to die in the hard-fighting 148th Pennsylvania during the war.[9]

Joseph Harrison Law (left) served with his brothers, Charles and Daniel, in the 148th Pennsylvania. The Story Of Our Regiment: A History of the 148th Pennsylvania Vols.

Moorehead buried Law on the battlefield. Later, he presented Harry's blood-spattered bugle to his brothers, who gave it to his widow. Years later, the relic was destroyed in a house fire. Law's remains, however, never made it back to Pennsylvania. Moorehead died shortly after the war, leaving the location of Law's grave a mystery.

"We know where he's not buried," Warner says.

He stands in a shallow area in a thin patch of woods, yards off the Old Jamestown Road. In 2021, Warner had deployed ground-penetrating radar to try to locate Law's remains. Nothing turned up, but he suspects the bugler rests near the "S"-shaped road.

Earlier that year, Warner had connected with Law's great-great-grandson, who supplied him with copies of dozens of wartime family letters and other information. Weeks after my visit, he walked the ground with Warner—a surreal, emotional experience for both.

---

9. Fox, William, *Regimental Losses in the American Civil War, 1861-1865*, Albany, N.Y., Albany Publishing Co., 1889

On the night of April 7, Ulysses Grant—commander of all U.S. Army forces—sent a messenger through the lines to Lee: *It's time to give up.*[10] Lee asked James Longstreet, his "Old War Horse," what he thought. "Not yet," the lieutenant general said.[11]

"That messenger rode right out here along the Jamestown Road and delivered the message by torchlight," Warner says.

Later that night, Lee's army withdrew by light of bonfires in the woods beyond Bad Luck Creek.

The Army of Northern Virginia could have surrendered *right here*. But no historical marker marks this battlefield.

"This place is forgotten," Warner says.

And so Dirk Warner dreams that someday, perhaps after both he and Jane rest in graves near the redbuds, this unheralded battlefield becomes a national park. He dreams his house becomes a visitors' center and museum. Relics unearthed on the farm become its centerpiece.

Meanwhile, he will admire the warm glow of battlefield sunsets and think of the stories that linger on his farm like wisps of musket smoke.

"This place," he says, "is so humbling."

I could spend days with Warner on his hallowed ground. But other Virginia battlefields await. It's time to explore the Shenandoah Valley and the Civil War's Mother Road.

---

10. *Official Records*, Vol. 38, Part 1, Page 47

11. Longstreet, James, *From Manassas to Appomattox*, Philadelphia: J.B. Lippincott Co., 1896, Page 619

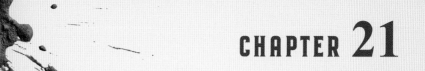

CHAPTER 21

Virginia's Shenandoah Valley

THE MOTHER ROAD

Cranky and tired after a freezing night in a restored farmhouse on the Cross Keys battlefield, I gulp what seems like four gallons of coffee at a bakery in Harrisonburg, Virginia. This is where Nathaniel "Bobbin' Boy" Banks—the incompetent political general, and *NO RELATION!*—set up his HQ in 1862.

I ask the early-20ish woman behind the counter if she knows about the building's Civil War significance.

"Sorry," she says, "I'm not from the South."

Then I'm off for the day to explore the Civil War's Mother Road, the Valley Pike.

Thousands of soldiers from both sides traipsed upon and fought over the pike, which wound through the Confederacy's breadbasket in the Shenandoah Valley. The 93-mile turnpike, from Winchester in the north to Staunton in the south, served as the key artery in Stonewall Jackson's Valley Campaign of 1862 and the U.S. Army's campaigns of 1864. The pike—nearly all macadamized—enabled swift movement of wagon trains, artillery, and troops even during rainy weather, when dirt roads became quagmires.

In the spring of 1862, Jackson marched his infantry through the Valley and gaps in the Blue Ridge, often befuddling Union commanders and whipping their army. Banks may still be quivering in his Massachusetts

177

grave at the thought of the oddball Confederate general attacking him in the Valley.

Elsewhere along the Civil War's Mother Road, the armies clashed at places such as New Market, Tom's Brook and Fisher's Hill, where I once was stared down by a gang of hoodlum cattle. "Depressed over the death of one of their own," a local woman later told me.

In 1840, six years after Virginia authorized the state legislature to create the Valley Turnpike Company, traveling the length of the pike cost roughly $4.38.[1] But I suspect the state collected no tolls from soldiers in either army during the war.

"The race course of armies," postwar newspapers called the pike. Nineteenth-century speed limit: 15 mph.[2]

In 1918, when the state took over the turnpike, tolls went by the wayside. Five years later, someone even wrote a glowing poem about the historic road:

> *Ninety miles and more it stretches*
> *Up the Valley, towards the south:*
> *Firm it is to wheel and hoof beat,*
> *Firm it holds in flood and drouth:*
> *And it links the towns and cities,*
> *Jewels on a silver chain,*
> *Shining in their emerald settings,*
> *In the broad and fertile plain.*
> *Straight it runs for leagues of distance,*
> *Here and there a crook or turn:*
> *Now it leaps a creek or river*
> *Or caresses bank and burn:*
> *But it never halts or falters,*
> *On it leads through night and day,*
> *Like a cheering path of promise*
> *"tis a fine old honest way!"*[3]

---

1. "The Valley Turnpike Company," National Park Service web site, accessed Dec. 24, 2022

2. *Richmond Times-Dispatch*, July 24, 1932

3. Wayland, John W., *A Scenic and Historical Guide to the Shenandoah Valley*, Shenandoah Press, Dayton, Va., 1923, Page 98

In the late 1920s, when cars became popular and folks aimed to stretch their legs well beyond their home base, the paved pike remained an important transportation route. The beauty of the ride captivated travelers, too. To the east stand the awe-inspiring Blue Ridge and Massanutten mountains. To the west loom the equally beautiful Alleghenies.

"One of the most inspiring drives in all the world of motordom," a reporter wrote in 1932 about a pike drive.[4]

By the 1950s, scores of kitschy accommodations such as the Tiny Town Motel, Blue Ridge Inn and Appleway Motel had risen along the pike for Valley tourists. Attractions such as the Endless Caverns in New Market, spring apple blossoms in Winchester and Shenandoah National Park lured them. But in the 1960s, the feds constructed four-lane Interstate 81 roughly parallel to the two-lane pike. As a result, tourism along the pike waned and battlefield preservation took a massive hit.

I-81 did more damage in the Shenandoah Valley than Sheridan, a local once told me. The interstate stuck a red-hot poker through the hearts of Cedar Creek, New Market, Winchester and other hallowed ground.

In the 21st century, I-81 turned beastly, fraying nerves and surely sending Valium sales upward. No sane person will write a poem about the interstate, but if they did, it would be full of expletives.

The pace of the Civil War's Mother Road—U.S. Route 11—is much more appealing. She often lures me with charms such as the smell of fallen walnuts on the Cedar Creek battlefield; the beauty of a huge, faux rooster outside a circa-1960s motel in Woodstock; butt-ugly pumpkins in Mount Jackson in the fall; and the intriguing odor of a decomposing bear in a small cave at Hupp's Hill near Strasburg, a strategic spot for both armies.

* * *

Near a circa-1929 filling station along the pike, six miles from Harrisonburg, a huge banner beckons, like an alluring lady in the corner of a smoky French Quarter bar:

"Melrose Civil War Caverns. Underground History of the Civil War."

---

4. *Richmond Times-Dispatch,* July 24, 1932

I have experienced Civil War vibes in cornfields, cow pastures, peach orchards and Confederate Gen. Gideon Pillow's smokehouse but never in a cave with inscriptions made by actual Civil War soldiers. I score a "VIP tour," code for "I do not have to pay." Jack Yancey, the late-20ish director of operations, greets me in the Melrose Caverns Lodge, a two-story, European ski chalet-like building without the trappings.

With no trappings at all, actually. The building is as cavernous as the cave. It housed a Civil War museum from 1929 until the late 1960s. In the 1970s and 1980s, the lodge became the party destination for college students and their assorted hangers-on. The place conjures images of a massive disco ball, blaring Bee Gees music, and hundreds chugging beer from 25 kegs. I like it.

Yancey's family owns the caverns, now a tourist attraction/wedding venue. Business is slow, but the family remains hopeful of a rebound. The caverns and the fabulous, adjacent farm have been part of their family since 1748. The circa-1859 farmhouse somehow missed a torching by marauding Yankees during "The Burning" in the fall of 1864.

"There are more than 300 signatures of soldiers in the cave, mostly Union soldiers," Yancey tells me. "Some were left after the war when soldiers returned after the war."

"Who counted them?" I ask.

"Not me."

My caverns guide is Andrew, a 20-something from South Carolina who seems to be in a hurry. He opens the bank vault-like caverns door, added years ago to deter nighttime intruders from descending into the darkness to cause mischief. Or worse. No one wants to get trapped 100 feet underground unless you're a Mafia turncoat dropped from the Witness Protection Program.

A couple from Florida accompanies us. Andrew—"one of our best guides," Yancey says later—flicks on the cave lights. We pass stalactites and stalagmites—stuff Ms. Smiley schooled me on in the fourth grade at Julia Ward Howe Elementary in suburban Pittsburgh. I annoy Andrew with a volley of questions.

"Now there's a cave below us," he says. "Don't step too hard or you may fall in."

In 1862, 4th Ohio Private John Hollabaugh inscribed his name on a wall in
Melrose Caverns.

Andrew is joking. For a second, though, he stares at me with the very
same grin I saw from Jack Nicholson when he broke down the door in *The
Shining*. I sweat even though the caverns temperature remains about 55
degrees year-round.

Andrew points out the first inscription, carved in 1862 by John
Hollabaugh, a 4th Ohio private. He included his last name, first initial and
company. It probably took him hours using his bayonet to make this lasting
impression in the limestone wall.

"One of this soldier's descendants came here to see this too," Andrew
says.

In a large, open area where they hold weddings, Andrew identifies a
huge column, formed by a stalactite-stalagmite marriage.

"Soldiers stuffed their ears with cotton and used the column for target
practice," he tells us. Then Andrew points to another stalactite, about 25
paces away.

"They stood over there."

Incredulous, I conduct a brief (three seconds) forensic examination on the column.

The soldiers fired muskets from *25 paces in a cave?!* Imagine the noise. Then a tiny, imaginary man on my shoulder whispers an old journalism maxim into my ear: *"If your mother tells you she loves you, get another source."* So, I vow to dig deeper, but not in the cave, because there could be another one below us.

We examine "cave sausage," "cave bacon," "cave popcorn," "cave soda straws," a lizard-like formation, a bored bat just hanging out—one of two said to lurk in the caverns—and an open area believed to have been used as sleeping quarters for soldiers. Dozens of initials, names, and regiments of soldiers mark the walls. Some soldiers used ash from torches for this cave artwork. One created a crude image of Abraham Lincoln, a labor of love, for sure.

"They would write with anything within their reach," Andrew says. Some soldiers apparently used the butts of their rifles to batter defenseless stalactites—"soda straws," our guide calls the victims.

We're joined by Jack and his Uncle Jim, a curly haired gentleman in his late 50s or early 60s. He wears jeans and a long-sleeve sweatshirt from a Canadian ski resort. Looks tired.

"I explored this place as a kid." Uncle Jim says. "Used a Bic lighter. Yankees controlled this area during the day, the Rebels ruled the night." He says that in the evenings, Union soldiers descended into the caverns and used it as an ammo dump.

"This place was a great, big *bomb*."

Then, while I examine an inscription, Uncle Jim inches a little closer. "Pardon the smell. I'm a chicken farmer."

The next 25 minutes are a blur of etched initials, stalactites and stalagmites and the story of a man who aimed to build a hotel over the caverns more than 100 years ago. (The venture failed.)

Back in the lodge, Uncle Jim nurses a bottle of Guinness while I suffer from the effects of only four hours' sleep and a bazillion cups of coffee. Yancey shows me an album of caverns wedding photos and a slip of paper from the old museum. It's evidence, he believes, that soldiers used the cave as a shooting gallery.

Then the tiny, imaginary man on my shoulder whispers in my ear: "It's time to ramble on."

* * *

Besides squirrels, opossums, deer, skunks (dead) on the road and camels (living) on the farm astride Port Republic Road near the Cross Keys (Va.) battlefield, I spot other wildlife on my Civil War travels. Along the Valley Pike in Rockingham County stands a gigantic turkey, a tremendous photo op. Naturally, I stop for a pic, enduring the smirks of locals, who probably wonder: "Why is the strange man shooting multiple closeups of our large bird?"

I often spot animals on road trips—live, dead and sometimes inanimate, like this huge turkey along the Valley Pike.

As it turns out, it is a faux turkey—"Welcome to Rockingham County. Turkey Capital," reads the plaque below the bronze bird. Now it's impressive and all, but maybe the county should invest instead in fixing that pike pothole before Edinburg, my next stop.

Edinburg, population roughly 1,300, still has a pay phone on the corner—a local call will cost you a quarter. Inside the town's 1848 gristmill along the pike, I meet 83-year-old Barbara Forsyth—a self-described "people person" and a telephone switchboard operator in the early 1960s. She's the mill's docent, receptionist and gift shop salesclerk.

"Come over here," she says.

Sweet Barbara points to charred floorboards in a corner on the first floor—evidence of Union Gen. Phil Sheridan's ugly work, discovered during a 1979 remodeling. To deprive the Confederate Army of resources, the cavalry of "Fightin' Phil" destroyed mills, barns, sheds, tanneries, furnaces and more in the Shenandoah Valley during "The Burning" from September 27-October 9, 1864. The U.S. Army drove off or confiscated livestock and destroyed foodstuffs and transportation equipment. As Ulysses Grant wished, the Valley became a wasteland "so that crows flying over it for the balance of the season will have to carry their provender with them."[5]

Nearly 120 years after the war, the mother of my college girlfriend harbored bitterness about what the Yankees did in the Valley. She lived in Luray, Virginia—about a half-hour drive over the mountain. At least one of their ancestors served in the Stonewall Brigade, one of the war's most celebrated combat units.

Shortly after noon on October 7, 1864, Union soldiers set the Edinburg mill ablaze. According to local lore, a bucket brigade that included the granddaughter of the mill's owner—a Mexican War veteran—saved the place. As another story goes, Sheridan ordered the fire put out after the pleas of the mill owner's granddaughters. *Now name a puppy after me*, Sheridan supposedly told the young ladies after the flames had been extinguished.

The Edinburg mill—saved by the town and a preservation group—now serves as a gift shop, restaurant and a three-floor museum stuffed with Shenandoah Valley antiques, photos and paraphernalia. Locals donate most.

"They fear if they leave it to their kids, it might end up on eBay," says Dan Harshman, the town's mayor since 1992. He creates the displays. I love the crazy-ace hornet's nest found in a pine tree on the old Wetzel property. The thing whispered to me. Sleep deprivation can be an ugly thing.

In the museum, I also spot a photo of a "prized hog" going to slaughter (that was quite the social event back in the day); a door from Hank Saum's hardware store; a hand crank paddle assembly from Mr. Dove's apple butter stirrer; a still; dozens of artifacts from the 1862 Battle of South Mountain in Maryland; a roll of names from Company K of the 12th Virginia Cavalry; the obligatory illustration of Robert E. Lee; and some beaded ladies' handbags.

In 1898, an Edinburg youngster suffered a mortal wound in an ax grinding accident in the mill. His spirit is said to lurk in the place. In 2011, a paranormal investigative team placed a flashlight on the steps of the mill and coaxed the ghost—his name is "Frankie"—to play with it. A less professional team of teen paranormalists using a Ouija board determined the ghost was a misogynist, peeving Sweet Barbara.

---

5. *Official Records*, Vol. 37, Part 2, Page 301

Burn marks on the floor of the mill in Edinburg, Virginia.

"You tell him," she told the teens, "that when I turn the lights on up there that I will not say good night to him."

* * *

Before arriving in Winchester, the "Apple Capital of the World," I pass the Kernstown battlefield, nearly hemmed in by modern development. The battlefield gate is locked. Closed for the day. *Damn*. It's enough to crush a battlefield tramper's soul.

"Our men fought bravely, but the superior numbers of the enemy repulsed me," Jackson wrote about a stinging defeat here on March 23,

1862—a rare "L" on the general's Civil War résumé. "Many valuable lives were lost. Our God was my shield. His protecting care is an additional cause for gratitude."[6]

Nearby, beyond Winchester's urban schlock, Jackson made his official headquarters in a residence on North Braddock Street from November 1861 to March 1862. It's a tidy residential area near the apple pressing plants today. But Jackson's HQ is closed, too. Around back, a man named Myron is prepping the place for its re-opening on April Fool's Day. He's a 65-year-old former apple juice presser, lifelong Winchester resident and longtime owner of his own masonry business.

"This place looks nothing like it did on the historical sign out front," Myron says of Jackson's HQ. In an 1861 letter to his wife, the general wrote that the walls inside are "covered with elegant gilt paper."

In 2003, producers filmed a scene from *Gods and Generals*, the awful Civil War movie, on this very ground.

"It was fricking wild," Myron says. "There were horses and carriages all over this place."

Nearby stands Sheridan's wartime headquarters, a former private residence that now houses a "roomy store featuring women's clothing, linens, china, crystal & home décor, plus bridal registries," according to sources. I don't think the gigantic faux apple in the front yard stood there the day "Little Phil" began his ride south on the Valley Pike to turn the tide at Cedar Creek.

But neither Jackson's nor Sheridan's HQs are the best reasons to visit Winchester, the northern terminus of the Mother Road. On the northeast side of town, less than a mile away, nearly 1,700 known Rebel soldiers rest in Stonewall Confederate Cemetery, part of Mount Hebron Cemetery. Most lay under small, slate-gray tombstones. Within sight across the street, beyond two stone walls, 1,349 Union soldiers rest under pearl-white markers in the national cemetery. Many died in battles along the Valley Pike, the Civil War's Mother Road.

In death, Yankees and Rebels remain divided.

In the Georgia section of the Confederate cemetery, I'm drawn to the marker for Francis Mobley, a 50th Georgia lieutenant. Years ago, I read his

---

6. Jackson, Mary Anna, *Life and Letters of General Thomas J. Jackson*, New York: Harper & Brothers, 1892, Page 247

wartime letters online. At Antietam on September 17, 1862, he suffered a bullet wound in the chest. By early October, Mobley lay in a Winchester hospital.

"[I]t was God's mercy that saved me from instant death," he wrote to his wife, Rhoda, in Nashville, Georgia.[7]

But on the morning of October 9, a doctor told Mobley to prepare to die. Struggling to communicate, he seemed unaffected by the grim news. That night, his voice "weak and faint," Mobley asked a friend to write three letters for him—one to his father-in-law, another to his father and one to "Rodey," his wife. He hoped his young son would be "raised up in the right manner and to live and fear the Lord." A Bible lay by his side. His pain sometimes proved excruciating. Mobley died that day. He was only 26.

"I have every reason to believe that he died trusting in his precious Savior," a Winchester woman wrote, "and his greatest dearest wish was that his precious wife and child might meet him in Heaven."[8]

Before departing the cemetery, I tap Mobley's grave. Remember one, someone once said, and you remember them all.

Twelve hours later, I am speeding north. In Sharpsburg, Maryland, I have a date with a cookie and a woman with an Abraham Lincoln obsession.

---

7.   Francis Lawton Mobley Papers, Atlanta History Center, ahc.MSS1008

8.   Ibid

CHAPTER 22

Sharpsburg To Frederick, Maryland

ABRAHAM LINCOLN AND THE OREO COOKIE LADY

Every time there's a Polar Vortex in the East, I can't help but think of the day I re-traced part of President Lincoln's October 1862 journey from Washington to the Antietam battlefield with the Sharpsburg, Maryland woman who owns an Oreo cookie with the profile of Abe in the white frosting.

Lincoln fanatic Laura Van Alstyne Rowland—the presidential cookie owner—didn't flinch on my whimsical idea despite unusually frigid spring weather. The 67-year-old retired clinical social worker embraces all things Lincoln with unbridled joy. Think a baby blowing bubbles with her momma; a puppy playing with a chew toy for the first time; me after getting Mrs. B's OK for another road trip.

Here's our loose in-the-footsteps-of-Lincoln itinerary, Rowland's *fourth* such journey: Harpers Ferry, West Virginia (Virginia in October 1862); the intersection where Lincoln met a Union corps commander; two farmhouses near Sharpsburg; and Frederick, Maryland, where the president comforted a wounded Union general and later departed for Washington.

Rowland's Oreo strikes me as the ultimate symbol of Lincoln fandom. An intern in a hospital whom Rowland supervised sculpted Abe with toothpicks and love in about 30 minutes. Then she gifted it to Rowland in 2014. "A one-of-a-kind gift for a one-of-a-kind person," its creator told me.

Like the 16th U.S. president, it isn't perfect—the cracks snaking through the chocolate wafer and the cookie's flaking frosting make it look care-worn. But in its own, quirky way, the thing exudes confidence, an aura even. And, besides, who else on the planet has one?

Rowland and her husband, Dave—also known as "Bear"—live in a 1782 house in Sharpsburg with their dog Jake, a half Siberian husky, half border collie mix. Bear, a retired bookseller, co-founded the Green Party in Utah, where the couple reared their four children, now adults. Laura is a descendant of a 150th New York corporal who was killed at Culp's Hill at Gettysburg on July 3, 1863.

From 2016-2019, the Rowlands leased the historic house on Main Street, across from the national cemetery, where nearly 4,800 Union soldiers rest. The couple embraced Sharpsburg and the battlefield. Beautiful, history-rich western Maryland enthralled them. Then they moved back to Utah for 10 months. But they longed for Sharpsburg, population about 750. In 2020, the Rowlands returned after purchasing the house they had leased. The move buoyed the Rowlands and Jake.

"When we moved back to Utah, he was so depressed," Laura says of the dog. "When we moved back, he remembered all the old places. He loves the battlefield."

Jake and Laura take frequent battlefield walks. On a stroll with Jake on Cornfield Avenue, near the epicenter of vicious fighting on the old David R. Miller farm, she had a strange experience. Laura noticed a man walking near the Mississippi and Georgia monuments.

"*Trego!*" he yelled into the distance. Rowland figured the man was calling for his dog.

Distracted by a National Park Service ranger in a car, she briefly turned away. When Rowland turned around moments later, the man had vanished. Curious, she researched this "Trego." As it turned out, a soldier named George Trego of the 128th Pennsylvania had suffered two wounds in the Bloody Cornfield, near where she was walking with Jake. A monument to Trego's regiment stands on Cornfield Avenue.

While ghosts may not occupy the Rowlands' residence, their house has a tragic history: During the Battle of Antietam on September 17, 1862, a Union artillery shell crashed into it, killing on impact a Confederate soldier drawing water at a well and two more Rebels inside the house with the subsequent explosion. One of those soldiers was discovered clutching onions, booty perhaps.[1] Wounded soldiers found succor in the house, also used as a hospital. Dark stains, believed to be blood, remain on the Rowlands' hardwood floor.

As we depart Sharpsburg at 9:56 a.m. in Murray, Mrs. B's vehicle, I consider the ability of the Oreo's frosting and chocolate wafer to withstand direct sunlight. I don't think the Rowlands' homeowner's policy covers the cookie. But we take no special precautions for our journey. No Oreo seatbelt. No portable Oreo vault. The thing travels in a shadow box frame Rowland bought for it in 2014.

Almost immediately, I quiz Rowland about her obsession.

"Well, my dad loved Lincoln," she says.

Dad went to Yale and became a constitutional law professor.

As a kid, Laura had a moderate interest in the 16th president. Rowland's Lincoln fandom skyrocketed, however, when her youngest child Trevor attended eighth grade. To keep up with his Lincoln studies, she absorbed all things Abe, mainly books. Then she branched out.

"I went to as many Lincoln-related sites as I could," Rowland says as I navigate a twisting backroad to Harpers Ferry.

Minutes later, we rumble over the town's cobblestone streets. In the historic section of Harpers Ferry, Rowland—who has an artificial right knee and hip—navigates the slope down to the Potomac River. Meanwhile, I slip and stagger behind her: "Hey, Lincoln could have stumbled here."

I stifle an urge to dig my hand into the historic mud.

At about noon on October 1, 1862, Lincoln—traveling by rail from Washington—arrived across the Potomac River from Harpers Ferry with a presidential party. The regular bridge had been destroyed by Confederates, so the president walked into town across a pontoon bridge. Steps away from us, iron rings that may have secured it remain embedded in stone walls—a possible hidden-in-plain-sight Lincoln link.

---

1. Reilly, Oliver T., *The Battlefield of Antietam*, Hagerstown, Md., self-published, 1906

Rowland looks wistfully across the river, toward towering and wooded Maryland Heights.

"I think this is so cool that this is the place where Lincoln arrived. To think of him crossing here."

In the afternoon, Lincoln and George McClellan, the Army of the Potomac commander, reviewed troops on Bolivar Heights outside town. Troops in Harpers Ferry greeted the president with "great enthusiasm."[2]

A hospital intern sculpted a profile of Abe Lincoln into the white icing of this Oreo. Then she gave the cookie to Laura Van Alstyne Rowland as a gift.

Lincoln and McClellan, who had led the Federal troops at Antietam, shared a mutual contempt. They both also shared the mental burden of knowing more than 3,500 young Americans had died two weeks earlier in the fields, woodlots and makeshift hospitals at Sharpsburg. Soldiers still were dying in makeshift hospitals on the very day of the presidential visit and for weeks afterward.

At night, Lincoln stayed somewhere in the area, perhaps in nearby Bolivar. No one knows for sure where. Rowland likes to think he slept at the hilltop Lockwood House, an imposing two-story with grand porches, instead of a less-presidential venue nearby. There, steps from a cemetery, we admire the commanding view of the town, the Potomac River, Maryland Heights in Maryland and Loudoun Heights in Virginia beyond. After the war, the house became part of Storer Normal School—one of the country's first schools for freed slaves.

During his visit, Lincoln started for the Maryland Heights summit astride a horse to visit troops. "I showed the way until we got to a path where it was right straight up, when Abraham backed out," a 2nd Massachusetts soldier recalled. "I think it must have reminded him of a

---

2. *New York Daily Herald*, Oct. 3, 1862

little story about a very steep place; at any rate, around they turned and went back down the mountain."[3]

My Fitbit, heart and lungs confirmed on previous hikes up the steep, rutted trail that the president was no laggard.

A circuitous route takes us back into Maryland. Then we travel the hilly, serpentine road taken by abolitionist and madman John Brown and his 21-man gang for their unsuccessful raid on the Federal arsenal at Harpers Ferry on October 16, 1859. Nearly three years later, Lincoln traveled the same road in a horse-drawn carriage.

"I wonder if he thought about it or even knew," Rowland says as we travel under a canopy of trees.

Besides Lincoln's sense of humanity and ability to analyze the Constitution, Rowland appreciates Lincoln's sense of humor. He often used it to put others at ease as well as to relieve stress or make a point.

"He seemed to have so much native intelligence without any formal schooling, and he was such a great people observer," she says. "He seemed to have a natural ability to connect with people.

"Politically, he was so respectful of the Constitution. Even though he didn't like slavery, he didn't feel like he could touch it. He tried to reassure the South over and over again that it would remain in the states where it already existed.

"He was prone to bouts of depression. I don't think he was an easy person to live with. He got lost in own thoughts."

Nearly lost in my own thoughts in the beautiful, rolling hills, I hang a left at a fork in the road. If I go right on Chestnut Grove Road, I'd soon arrive at the Kennedy Farm cabin, launch point for Brown's infamous raid. Minutes later, we arrive at the corners of Mills and Harpers Ferry roads, where I park.

Euphoric, Laura, smiling as usual, breathes in the crisp, country air and history. We try to imagine the 1862 scene—flags fluttering, Lincoln stepping from his carriage, a presidential handshake with bewhiskered Ninth Corps commander Ambrose Burnside, fields filled with white tents and Union soldiers, the awesome aroma of smoke from hundreds of campfires.

---

3. Frye, Dennis, *Harpers Ferry Under Fire*, The Donning Company Publishers, Virginia Beach, Va., 2012, Page 111

At the Grove farm near Sharpsburg—one of our stops—Alexander Gardner photographed Lincoln, George McClellan and other U.S. Army brass in October 1862. Library of Congress

"There's something about this road that I'm drawn to," Rowland says.

No marker denotes the historical significance of this unremarkable country intersection. This moment merits special recognition. Rowland and her framed Oreo become subject matter for a photograph, occasional traffic be damned. The cookie appears unharmed despite its rare road trip. This sure isn't how Shelby Foote and Bruce Catton experienced Civil War history.

The intersection is Rowland's favorite in-the-footsteps-of-Lincoln tour stop … until the next stop changes her mind.

On the afternoon of October 3, 1862, about a mile west of Sharpsburg, Lincoln stopped at Mount Airy, the home of Stephen Grove. His impressive brick house became a major Confederate hospital in the aftermath of Antietam. Wounded Union soldiers received care here, too. The president may have put his large hand on the head of the Groves' seven-year-old daughter and apologized to her parents for the destruction the war had wrought.[4] In a field here, Richard Clem—my Civil War poppa—unearthed a bullet carved into a top hat by a soldier, perhaps a tip of his kepi to the president.

At the Grove farm, the president conferred with McClellan, reviewed troops and posed for an image by Alexander Gardner, one of Mathew Brady's photographers. A photograph with "Little Mac" and other U.S. Army brass in front of the house became one of the war's most famous images. A chimney of Grove's house peeks from behind the subjects in Gardner's image. The photographer captured something else: palpable tension between the president, wearing his stovepipe hat, and the much smaller McClellan.

Lincoln considered "Little Mac" much too sluggish in his post-Antietam pursuit of Robert E. Lee's Army of Northern Virginia. Lincoln's sad appearance struck Union soldiers. "Careworn," a Pennsylvania soldier described the president.[5]

"We could see the deep sadness in his face, and feel the burden on his heart," recalled Joshua Lawrence Chamberlain of the 20th Maine.[6]

The Grove farm is private property—DO NOT TRESPASS—but an acquaintance of mine relic hunts the grounds and is cordial with the owners. A phone call with him and in-person schmoozing with an owner earns us a brief outside visit. This up-close inspection, Rowland's first, prompts a revision of her in-the footsteps-of-Lincoln tour rankings.

"I think this may top them all," she says.

The original steps Lincoln probably trod upon to visit inside with Confederate and Union wounded are long gone, replaced by wooden ones. Oh my, how we would love to walk in Lincoln's footsteps inside this historic treasure. An owner of the place, it is said, used a live, 20-pound Parrott shell inside as a doorstop.

---

4. Source is the papers of the Grove Family, Sharpsburg and Hagerstown, Md. John Schildt, a longtime Sharpsburg area resident and historian, examined these papers years ago while researching his privately published book, *Four Days in October*. The whereabouts of the papers are unknown today.

5. Oct. 3, 1862, diary entry of 100th Pennsylvania soldier Christopher Columbus Lobinger via Spared and Shared web site.

6. *Ceremonies in Commemoration of the One Hundredth Anniversary of the Birth of Abraham Lincoln*, Military Order of the Loyal Legion of the United States Commandery of the State of Pennsylvania, Philadelphia, 1909, Page 23

Surgeons used a rough-hewn table inside for operations. An area behind the barn, near a stone fence, became a dumping ground for amputated limbs. Surgeons in both armies shared quarters in Grove's attic, where they "ate together ... drank together, and had a high old time."[7]

In 1934, Fred Cross, a Massachusetts historian, accepted an invitation from the "lady of the house" to look around. In the parlor, she lifted a rug, revealing a large bloodstain.

"I have washed and scrubbed that spot again and again until I have thought I had got it all out," she told Cross, "but as soon as the floor dried that spot would reappear as plain as ever."[8]

On October 4, 1862, 4.5 miles northeast of the Grove farm on the Shepherdstown Pike, Lincoln stopped at the Philip Pry house to comfort Union Gen. Israel Richardson, who had suffered a shrapnel wound at Antietam. ("Fighting Dick" died a month later.) According to local lore, Pry and one of his slaves buried cannonballs somewhere near the barn, which still stands.

After leaving Richardson, Lincoln's party stopped at a house where many Confederate wounded lay. The president said he bore the men no malice and shook their hands. "It was a moving scene," a reporter wrote, "and there was not a dry eye in the building."[9] We can only speculate where this epic moment occurred.

At Frederick, 40 minutes east of Sharpsburg, my only concern is the @#$%&! traffic. Upon entering the town, the president received a 21-gun salute. A cheering crowd waved flags and handkerchiefs during his visit.[10] Ours includes far less fanfare. I receive an angry glare during a lane change.

At the Ramsey House on Record Street, Lincoln visited with Union Brig. Gen. George Hartsuff, who had suffered a bullet wound in the pelvis at Antietam.

---

7. Nelson, John H, "As Grain Falls Before The Reaper: The Federal Hospital Sites And Identified Federal Casualties at Antietam," Privately published CD, Hagerstown, Md., 2004. (Nelson cites the source of the farm's use as a hospital as Stephen P. Grove's granddaughter. See John Philemon Smith file in the Antietam National Battlefield Visitor's Center Library.)

8. *Hagerstown (Md.) Daily Mail*, March 12, 1934

9. *Herald of Freedom & Torch Light*, Hagerstown, Md., Oct. 15, 1862

10. *Washington Evening Star*, Oct. 6, 1862

Laura Van Alstyne Rowland, standing with the Lincoln Oreo in the Lincoln Room of her house, relishes walks on the Antietam battlefield.

"Three cheers for the hope of America!" someone shouted from the huge crowd as the president left the house.

"Speech!" cried another.

But the president demurred.[11]

I tap the historical sign outside the Ramsey House, now the Lincoln Condo, and briefly commune with the president's spirit.

Minutes later, Rowland leans out the window of Mrs. B's SUV to shoot a pic with my iPhone of the train station where Lincoln gave into the crowd's request for a speech. The station now houses an agency where the area's homeless and low-income families receive services.

"I think the president would approve, Laura."

She nods approvingly. Even the Oreo, resting comfortably on the floor of Murray, seems pleased.

---

11. *National Republican*, Washington, D.C., Oct. 7, 1862

Close your eyes (but not while driving), and perhaps you can imagine the president's brief speech on that rainy, windy afternoon in 1862.

> *I return thanks to our soldiers for the good service they have rendered, for the energies they have shown, the hardships they have endured, and the blood they have so nobly shed for this dear Union of ours. And I also return thanks not only to the soldiers, but to the good citizens of Maryland, and to all the good men and women in this land, for their devotion to our glorious cause.*[12]

Nearly six hours and 85 miles after our journey began, The Oreo Cookie Lady and I arrive back at home base. Bear, Rowland's husband, and Jake, the mixed breed, greet us.

In the Rowlands' living room—the Lincoln Room—we decompress. In one corner sits a life-sized, painted plaster bust of the president. On the wall, near where the Oreo cookie usually hangs out, they display framed clippings of snippets of hair of Abraham and Mary Lincoln.

"It's certified by Christie's auction house, but who knows if this is real?" Laura says. Dozens of Lincoln books fill a bookcase.

I coax my host to remove the Oreo from its frame home for a photo.

"Don't let Jake eat it!" Bear warns his wife while Laura performs the delicate task.

For history's sake, no one wants to see this remarkable cookie crumble.

But it's time to go. I have unfinished business on the Mother Road in the Shenandoah Valley.

---

12. *New York Tribune*, Oct. 6, 1862

CHAPTER 23

Middletown, Virginia

RAMBLING WITH
THE CHIEF
AT CEDAR CREEK

After a strenuous morning with a framed Oreo cookie riding shotgun, I doze for a few minutes in Murray at the Cedar Creek battlefield in Middletown, Virginia. Then a bigger and much better SUV rumbles into the gravel parking lot. It's Nick Picerno, my friend and today's tour guide.

Everything about Picerno is *big*. Big personality. Big Civil War collection. Bigtime battlefield preservationist. Big aspirations. Big guy, *period*. He stands 6-foot-8 and weighs about 325. He's a 67-year-old retired police chief. Naturally, subordinates called him "Chief."

Lucky for me, the Chief has a sense of humor, too.

Big Nick occasionally puts me up in the Widow Pence farmhouse on the Cross Keys battlefield, where Stonewall Jackson earned a big victory during his 1862 Valley Campaign. The farm serves as home base for the Shenandoah Valley/Lincoln Oreo cookie leg of this road trip. The previous owners—a doctor and his wife—lovingly restored the farmhouse and gave it and surrounding battlefield to the Shenandoah Valley Battlefields Foundation. Picerno is the preservation organization's longest-serving board member. The Chief has pull.

As I drove up the gravel road to the Widow Pence farmhouse during a previous visit, I spotted several angry cows and a snorting bull yards away. Woozy from a day of battlefield tramping in Maryland, I slammed on the brakes, threw the car into reverse and plowed into an unforgiving post, crumpling a rear panel and causing a temporary rift in my marriage. Duct tape put the panel back together, but my psyche remains scarred to this day. To compound my angst, a towel rack in the farmhouse bathroom fell at three the next morning, rousing me from a rare, restful sleep.

I recount the sorry details of this cow and bull intimidation story to Picerno, who chuckles and offers half-hearted condolences.

While Picerno drives (of course), we explore Cedar Creek, site of a come-from-behind Union victory on October 19, 1864—I never forget the date because it happens to be Mrs. B's birthdate (but not the same year). We also make a side trip on Banks Fort Road in nearby Strasburg to view the remains of earthworks constructed by U.S. Army troops in 1862 under Gen. Nathaniel Banks, who, as you know, is absolutely no relation.

Picerno's interest in the Civil War dates to 1966, when his family took a trip to Florida and stopped in Fredericksburg, Virginia, site of the Union Army's epic December 1862 defeat.

"I was amazed that such places exist," he says.

When he was about 18, Picerno traveled with his family from their home in New York to a harness racing track in Delaware. The Picernos dabbled in the sport, having owned a couple of horses. But the Chief took the family car for a side trip to Gettysburg instead. On the second date with his future wife, Kathy, he took her to … *Gettysburg*.

"I wanted her to know what she was getting involved with."

In the 1960s, when he was a teen, Picerno began acquiring Civil War artifacts—canteens, cartridge boxes, artillery shells and other stuff Mrs. B won't let into our house. In the late 1970s, he became laser-focused on collecting anything from the 1st, 10th and 29th Maine regiments—29th Maine Lt. John Gould eventually became almost his alter ego.

Years ago, during a visit to his house in New Market, Virginia, Picerno played for me a music box that Gould had swiped from a house during the Red River Campaign in Louisiana. "I was wicked enough to take [it] myself," Gould wrote, "knowing very well that if I didn't someone would, and the story I heard of the condition of the house an hour after my visit confirmed me in this idea."[1] Picerno had acquired the relic from the soldier's descendant.

The Chief also made me squirm when he showed me a close-up *carte de visite* (CDV) from his collection of a Civil War soldier's, ah, *derriere*. I am amazed that such photos exist. Perhaps a disease-riddled veteran used the risqué image in a pension request.

Like all the great collectors, the Chief has some magical magnetic field around him that attracts Civil War artifacts and memorabilia. Kathy calls it "divine providence." Exhibit A: A descendant of 10th Maine Private Asa Reed discovered Picerno had several hundred images of other soldiers from the regiment. "Asa," the man said, "belongs with his buddies." And so he gifted Picerno a CDV of Reed, who had been killed at Antietam.

Picerno also has mastered the art of persuasion. I know. He bulldogged me for a remarkable set of six images taken by Gould's son at Antietam in 1891. On the back of the frame for each image, John Gould had written detailed descriptions of the location for the photograph—pure gold for historians and photos aficionados like us. We completed the deal on the Widow Pence farmhouse porch on September 17—the anniversary of the Battle of Antietam.

"The great thing about this is the hunt," Picerno says about Civil War collecting. "The greatest thing is sharing it with others." His collection includes thousands of items, from swords and pistols to diaries and letters.

On a road trip with Kathy in 2022, Picerno logged 4,000 miles and visited battlefields in Mississippi, Missouri, Arkansas, Oklahoma, Tennessee and Kentucky. So the Chief and I are kindred spirits.

As we tool around the battlefield, Picerno talks about his other passion —battlefield preservation. He enjoys picnicking with Kathy at Cedar Creek, a crazy quilt of preserved and developed land. (His favorite battlefields are Third Winchester and Antietam.) Picerno gestures toward a housing development on the west side of Valley Pike.

"A year ago that was battlefield."

---

1. *The Civil War Journals of John Mead Gould, 1861-1866*, Edited by William B. Jordan, Baltimore, Md.: Butternut & Blue Publishers, 1998

At the Cedar Creek battlefield, Nick Picerno—"the Chief"—poses with the sword of 29th Maine Major George Nye, a prized relic from his vast collection.

Later, he points to a tree where he had posted a "No Relic Hunting" sign on ground preserved by the Shenandoah Valley Battlefields Foundation.

"Look, they took it down."

Picerno suspects "they" may be unscrupulous metal detectorists, the bane of most battlefield preservationists. In 2021, Picerno led a successful effort in Virginia to make relic hunting on preserved battlefield land a crime.

As we rumble along a gravel road, the Chief tells a story about tensely named Uranus Stacy of the 29th Maine. Shortly before the Third Battle of Winchester, one of his commanding officers had a premonition of death. "He was telling us to shoot down a rebel flag when he was hit," wrote Stacy. "Poor fellow, he was a brave man and clever officer."[2] The major died the next day. Early in the battle at Cedar Creek, the Rebels drove Stacy's comrades "like sheep," he wrote his mother.

Fifteen minutes later, the Chief points to an open field to our left—preserved land—where Gen. Phil Sheridan led the grand counterattack that turned Union defeat into victory. Nearby, we meet a farmer named Jesse, the mid-30ish owner of dogs named Stella and Hank and an aloof, 325-pound boar named Louie. The animal has gleaming white tusks his veterinarian must love. I briefly interview the boar, who only grunts.

"What does Louie eat?" I ask.

"Whatever he wants," Jesse tells me.

With his dad, Jesse farms battlefield leased from the Shenandoah Valley Battlefields Foundation. Like Picerno, he's bummed about 21st-century developers scoring so many recent victories in the Valley.

On the battlefield, Jesse leases the circa-1780s Dinges house. Next to his bed one morning, he woke up to a five-foot black snake.

"Disgusting little animals," he says.

Jesse sometimes dispatches them to reptile heaven with firepower. The animals are one of the perils of living at the historic residence, probably used as a makeshift hospital during the battle.

Like every battlefield, Cedar Creek teems with stories. Most you can only fully appreciate by walking the ground. One of my favorite dramas occurred on the east side of the Valley Pike. On the foggy morning

---

2.   Stacy letter to his mother, Oct. 5 and 22, 1864, Picerno collection

Louie, what a boar.

of October 19, 1864, Union brass ordered Colonel Stephen Thomas'
1,500-soldier brigade to delay a surprise attack by an overwhelming Rebel
force—an impossible job. Predictably, the Confederates crushed Thomas'
brigade, which suffered 70 percent casualties (1,050 men). But the effort
and bravery of Thomas' soldiers bought the U.S. Army nearly 30 crucial
minutes.

In brutal, often hand-to-hand fighting, the 8th Vermont defended a
deep ravine and stretch of woods, suffering 110 casualties out of 164 men
engaged. Three of its color-bearers fell.

"Men seemed more like demons than human beings, as they struck
fiercely at each other with clubbed muskets and bayonets," recalled a
Vermont soldier. "But in that vortex of hell men did not forget the colors."[3]
The 8th Vermont monument, dedicated in 1883, is something to behold. (So
is the smell of fallen green walnuts in a nearby field.)

---

3. Carpenter, George N., *History of the Eighth Regiment Vermont Volunteers 1861-1865*, Boston: Press of Deland & Barta, 1886, Page 215

After the Union Army rapidly retreated, regrouped and finally routed the Rebels, the 2nd Connecticut Heavy Artillery aided its wounded and buried the dead. The next morning, the regiment's assistant surgeon spotted near a stone wall the bodies of corporals George W. Page, 25, and Charles Reed, only 19.

The two friends in Company G had crawled "quite a distance to each other from where they were hit," a 2nd Connecticut Heavy Artillery officer wrote, and were clasped in each other's arms.[4]

A burial crew tossed Page and Reed into a trench with the rest of the regiment's dead. "[M]any a rough and war worn veteran's face was washed with tears as he turned away from so affecting a sight," recalled an assistant regimental surgeon.[5]

On the battlefield, comrades discovered the body of 2nd Connecticut Heavy Artillery Corporal George Page clasped in the arms of another dead soldier. Donald Serfass collection

When we lived in Connecticut, I visited Page's damaged marker in an off-the-beaten path cemetery. The stone carver had misspelled his place of death as "Seder Creek."

Picerno points out of where the Heavies fought, near Belle Grove, used by Sheridan as a headquarters. That stone wall where Page and Reed lay clasped in each other's arms is long gone.

Nearby on the morning of October 19, 29th Maine Major George Nye viewed the battle from astride his horse. As a civilian, he managed operations at a textile mill. With thick mutton chops Nye stood out. Confederate lead crashed into the right side of his nose, knocking out two teeth and lodging in his mouth. To repair the damage, surgeons gave Nye a shave.

---

4. 2nd Connecticut Heavy Artillery Lt. Michael Kelly diary, Connecticut Historical Society collection, Hartford, Conn.

5. Vaill, Theodore, *History of the Second Connecticut Volunteer Heavy Artillery*, Winsted, Conn.: Winsted Printing Company, 1868, Page 323

The major, a tough man, pocketed the bullet.

"I bled like a stuck hog," Nye wrote. "I think I must have bled all of a pint."[6]

After crisscrossing the battlefield, Picerno parks on preserved land near where Nye suffered his wound. The exact spot long ago became a victim of a limestone quarry operation. Nye, like Gould, is one of Picerno's guys.

From the back seat of his SUV, the Chief carefully pulls out Nye's inscribed sword—the first time it has returned to the field since the battle. Talk about a Civil War high. The sword was a gift to Picerno from Nye's descendants, who had no other family. The Chief owns hundreds of

A wartime image of 29th Maine officer George Nye, who survived a bullet wound to the mouth at Cedar Creek. Nicholas Picerno collection

Nye's wartime items, mostly letters—including the one in which the officer described his gruesome Cedar Creek wound. In 1908, the sword lay atop Nye's casket during his funeral at Arlington National Cemetery. In March 1865, he had been promoted to brevet major general.

"They wanted it to be where it would be most appreciated," Picerno says of the descendants and the sword, "and as long as I told the general's story."

Afterward, the Chief and I decompress at one of his favorite haunts, an Italian restaurant near the battlefield.

"My northern office," he says of the place.

Alas, stuffed with an Italian sub and battlefield knowledge, I must depart for my southern office. Among million-dollar homes in suburban Nashville, I'm going to tramp upon a battlefield lost.

---

6. Nye letter to wife Charlotte Nye, Oct. 19, 1864, Picerno collection

CHAPTER 24

Nashville, Tennessee

A WALK WITH AN EX-ROADIE IN AN ALL-GIRL BAND

Steps from oncoming traffic, Ross Massey and I straddle a thin strip of grass along Granny White Pike in Nashville—an important battlefield artery in 1864, more like a two-lane drag strip today. Our immediate goal is to make it to the other side of the road alive. Then, if we do, determine where a young Minnesota officer captured a Confederate flag and thus earned a Medal of Honor.

Massey, a descendant of Confederate soldiers, grew up in a house that bordered the battlefield. Today, 95 percent of it has been overrun by residences, commercial developments and streets and freeways traveled by all those bachelorettes who visit "NashVegas."

When he was seven, Massey's mom took him to the 100th anniversary reenactment of the Nashville battle at a steeplechase track—"best reenactment I ever saw," he says. Massey is proud of his Southern roots. (*Psst*: I think he considers Philadelphia foreign territory.)

For years, Massey tried to determine if real soldiers had fought in his own backyard. They had not.

206

"So now I spend time figuring out if anything happened in anyone else's backyard," he says. He the author of a book on the vast Nashville battlefield and its nooks and crannies.

Besides his battlefield expertise, I admire Massey for his thick, white mane and ability to handle high-pressure situations such as our Granny White Pike crossing in busy traffic. Perhaps he honed that quality in the late 1970s, when he served as a roadie for an all-girl band called Maiden Voyage. The intense gig involved insanely late nights, late breakfasts and experiences unimaginable to me as a teen.

"Did you like it?"

"It was *fantastic*," the mid-60-ish Massey says while two SUVs barrel past us.

Slightly flustered, I steer the conversation to our mission. On Granny White, named for a woman who ran a humble roadside inn during the 19th century, million-dollar-plus residential properties occupy ground where farmers, laborers and slaves once tended to crops. Along the pike, two historical markers explain its Civil War significance. But those who dare slow to read them risk a visit with their insurance agent.

I briefly stare at a hole in ground, wondering what battle relics may rest inches beneath the soil. Locals occasionally find a bullet or two on the surface or an artillery shell or U.S. belt buckle in their gardens. But Massey doesn't think much remains underneath the turf along Granny White Pike.

"Now you'd probably only find a fence that fell over, tools, beer cans and some other garbage," he says.

This is how a piece of my soul dies.

Over our shoulders, above the mansions in a cul-de-sac, looms Shy's Hill, Nashville's humbler version of Gettysburg's Little Round Top. For much of the 19th century, the landmark was known as Compton's Hill, after slave owner Felix Compton, who owned a 760-acre farm. After the battle, it became known as Shy's Hill, for 20th Tennessee Colonel Bill Shy, who was fatally wounded defending it.

In the 1950s, the construction of a water tower (since removed) flattened earthworks and the crest of the hill, which developers ringed with residences. After the war, most Nashvillians had little interest in saving anything to do with a major Confederate defeat.

But in the early 1990s, preservationists created a small battlefield park on Shy's Hill, enjoyed now by neighbors, hikers, tourists, deer and the occasional nighttime amorous adventurers. As a teen in the early 1960s, Hank Williams Jr.—the future country music superstar—unearthed battle relics with his rowdy friends in the neighborhood.[1]

At Nashville on December 16, 1864, the Union Army, commanded by George "Pap" Thomas, continued its pummeling of John Bell Hood's Army of Tennessee. The previous day, Thomas had pushed the vastly outnumbered Confederates from countryside south of the U.S. Army-occupied Tennessee capital, one of the war's most heavily defended cities.

On Day 2, Hood anchored his extreme left on Shy's Hill, the extreme right roughly 2.5 miles east at Peach Orchard Hill.

The weather that day was gloomy—misty, overcast, the temperature hovering in the 50s. For the Floridians who helped defend Shy's Hill, it was no day at the beach. Ill-equipped, tired and ornery, Army of Tennessee soldiers longed for grub.

Wrote an Alabamian: "It is seldom the case that an army is in worse condition for meeting its enemy in battle's dread array than ours is at this time."[2]

At about 3:30 p.m., three U.S. Army brigades in Gen. A.J. Smith's division attacked the Confederate left. Under relentless fire, Lt. Thomas Parke Gere and his 5th Minnesota comrades advanced through a muddy cornfield along Granny White Pike. A thin line of Rebels awaited behind a stone wall protected by a ditch and abatis—hastily made fortifications of tree branches and limbs.

Only 22, Gere already was a seasoned soldier. As a 19-year-old in Minnesota Territory in August 1862, he took over a fort after the commander had drowned during a fight against the Dakota. By May 1863, he was fighting in Mississippi during the Vicksburg Campaign. In Nathaniel Banks' 1864 Red River Campaign in Louisiana, the 5th Minnesota guarded supply trains, served as a rearguard and fought in such godforsaken places as Yellow Bayou, Campti and Sabine Crossroads.

1. *The Nashville Tennessean*, Dec. 6, 1964
2. Cannon, James P.; Crowson, Noel; Brogden, John V., *Bloody Banners and Barefoot Boys: A History of the 27th Regiment Alabama Infantry*, Shippensburg, Pa.: White Mane Publisher, 1997

Ross Massey, standing at Shy's Hill on the Nashville battlefield, is proud of his Confederate roots.

"Composed of hardy frontier citizens, long accustomed to hardship and privation, probably no finer organization has ever been sent into the field," a Minnesota newspaper wrote about the regiment.[3]

At Nashville, Gere and the 5th Minnesota faced their stiffest test of the war. But still reeling from their Day 1 whipping, the beleaguered Rebels eventually scattered. Hundreds became prisoners. "[T]he most complete rout of the enemy that I have ever witnessed," Gere later said.[4]

When Gere reached the Rebel works, his horse refused to cross the abatis and stone wall. In the maelstrom, he spotted the frazzled 4th Mississippi flag-bearer skedaddling without his colors. Gere couldn't reach the prize,

3. *The Goodhue Volunteer*, Red Wing, Minn., July 6, 1864

4. The Bravest 500 of '61, *Their Noble Deeds Described by Themselves*, compiled by Theo F. Rodenbough, New York: G.W. Dillingham Publishers, 1891, Page 101

so he ordered the soldier to hand him the trophy. His loaded revolver compelled the man to deliver it ASAP.

"I was lucky enough," Gere recalled later, "to get the battle flag of the Fourth Mississippi regiment in the charge."

In its deadliest battle of the war, the 5th Minnesota suffered dozens of casualties. Among those killed were Private Lysias Raymond, the married father of girls ages 1 and 4, and Irish-born Patrick Byrnes, a widow's son.[5] One of Gere's friends, English-born William Sargent, a 24-year-old lieutenant in the 8th Wisconsin, took a bullet through the heart.

"The fighting was the heaviest in our front," Gere wrote in his diary. "It was indeed a desperate thing to go through that storm of grape, canister and musket balls—we who got through wonder how we escaped! Our feelings can not be described! But we won the victory!"[6]

Using a map and finely honed instincts, Massey points out the general area of the flag capture. Heavy traffic and modern development kill the battlefield vibe, so I'm tempted to shake my fist and yell at the passing vehicles: *"Don't you know this is hallowed ground?!"* But the fear of an altercation and the dread of ruining the family name and embarrassing Mrs. B stifle the urge.

Antebellum, dry-stack stone walls line stretches of both sides of the pike. Near one of them, soldiers in a Union regiment captured mud-caked Confederate Gen. Henry Jackson, who had slogged through the fields south of Shy's Hill. But the remains of the battlefield wall where Gere acquired his prize may be part of someone's stone walk to a backyard pool.

"That's where it was," Massey says of the wall, site of the flag handover.

He points to a stand of trees and brush across the road. We poke around there, hoping to find stones from the battlefield wall or perhaps a stray artillery shell Hank Jr. had overlooked.

To our left stands a large, one-story ranch house.

"They probably just bulldozed the earthworks here when they put this up," Massey says, wistfully.

---

5. Raymond and Byrnes pension files, National Archives and Records Administration, Washington, D.C.

6. Thomas Parke Gere's wartime diary (typewritten copy), Minnesota Historical Society, (Battle of Nashville text courtesy Tim Bode, 5th Minnesota Research Group on Facebook)

In the distance, across the pike, Confederates defended ground behind a stone wall on what was John Lea's estate in 1864. Now it's part of the wealthy Nashville suburb of Oak Hill, where an acre goes for a million bucks.

An antebellum plantation wall survives in Oak Hill, snaking behind a tennis court and through backyards. A rare battlefield "witness" tree, a huge oak, stands in the front yard of a modern house, near the location of a Rebel battery. The oak is missing a chunk of its top, perhaps caused by Union artillery fire.

Thomas Gere of the 5th Minnesota earned a Medal of Honor by capturing a 4th Mississippi flag at the Battle of Nashville. Minnesota Historical Society

True story: After a violent storm, I noticed limbs from the witness tree scattered about. So, I called a friend, a lawyer who lives in Oak Hill. He owns a metal detector and a real Civil War cannon—it stands guard in his front yard. I'd like one. My friend called the property owner, who let us inspect fallen limbs with his detector during a tree trimming.

"You get this one," my friend told me.

Several waves of his detector determined no wartime metal embedded in my hunk. Then he had five or six other large hunks of witness tree hauled away. A few waves of his magic wand over them indicated the presence of… well… *something* inside each.

Weeks later, he had the hunks X-rayed at his veterinarian's office, expecting the things to "light up like a Christmas tree" with battle relics. The result: Zip. My lawyer friend looked like his dog had just died. One of my hunks, probably filled with wartime lead, still rests in our garage.

I tell the tree story to Massey, who seems slightly dubious. He steers our conversation to a Confederate commander who lost his leg somewhere on the battlefield. But I'm thinking about Gere, the young, mustachioed Minnesotan.

Weeks after the battle, George Thomas—"The Sledge of Nashville"—
ordered him to lead a detachment to Washington for a special ceremony.

On February 22, 1865, Gere found himself in the gloomy War
Department building, a short walk from the White House. Fourteen other
bronze-faced U.S. Army soldiers joined him. Each was based in Tennessee,
at least one had served in the Mexican War, and all but two had captured an
enemy flag at Nashville.

Eagerly anticipating the event, the soldiers pushed through a massive,
green leather door and filed into a large reception room. Members of
Congress, foreign dignitaries, governors and other guests—roughly 100 in
all—stood in a horseshoe formation steps from the soldiers. Displays of
upright muskets near the walls gave the setting a martial air.

Conversations abruptly stopped when Secretary of War Edwin Stanton,
a short, square-shouldered 50-year-old, entered the room. After a short
speech, the bearded and bespectacled bureaucrat read aloud the names of
the soldiers:

Corporal J.W. Parks, 11th Missouri.
Private W. May, 32nd Iowa.
Private G. Stokes, 122nd Illinois ...

Finally, Stanton summoned Gere. Holding his tattered Nashville trophy,
the officer eyed his impressive audience.

"Mr. Secretary," he began, "I have the honor and pleasure to present to
you the colors of the 4th Mississippi Infantry, C.S.A."

In the cavernous room, Gere emphasized the team effort involved in the
capture of the colors and the valor of soldiers of Lucius Hubbard's brigade,
John McArthur's division of A. J. Smith's detachment.

"It was the result of the final charge upon the enemy's works by that
invincible command in the second day's battle," the slender, earnest-looking
Gere said. "Every soldier who participated in that assault shares the credit of
the captured colors."

After Gere told his Nashville story, other soldiers recounted the capture
of their flags. Not every story teemed with heroism.

On December 16, 1864, Corporal Frank Carr of the 114th Ohio
re-captured a Federal cavalry guidon. During his regiment's retreat, he got
stuck in abatis. Then "a fellow came up and asked me to surrender," Carr

told Stanton. "I wouldn't do it, but put on my bayonet and was going to stand a fight when the fellow ran and dropped his flag."[7]

Private Wilbur F. Moore of the 117th Illinois captured a flag from a Confederate battery. "The color-bearer was in a small line of rebels," he recalled, "and was trying to climb the hills. I shed my knapsack to go out for him and captured him and a captain of the same regiment, too."[8]

Each soldier at the ceremony handed a captured flag to a Mexican War veteran, who placed the war trophy atop a display of muskets. "[W]hen the last silken standard had been placed there, the effect was brilliant and thrilling," according to an account. "The varied hues of the rainbow lighted up the sombre apartment in a blaze of color."[9]

Clearly impressed with the soldiers, the gruff Stanton shook each man's hand. Then he briefly expressed appreciation: "On behalf of the Government of the United States I return to you its thanks and the thanks of the people, for your noble gallantry. Accept also the gratitude of the department for yourselves and companions in arms."

Each soldier received a 30-day furlough and an advance of a month's pay. Later, they received another award from a grateful government: a Medal of Honor, the nation's highest military honor.

Before they departed the War Department, Gere and his Tennessee detachment saluted Stanton. The man who managed the U.S. Army war machine waved back ... and wept.

The whoosh of traffic along Granny White snaps me back to reality. Then the eclectic Massey weighs in on balalaika music at a low-watt radio station in Pittsburgh that he listened to decades ago.

"You know," he says, zeroing in on the Civil War again, "it seems like for a while they were bulldozing something here in Nashville every year."

It breaks the hearts of history lovers.

Steel yourself for more heartache. Thirty miles southeast, in Murfreesboro, Tennessee, the 21st century is kicking the 19th century's butt.

---

7. *Washington Evening Star*, Feb. 22, 1865
8. Ibid
9. *The Bravest 500 of '61*, Page 105

CHAPTER 25

Murfreesboro, Tennessee

CARNAGE IN A CONSTRUCTION ZONE

On a raw afternoon, earth movers at a construction site snort and grunt as they pound and pulverize the meager remains of a lunette at Fortress Rosecrans. It makes my heart hurt. My head hurts, too. I'm battling a cold, which isn't helped by a biting wind that chaps my face and hands.

Nearby, drivers barrel down a four-lane parkway, oblivious to the carnage in the construction zone. In the far distance, a huge crane hovers next to the skeletal frame of a high-rise. A brilliant orange sun begins its slow descent—a metaphor, perhaps, for Civil War ground in Murfreesboro.

I'm here for a relic hunt at the invitation of Stan Hutson. He's a bearded, 40-something native of Alabama, an Afghan War veteran with a deep appreciation for Civil War and family history.

Hutson descended from a passenger on the *Mayflower*. His Civil War ancestors fought on *opposites sides* at killing fields along the Old Nashville Pike at Stones River and on the rocky ridge of Little Round Top at Gettysburg—a Tennessean against an Ohioan; Alabamians against soldiers from the 83rd Pennsylvania and the famous 20th Maine. Hutson's great-great-great-grandfather served as a guard at the notorious Andersonville POW camp, where a U.S. Army soldier ancestor of his died of disease.

In his day job, Hutson is a maintenance employee at the Stones River National Battlefield nearby. In his free time, he often goes relic hunting for Civil War artifacts in the few sites remaining in Murfreesboro.

"They don't want to leave any sliver," Hutson says.

He's talking about ravenous developers, who show no mercy for almost any open ground in Murfreesboro.

Only 680 acres, about 15 percent of the vast Stones River battlefield, are preserved by the National Park Service. The rest lies underneath car dealerships, restaurants, residential developments and other urban schlock. Lots of luck interpreting the battle, which resulted in nearly 25,000 casualties in late December 1862 and early January 1863.

"Good grief," Hutson says. "I don't know if Americans know what they've lost. We have a McDonald's on every corner. Do we really need another one?"

In 2019, on the site of the opening action at Stones River, Hutson unearthed three rare Confederate droop eagle buttons and seven ball buttons. Some still had the uniform cloth attached. "The find of a lifetime," he told me then about the discoveries at the construction site. Months later, an apartment complex occupied the site.

Nearby, within spitting distance of a dumpster behind a chicken restaurant, Hutson had uncovered a six-pound Confederate solid shot buried in three inches of soil.

Much of Fortress Rosecrans has shared the fate of the Stones River battlefield. Only pockets remain—including earthworks preserved by the National Park Service along the Old Nashville Pike. It's not surprising. The war's largest earthen walled fort covered 200 acres, roughly the footprint of 40 Walmart superstores. Few historic preservationists would advocate for saving it all.

In the aftermath of Stones River, the U.S. Army wanted a heavily protected fort to stockpile supplies for Western Theater campaigns and as a fallback option in case the Rebels got frisky in Middle Tennessee. Beginning in late January 1863, thousands of soldiers, as well as the formerly enslaved, labored around the clock to create Fortress Rosecrans.

Laborers built earthen walls as high as 15 feet and dug ditches as deep as 10, fronting them with sharpened stakes. Around the fort for hundreds of yards, they felled scores of trees, clearing fields of fire for artillery. "A wilderness of timber has disappeared and in its place [is] a large prairie waste," a local citizen wrote.[1]

A brigade of engineers, mechanics and skilled laborers—the Pioneer Brigade—pitched in. "[They] could throw up defenses [and] span rivers with bridges almost like magic," an account noted about the unit.[2]

The brigade was the brainchild of Army of the Cumberland commander William Rosecrans, the fort's namesake. The 43-year-old general was a headstrong West Pointer with a tendency to get excitable in battle. Colleagues called the Ohioan "Old Rosy."

But the real brains behind the construction of Rosecrans' fort was 33-year-old James St. Clair Morton. He was the Pioneer Brigade commander and son of a Philadelphia physician who collected human skulls from around the world. In the construction of his stone-walled Fort Negley in Nashville, hundreds of impressed Black laborers—men, women and children—died from hunger, disease and exposure.[3] Morton wouldn't see the end of the war. In June 1864, a Rebel bullet killed him at Petersburg, Virginia.

Upon completion, Fortress Rosecrans included steam-powered sawmills, quartermaster depots, warehouses, magazines and a 50-acre vegetable garden. Through the grounds ran a line of the Nashville and Chattanooga Railroad. The railroad delivered supplies that fed a gluttonous war machine for advances toward Chattanooga later in 1863, Atlanta in 1864 and elsewhere. It was said the fort was big enough to protect an army of 50,000 soldiers.

Fortress Rosecrans, of course, bristled with artillery. In lunettes—angled, earthen fortifications—the U.S. Army placed heavy weaponry such as siege howitzers, James rifled field guns and massive Parrotts, which produced a deafening roar when fired. In four redoubts, actually mini forts within the fort, the Yankees positioned even more artillery. One of the

---

1. Spence, John C.H., *A Diary of the Civil War*, Murfreesboro, Tenn.: Rutherford County Historical Society, 1993

2. *The Philadelphia Inquirer*, June 21, 1864

3. "Testimony by the Commissioner for the Organization of Black Troops in Middle and East Tennessee before the American Freedmen's Inquiry Commission," Nov. 23, 1863, Freedmen and Southern Society Project (www.freedmen.umd.edu)

"If we don't save it, it's gone," relic hunter Stan Hutson says of artifacts uncovered at Fortress Rosecrans.

fort's big guns pointed to the nearby courthouse in Murfreesboro in case the locals rose up against the occupiers.[4]

"Astonishing," a Union veteran called Fortress Rosecrans, "… equal in magnitude and strength to those which defend great cities in Europe."[5]

"Impregnable to assault," another wrote.[6]

The Rebels roaming Middle Tennessee rarely tested it.

"Enemy had marched out and offered battle under the guns of their strong works [at] Fort Rosecrans," a Confederate general wrote on December 7, 1864. "We took 5 different positions and declined the invitation to fight."[7]

---

4. Zimmerman, Mark, *Fortress Nashville*, Nashville: Zimco Publications LLC, 2022, Page 170

5. *The National Tribune*, July 12, 1906

6. Ibid, Aug. 6, 1903

7. 1864: Diary of Brig. Gen. Claudius Wistar Sears, Dec. 7, 1864, Spared & Shared web site. Accessed Oct. 29, 2022

Close your eyes and blot out the drone of traffic today and you can imagine fresh-faced U.S. Army soldiers passing through Fortress Rosecrans toward the front.

"[T]he passionate kisses of their mothers scarcely cold upon their lips, they pass onward in the cause of freedom," an Indiana artillery soldier wrote of just such a scene.[8]

Shortly after the war, the U.S. Army abandoned Fortress Rosecrans. Then nature claimed some of it. As Murfreesboro exploded from a town of 19,000 in 1960 to a city of nearly 200,000 today, development claimed much of the rest.

At the unmarked site of Lunette Negley—named for Union Gen. James Negley—Hutson sweeps a Fisher F75 metal detector across the nearly barren, lunar-like landscape. Meanwhile, Dave—Hutson's friend and relic hunting pard—pokes at the deep-brown soil with a shovel. Hutson wears a gray hoodie, blue jeans and work boots. Dave is clad in a light blue long-sleeved shirt and camouflage pants. I wear a light jacket too thin to brace the biting wind and a smile.

I don't own a metal detector, but what history-minded adventurer wouldn't want to be here—even in 35-degree wind chill?

"This was a city dump for a while," says Dave, a lifelong Murfreesboro resident.

Twenty yards away, a mound of earth roughly 40 yards long is all that remains of Lunette Negley's once-imposing earthen walls. Hutson and Dave hope to recover artifacts before building foundations sprout like goosegrass and carpetweed.

This isn't Hutson's first time at the site. On previous hunts—always with permission, of course—he has unearthed pieces of a mangled U.S. Federal cartridge box plate, a dozen Yankee eagle buttons and shards of period glass from an 1860 Drakes Plantation X Bitters bottle. At a wartime firepit cow bones and hog tusks have turned up.

Elsewhere on the well-hunted site, he and Dave have unearthed Williams cleaner bullets, a Schenkl artillery shell fragment, a period watch cap, a piece of a harmonica and a musket lock plate and barrel band.

"If we don't save it, it's gone," Hutson says.

---

8. *The Nashville Daily Union*, April 10, 1864

Cow bones, hog tusks … bullets. I *love* this stuff.

My own relic hunting career ended ignominiously after two or three hunts in the early 1980s. A total haul of five beer can tabs, a rusty Coke can and a solitary plow-scarred three-ringer from the David R. Miller farm at Antietam failed to impress any of my friends. Of course, I didn't have a prayer with my cheap detector purchased at a Gettysburg store that also sold Bibles and other religious goods.

Compared to modern detectors, with their digital technology, my machine was a rake. Modern detectors find relics missed by previous generations of diggers through discrimination technologies that can separate, say, a brass button that's right beside an iron nail or by penetrating much deeper into the ground.

Without these advantages it would be difficult to find much these days. In the glory days of hunting, from the 1960s-1980s, relic hunters such as Richard Clem—my Civil War poppa—found artifacts just beneath the surface or even by eyeballing them on the ground.

Like people, relic hunters fall into classes. Let's call them "The Virtuous," "The Vile" and "The Somewhere in Betweens." It would be four if I allowed a friend of mine, a Virginia battlefield preservationist and historian, to weigh in.

"They're all vermin," he has told me often and with great disgust.

Many archaeologists view relic hunters with similar disdain. Take a relic from the ground, they say, and we lose the ability to fully interpret what happened there.

"The Virtuous," like Clem, always ask permission to hunt ground. They might document all their finds in a notebook, as Clem did for decades. "The Vile" follow their own rules, even hunting in national military parks, which is illegal. "The Somewhere in Betweens" fall in the middle, skirting the unwritten rules every now and then.

Maybe another class is required, an "If We Don't Save It, It's Gone" group, inspired by Hutson. Put me in that one. Open ground in Murfreesboro disappears like wisps of gun smoke on a windy day. So what's wrong with retrieving relics from what will soon become a parking lot?

Beep, beep, beep … *beeeeeep, beeeeeep!*

A round ball unearthed at the site of Fortress Rosecrans.

Minutes into his relic hunt, the sounds from Hutson's machine change tone, an indication of metal in the earth. He scoops out about two inches of soil with his shovel, reaches down and picks up an unusually shaped object roughly 6½ inches long.

"I cannot believe this. Holy cow!"

Hutson is jazzed.

The 19th century has finally let go of a trigger guard for a musket, perhaps an Austrian Lorenz or Enfield, used by soldiers on both sides in the Western Theater. Maybe the weapon belonged to a soldier who served under 75th Illinois Captain David M. Roberts, who commanded a battery at Lunette Negley. He had two six-pounders, a three-inch gun, a six-pounder James rifle field gun and an eight-inch siege howitzer at his disposal.

Minutes later, Hutson still is on a relic hunter high.

"I'm gonna get cotton mouth," he says.

A close examination of the ground reveals an interesting mosaic: soil, stone, shards of opaque glass, ancient nails and small porcelain chips, probably from dishes. To our untrained eyes, most of the artifacts seem to date to the Civil War era.

Months earlier, Dave had unearthed at the lunette site a .54-caliber bullet mold, perhaps Confederate.

"It's like Christmas every time I dig," he says. "You don't know what you're going to get when you dig it up."

Probing at the ground after a hit on his metal detector, Hutson uncovers another piece of metal.

"What do you think this is?" he says. "A door handle?"

Hutson tosses his finds on a mound of dirt pushed aside by the construction crew. On the surface, Dave picks up a porcelain button, probably from a soldier's blouse. Later, he uncovers a .69-caliber round ball.

At the remains of a fort firepit, Hutson points out in the soil the telltale black marks from the burning of a log. Then he recovers a large iron hook.

"This might have been used by soldiers to hold a pot for cooking," he says, holding it up for my inspection.

Scattered about are old nails, bolts and bricks. Hutson uncovers a piece of glass.

"That probably hasn't seen the light of day since the war," he says.

Hutson speculates the bricks could be the work of slaves. Fifteen minutes later, he uncovers an ancient piece of a hoe eight inches deep.

About an hour before dusk, the shadows of diggers dance on a bank of soil richly illuminated by the sun. Yards away, the faceless and merciless construction crew continues its work. The 21st century sounds the death knell for the 19th.

Another relic hunt is nearly over.

Time is rapidly running out, too, for another Civil War site in Murfreesboro.

In far-off western Maryland, meanwhile, stands a house with a presidential connection.

What will I find there after my knock on the door?

CHAPTER 26

Middletown, Maryland

A LOVE STORY
IN A HOUSE WITH A
PRESIDENTIAL SUITE

"**M**ay I see your bedroom?"

Shortly before a visit to a historic private residence in Middletown, I mentally practice words that would make Mrs. B cringe. I am deep in Civil War country in western Maryland. Roughly five miles northwest is Fox's Gap at South Mountain, where the armies clashed on September 14, 1862. Three days later, they fought a much-bloodier battle 15 miles west near the banks of Antietam Creek.

On the opposite side of Main Street, about 350 yards away, stands an antebellum Lutheran church with a gleaming white steeple. It served as a hospital for both armies during the war.

Hoping for the best, I knock on a front door of the two-story, red-brick house.

"I understand this is the Hayes house. May I come in for a visit?"

A white-haired woman with a distinctive Maryland accent waves me inside after a slight hesitation. Her name is Lois Shank. Donald, her husband, sits in a comfy chair covered with a striped quilt. He wears a checkered flannel shirt, glasses with aviator rims and a frown.

In an upstairs bedroom in their unpretentious house, 23rd Ohio Lt. Col. Rutherford B. Hayes—the future U.S. president—recovered from a battle-field wound suffered at South Mountain. Few visitors knock on the Shanks' door to inquire about Hayes, and no markers on the circa-1840 house denote any historical connection. Years ago, a man from West Virginia took pictures of the place.

"But that's about it," Donald says.

Before broaching my question about a stairway to historical heaven, I gather information on my hosts. Shank, a Maryland lifer, and his three sisters were born in the upstairs bedroom—perhaps in the same room where Hayes' doting wife cared for him while he convalesced in the fall of 1862. Lois and Donald have lived in the house since 1960, the year they wed. From 1953-55, he served in the U.S. Army. Lois is in her 80s now; Donald's pushing 90. He warms to my questions.

"So, what's it like to live in a house where a president slept?"

"To us," says Donald, "Hayes is just another person."

Oh, my, if the walls of their place could talk. What a story they could tell about Hayes. It's a love story, really.

As he was giving a command to charge at Fox's Gap, the 39-year-old Hayes suffered a serious wound—a "stunning blow" from a musket ball just above his left elbow.

"Fearing that an artery might be cut, I asked a soldier near me to tie my handkerchief above the wound. I soon felt weak, faint and sick at the stom-ach," he recalled. While Hayes lay helpless, bullets passed by his face and burrowed into the earth around him.

As the battle raged, Hayes struck up a conversation with a wounded Confederate soldier. "I gave him messages for my wife and friends in case I should not get up," he remembered. "We were right jolly and friendly; it was by no means an unpleasant experience."[1]

Then, after the firing had briefly died down, Hayes cried out to his sol-diers: "Hallo Twenty-third men, are you going to leave your colonel here for the enemy?" A half-dozen or more Ohioans immediately bounded for-ward to carry Hayes away. But their bold move drew fire from the Rebels,

---

1. *Diary And Letters of Rutherford Birchard Hayes, Vol. 2, 1865-1881*, Edited by Charles Richard Williams, The Ohio State Archaeological and Historical Society, 1924, Pages 356-57

igniting return fire from the Yankees. Hayes ordered the men to seek cover because they were risking their lives and his. Finally, a Union lieutenant carried Hayes from the battlefield, placing him behind a large log with a canteen of water "that tasted so good."[2]

After Hayes had his wound dressed, he walked a half-mile down the mountain to the small house of a widow named Elizabeth Koogle, where he remained for two or three hours. Aides took Hayes, still faint from blood loss, via ambulance three or four miles into Middletown, which had thrown open its churches, houses, schools, barns and other buildings for Union wounded. The town had earned the nickname "Little Massachusetts" because of its pro-Union sentiment.

At about sunset, the ambulance carrying Hayes and army surgeon Joseph Webb, Lucy's brother, arrived at the house of Elizabeth and Jacob Rudy on the National Pike, near the town's western edge. The day before, Captain Jacob—a prominent merchant and farmer—served as a volunteer guide for the Union Army.[3]

The Rudys, who lived in the house with seven of their children, were enduring their own health crises. Twenty-one-year-old Daniel Webster Rudy, the couple's eldest son, suffered from smallpox. Daughters Laura, 11, and Ella, 9, had scarlet fever.

Men carried the disheveled and mud-splattered Hayes up a narrow staircase. They placed him in a bed near the room where Daniel lay ill. His mattress rested on a solid wooden board instead of the usual rope cords, which tended to sag. Hayes preferred a firm bed.

Webb and his brother, James, also an army surgeon, tended to Hayes' wounded arm. The Rudys called them "Dr. Joe" and "Dr. Jim." A respected local physician named Charles Baer aided them. Two Black servants, who had accompanied Hayes and Joseph Webb in the ambulance to Middletown, slept on the floor of Daniel's room.

While he recovered, Hayes felt "snug as a bug in a rug" in the Rudy house.

"I am comfortably *at home*," he wrote his mother the day after the battle, "with a very kind and attentive family here named Rudy."[4] He had

---

2. Ibid, Page 357

3. *Omaha (Neb.) Daily Bee via Cincinnati Commercial*, Oct. 4, 1881

4. *Diary And Letters of Rutherford Birchard Hayes*, Vol. 2, 1865-1881, Pages 353 and 355

telegraphed Lucy, whom he hoped was on her way from the couple's home in Ohio. From the house on September 17, Hayes heard cannons boom while a battle raged near the banks of Antietam Creek.

Hayes remained pain-free early in his recovery so long as he lay still. He delighted in sampling Elizabeth Rudy's currant jellies and chatting with the family's youngest son, eight-year-old Charlie. The boy enjoyed describing for Hayes the U.S. Army troops as they marched past the house on the busy National Pike—Main Street and U.S. Route 40 today.

"Charlie, you live on a street that is much traveled," Hayes said.

"Oh, it isn't always so," the youngster replied. "It's only when the war comes."[5]

More than a week after Hayes' wounding, a worried Lucy finally arrived after a circuitous journey. She first went looking for Rutherford in the hospitals of Washington. Elizabeth Rudy made an instant connection with the mother of five young sons.

"The moment she crossed our threshold," she said, "I knew she was a good woman and a natural lady… She was relieved to know that his wound was not so dangerous as she had imagined it." Early the next morning, she cooked Hayes' favorite breakfast in Elizabeth's kitchen.[6]

Hayes never used a cross word regarding the Rebels and "never liked to hear others do so" either, said Ella, one of the Rudy's five daughters. And he did his best not to be a burden to a family facing its own hardships.

"He not only wouldn't be cross—he wouldn't allow any extra trouble to be taken on his account," Ella remembered. "Mother used to ask him if she could not 'do something' for him. He always thanked her, but said no."[7]

By late September, Hayes had become well enough to walk about Middletown with Lucy, who often took grapes and other delicacies to wounded soldiers in the town's hospitals. "Comes back in tears," Hayes said of his wife, who later earned the nickname "Mother Lucy" for her devotion to wounded, sick and dying soldiers in the 23rd Ohio.[8]

---

5. Ibid, Page 354

6. *New York Herald*, April 9, 1877

7. Ibid

8. *Diary And Letters of Rutherford Birchard Hayes*, Page 359 | While First Lady in the White House from 1877-81, Lucy—a teetotaler—became known as "Lemonade Lucy" for her refusal to serve alcohol.

Dwelling in West End of Middletown, Md. where Gen. Rutherford B. Hayes lay wounded after the battle of South Mountain. He became the 19th President of the U. S.

An old postcard of the house where future U.S. president Rutherford Hayes recovered from his Battle of South Mountain wound.

In early October, he and Lucy visited the Lutheran church cemetery, where they would watch sunsets and admire dazzling fall foliage. Hayes preferred the unpaved south side of the street, sometimes sloshing through shoe-deep mud, instead of the paved north side, causing the town's tongues to wag.[9]

On his 40th birthday on October 4, Hayes and Lucy traveled with Jacob Rudy and two other men to the South Mountain battlefield. "Hunted up the graves of our gallant boys," Hayes wrote in his diary.[10]

Later that month, Hayes returned with Lucy to their home in Cincinnati. Weeks after Hayes' departure, every Rudy family member had contracted smallpox. Charlie died from the disease on November 4, 1862.

In the summer of 1864, with the U.S. Army in western Maryland to check Jubal Early's advance into the state, Hayes found time to visit again with the Rudys. He ate breakfast with the family in their house. "They

9. *New York Herald*, April 17, 1877

10. *Diary And Letters of Rutherford Birchard Hayes*, Page 361

were so kind and cordial," he wrote to Lucy. "They all inquired after you. The girls have grown pretty—quite pretty."

Jacob Rudy remained devoted to the soldier he took into his home in 1862. "Mr. Rudy said if I was wounded, he would come a hundred miles to get me," Hayes wrote Lucy.[11] Hayes remained close to the hearts of the rest of the family, too.

"So you all fell in love with the patient Colonel?" a New York newspaper reporter asked Elizabeth Rudy in 1877—the year Hayes became the 19th president.

"We fell in love with him directly," she replied.

Ella even showed the reporter the bed where Hayes slept, hers since the president had left the house 15 years earlier.

Rutherford Hayes never forgot the kindness of the Rudy family.
Hayes Presidential Center

"I've never had a bad dream in it," she said. "Never."

In 1884, three years after Hayes' term as president had ended, his memories of the Rudys and the Battle of South Mountain remained fresh. "Recalled my experience in the little brick house of Jacob Rudy at Middletown, Maryland, when twenty-two years ago I lay wounded, listening all day and until after dark to the sound of battle," he wrote in his diary on September 17, the Antietam anniversary.

In the late 19th or early 20th century, one of Hayes' sons visited the house where his father convalesced. He presented to its owner, Donald's grandfather, an 1865 image of his father in uniform.

"Do you want to see it?" Donald asks me.

Shank finds the old photograph, in an ancient frame, showing Hayes as a general, a rank he attained in the fall of 1864. In period writing on the reverse, someone wrote: "Of the presidents of the United States, from Washington to Wilson, fifteen served as officers in battle; but with the exception of James Monroe, when serving as a lieutenant in Trenton,

---

11. Ibid, Page 489

none other than General Hayes was wounded in battle."

Then I sheepishly pop the question to Lois: "*May ... I ... see ... your ... bedroom?*"

"Well, it's a mess up there. But OK."

I walk the narrow steps to the bedrooms. Upstairs, I imagine Lucy gently propping up Rutherford's head up with pillows, the same one Daniel used. Lucy apparently had no fear of smallpox. I briefly peer through the window for a view of the National Road, just as eight-year-old Charlie did. I feel the stares of the Black servants.

Donald Shank holds an image of Rutherford Hayes given to his grandfather by Hayes' son.

I see no mess at all.

One hundred and seventy miles south, near the former Confederate capital, a former slave made history. It's time to shine a light on his story.

CHAPTER 27

Henrico, Virginia

GUARDIAN OF A LEGACY

On Father's Day weekend, I drive east through the Shenandoah Valley and past Charlottesville, Gum Spring, Oilville and Short Pump and on into Richmond. Seated shotgun is my rock, a fist-sized lump of stone into which my dad—"Big Johnny"—crudely carved his initials "J.B." as a teen in 1948. In 2016, a stroke did him in at 80. "Big Johnny" loved history, so his spirit—in the form of the rock—makes this swing through the Eastern Theater of the Civil War with me.

Our first destination is Fort Harrison, southeast of the city, and roughly a mile from the James River. I'm here to meet with a direct descendant of a U.S. Colored Troops soldier who earned the Medal of Honor for valor in the Battle of New Market Heights nearby.

In September 1864, Fort Harrison served as one of the many obstacles to the Union Army, which had nonetheless put Richmond in peril. The previous two years, the Confederate military had impressed slaves for the construction of forts and trenches, making Richmond the Confederacy's most heavily fortified city. Alongside Battlefield Park Road, my route to the fort today, ribbons of undulating earth are reminders of their work.

Except for an occasional bicyclist, no one else appears on the grounds as I pull into the parking lot at Fort Harrison, named after a Confederate engineer. A steady breeze blows through the trees. Huge mounds of earth covered with grass—the remains of the fort's defenses—curl into the distance.

From a black Silverado pickup strides Damon Radcliffe, a 6-foot-4, 290-pound lieutenant in the sheriff's office in Yorktown, Virginia. He wears blue jeans, a black T-shirt, sunglasses, black Crocs and a silver chain around his neck with a gleaming religious cross. Flecks of gray sprinkle his goatee. Five inscribed metal bands loop the 45-year-old Radcliffe's right wrist and forearm, in memory of law enforcement officers who have died in the line of duty. He relishes his job despite its inherent dangers.

"You know the old saying," Radcliffe says while dipping a pinch of snuff. "When you love something you do, you never have to work a day in your life."

When Radcliffe was 23, less than six months into his career as a cop, he and his partner stopped a man for DUI. Radcliffe reached into the car to grab the keys in the ignition. Then the suspect threw the car into gear and raced off. Radcliffe miraculously escaped physically unscathed.

"Now I don't believe in ghosts," he says. "But I felt something pulling on my belt and away from danger."

Radcliffe is a fan of the old law enforcement TV shows *CHiPs* and *Miami Vice* and the epic 1989 Civil War movie *Glory*, about the 54th Massachusetts, the famed Black regiment.

"I've watched that maybe 100 times, at least," he says.

As a teen, Radcliffe had a large "54" tattooed on his beefy right bicep, above a tattoo of a Superman emblem, in honor of the regiment. At the time, he thought his great-great-grandfather had served with the 54th Massachusetts, too.

The Radcliffe family is steeped in military service. His younger brother, Edward, is a master sergeant in the Marines. His grandfather served in Europe in the U.S. Army during World War II. His paternal great-great-grandfather, former slave Edward Ratcliff, earned the Medal of Honor during the Civil War. Ratcliff's great-great-grandson serves as a family spokesman and a guardian of the legacy of one of the more remarkable soldiers of the war.

"We've always had a sense of pride in him," Radcliffe says.

On his right arm, Radcliffe sports tattoos of a Superman emblem and "54" — homage to the 54th Massachusetts, the famed Black regiment.

In grade school, Damon Radcliffe enjoyed lunch—"I always got an 'A' in lunch"—gym and history classes. But despite a love for the last, he had made only cursory attempts over the years to investigate his great-great-grandfather's background. The surname "Ratcliff" didn't become "Radcliffe" until early in the 20th century, throwing off his online searches. But the family knew it had a Medal of Honor recipient among its lineages.

As a child, Damon's grandfather—also named Edward—saw a faded photo of Ratcliff, clad in his Union Army uniform, hanging in his mother's house. Damon's mother spent hundreds of hours researching Ratcliff's life, tracing as far back as his birth. But the family didn't have the most complete story until 2006, when an eight-part series on Ratcliff appeared in a local newspaper.[1]

On February 8, 1835, Edward Ratcliff was born into slavery on the Hankins family's 700-acre plantation outside Williamsburg, Virginia. His father may have been white. On a bright, blazing-hot summer day in 2021,

---

1. The excellent series by Stephanie Heinatz appeared in *The Daily Press* of Newport News (Va.) from July 23-30, 2006.

Radcliffe visited the plantation in James City County, about an hour's drive south of Fort Harrison. Only a fraction of the grounds remain with the family of the original owner.

"My heart was fluttering," he says.

Near a golf course, the two-story antebellum plantation house still stands among walnut trees. Radcliffe felt a special vibe that day, not unlike the early morning when the unseen force yanked rookie cop Radcliffe from the DUI suspect's car.

"This is where it started, young buck," he thought. "This is where it started."

In January 1864, Edward left his wife and young daughter behind on the plantation to enlist in Yorktown as a private in the 38th U.S. Colored Troops, a three-year regiment. According to family lore, Ratcliff walked from the plantation to Yorktown along the York River, a trip of roughly 25 miles. At his enlistment, the army noted his height (5-foot-11), complexion (yellow), hair color and eyes (black).

By September 1864, most Black troops in the Union Army had transitioned from use almost exclusively as laborers to fighting men. Five months earlier, at Fort Pillow on a bluff above the Mississippi River in Tennessee, Confederates under Nathan Bedford Forrest massacred USCT after they had surrendered.

In late September 1864, Army of the James commander Benjamin Butler hatched a bold plan: Make a sudden crossing over a pontoon bridge on the James River with the Union Army's 18th Corps for a two-pronged attack at New Market Heights. The Black troops, including Ratcliff's 38th USCT and four other regiments, would carry the heaviest burden. The goal: Defeat the Rebels and march into Richmond on the New Market Road. Maybe they could end the war.

As the Black troops prepared for the assault, the politically savvy Butler—a USCT advocate—provided inspiration: "Your cry, when you charge, will be, 'Remember Fort Pillow!'"[2] Only white officers commanded USCT units. The U.S. Army deemed Black soldiers unable to lead themselves, an act of racism prevalent at the time.

---

2. Speech of Hon. Benjamin F. Butler, of Massachusetts, in the House of Representatives, Jan. 7, 1874, Government Printing Office, 1874

Behind breastworks and entrenchments awaited two thousand-some veteran fighters in the Texas Brigade under Brig. Gen. John Gregg. In front of their line stood a double line of sharpened tree branches called abatis and wooden _chevaux de frise_, the distant ancestor of barbed wire. Marshy Four Mile Creek, which ran below the ridge, provided another impediment. Rebel artillery commanded the north and south ends of New Market Heights.

In the pre-dawn darkness, a thick, eerie fog enshrouded the battlefield. The initial assault, at roughly 5:30 a.m. on September 29, 1864, was cut to pieces. At about 7:30 a.m., a brigade that included the 38th, 36th, and 5th USCT—approximately 1,300 soldiers in all—advanced across the same ground, strewn now with the bloody and broken bodies of bluecoats.

"When they charged," a Confederate soldier said, "...the fun began."[3]

Pfft.

Thump.

Pftt.

Thump.

Rebel Miniés plunged into trees and humans, the ghastly cacophony of battle.

"It was slow work," a white U.S officer recalled of the advance, "and every step exposed us to the murderous fire of the enemy."[4]

After his commander suffered a mortal wound, Ratcliff—who had been promoted to sergeant months earlier—took over and pushed on. He became the first Union soldier to breach the works of the outnumbered Confederates, who eventually abandoned their defenses. In all, the 38th USCT suffered 33 dead and 75 wounded among nearly 500 soldiers in the command.

"Think of what he had in battle—a musket with a bayonet," Radcliffe says of his ancestor. "I have a modern gun, body armor and a ballistic helmet to protect me."

Although the Army of the James had stalled before Richmond, the USCT proved to comrades and newspaper reporters alike that they could fight well—and bravely.

---

3. Price, James S, _The Battle of New Market Heights_, Charleston, S.C.: The History Press, 2011, Page 60

4. _The Jeffersonian-Democrat_, Brookville, Pa., July 15, 1915

"We've always had a sense of pride in him," Damon Radcliffe says of his great-great-grandfather, a USCT soldier who earned a Medal of Honor.

"The darkies advanced in solid column, and never flinched," wrote a New York correspondent from Fort Monroe, a U.S. hospital site at the tip of the Virginia peninsula. "The large number of wounded brought down here of these soldiers attests the valor displayed by them."[5]

"The standing of the colored troops in this army is of the best kind," a white U.S. Army soldier wrote. "All praise their noble behavior in the thick of the fight. A man would be hooted at here that would even hint that the colored troops will not fight."[6]

In the aftermath of the battle, Butler rode his horse among the wounded and the dead. In an area of roughly 80 feet by 300 or 400 yards long, bodies littered the ground.

"I felt in my inmost heart," Butler recalled, "that the capacity of the negro race for soldiers had then and there been fully settled forever."[7]

5. *New York Daily Herald*, Oct. 2, 1864

6. *The Tiffin (Ohio) Tribune*, Oct. 27, 1864

7. Butler, Benjamin F., *Autobiography and Personal Reminiscences of Major-General Benj. F. Butler*, Boston: A.M. Thayer & Co., 1892, Page 733

Radcliffe and I stand by an outer wall at Fort Harrison, renamed Fort Burnham in honor of the Union general who was killed during the successful attack on September 29. Beyond the tree line, about three miles away, his great-great-grandfather charged in 1864.

"Surreal," he says as he props his arm on a cannon.

A large swath of the battlefield is private property, inaccessible for us today.

Damn.

Henrico County has preserved a portion of the rest of the battlefield. But a postwar gravel pit destroyed a significant section of the battlefield. Only a few historical signs mark this nearly forgotten hallowed ground.

After the Battle of New Market Heights, Fort Burnham served as a U.S. Army garrison through the end of the war. Before the year was out, Ratcliff had been promoted to sergeant major.

But no matter Ratcliff's status in the army, his race disqualified him from casting a ballot in any U.S. election. At Fort Burnham on November 8, 1864, white soldiers voted in the presidential election pitting Abraham Lincoln against George McClellan, the former commander of the Army of the Potomac. White Americans forbade Black Americans from voting until after the passage in Congress of the 15th Amendment in 1870.[8]

Following the victory at New Market Heights, Butler forwarded a list of soldiers he considered deserving of the Medal of Honor to Lt. Gen. Ulysses S. Grant. The general's staff reviewed it and sent the list to the War Department.

On April 3, 1865, the day after the Confederate evacuated Richmond, the USCT marched into the capital after white troops had entered the city. Three days later, after the issue had languished for months, the government issued a Medal of Honor to Ratcliff and 13 other USCT soldiers who fought valiantly at New Market Heights. Two of them served in Ratcliff's regiment.

"Commanded and gallantly led his company after the commanding officer had been killed; was the first enlisted man to enter the enemy's works," read Ratcliff's Medal of Honor citation.

---

8. By Ohio law in 1864, a man of mixed ancestry could vote if he had more white than Black blood. The 5th USCT, mostly composed of Ohio soldiers, cast all of its 194 ballots for Lincoln, who easily won reelection. See: Versalle F. Washington's *Buttons: A Black Infantry Regiment in the Civil War*, University Press of Missouri, 1999.

Butler paid for the creation of his own medal to honor nearly 200 Black soldiers who fought in the battle. He awarded nearly all the Butler medals himself.

"Since the war I have been fully rewarded by seeing the beaming eye of many a colored comrade as he drew his medal from the innermost recesses of its concealment to show me," the general wrote.[9]

The whereabouts of Ratcliff's medals today are a mystery. Radcliffe's brother Edward—the Marine—suspects the Medal of Honor may rest with Ratcliff, who died in 1915, in the grave in Cheesecake Cemetery on the Virginia Peninsula. Or perhaps the medals may be somewhere in Philadelphia, where Edward's first wife lived. The original wartime image of their great-great-grandfather is lost to history, too.

As we walk the pathway inside Fort Harrison, Damon Radcliffe talks of his family's military service. When his brother retires from the Marines, he plans to have the ceremony held at Fort Harrison on September 29—the anniversary of the Battle of New Market Heights. The brothers embrace their family's legacy.

"And my purpose," Damon Radcliffe tells me, "is not to mess it up."

My immediate purpose is to get back on the road, but I vow to walk the New Market Heights battlefield someday.

But it's time for a drive to Cold Harbor, 10 miles east of Richmond. In a two-story log cabin near Turkey Hill lives a legendary relic hunter, who knows the blood-soaked battlefield better than anyone else.

---

9. *Autobiography and Personal Reminiscences of Major-General Benj. F. Butler,* Page 743

CHAPTER 28

Mechanicsville, Virginia

TALKING TURKEY HILL
AT COLD HARBOR

On a sultry Virginia afternoon, I plop onto a couch in the living room of Gary Williams' two-story log cabin, the nerve center of his Civil War belt plate-making operation on the Cold Harbor killing field. A bullet-riddled wooden beam from the wartime Grapevine Bridge serves as a mantle above his fireplace. Nearby, under a Plexiglas covering, rests the 1,000-bullet Union Army ammunition crate Williams had unearthed years ago on the battlefield.

On his desktop computer, Williams checks for belt plate orders, which arrive from around the globe—Germany, England, Austria and elsewhere.

"Italy is big," he says in a drawl as thick as cold pancake syrup. Texans love his reproduction plates, too.

"They want 'em bigger there," says Williams, a pony-tailed, 78-year-old Elvis Presley fan.

Williams runs Hanover Brass Foundry with his wife and son. He casts 30-50 buckles a day in a small foundry building on his property—about a quarter mile from Turkey Hill. It's the stretch of high ground where the Battle of Cold Harbor raged in early June 1864. Williams' belt plate-making business has thrived since it began in 1967, the year before his discharge from the Marines.

Williams lives in a two-story log house with his wife, Teresa, a Georgia native who has a doctorate in education. They met while relic hunting in Virginia in 1974. Two years later, on the Fourth of July, they married in Gettysburg during a battle reenactment weekend. The couple reared three children: Gary Jr., better known as "Bubba"; a daughter named Presley (after Elvis); and a son named LeeBrook, who died of cancer in 1991 at age nine. Williams thinks about him every day.

For decades, Williams—born and raised on the Cold Harbor battle-field—hunted for real Civil War buckles and other relics on Virginia battlefields and campsites using a "Double Eagle Deep Seeker" metal detector with a custom-made 38-inch search coil. He amassed one of the country's finest dug collections, more than enough to display in a large private museum he ran in nearby Williamsburg from 1982-1996.

Williams—a legend in relic hunting circles—still hunts for Civil War artifacts, just not nearly as frequently as in his glory days. Relic hunting has taken a physical toll. Williams complains of arthritis in his knee. He can't make a fist anymore. His feet and hips ache. He walks with a slight stoop. Williams is hard of hearing, too. But that's a result of aging, not lugging a 100-pound Parrott shell through tick-infested woods.

"Relic hunting," he says, "ruined me."

But it also provided nearly a lifetime of memories.

As a youngster growing up on the Cold Harbor battlefield, Williams would often pick up Miniés while searching fields for arrowheads. He eyeballed his first Civil War relic, an Ohio Volunteer Militia belt plate, in a field when he was 10. The battlefield, 10 miles from Richmond, was mostly countryside then.

For Christmas in 1955, Williams' parents gave him his first metal detec-tor, a Fisher T-10, packaged in a flimsy cardboard box. It cost $90.

"It was bigger than me, and probably weighed more than me," he says.

Williams hunted nearly every day, often on sites virtually untouched since the Civil War.

"When I first got into relic hunting," Williams says, "I just wanted to find buckles."

In the 1960s, while he attended high school, Williams' hobby grew into a business. He gave battlefield tours and sold relics from a small one-story building on Cold Harbor Road—the same route the armies used in 1864. Later, Williams ran a small Civil War museum in nearby Lightfoot.

A half-century ago, relic hunters found artifacts almost everywhere in the fields and woods at Cold Harbor and the immediate surrounding area. Kids in Henrico County got a metal detector before a bicycle. In the late 1950s, war relics sold for a fraction of what they cost collectors today.

"We found bullets around here like crackers," Williams says.

A fired bullet would sell for two cents, a drop for a nickel. Eagle breast-plates could be had for a buck. Williams considered unearthing 50 bullets a slow day.

Preferring a smaller-sized load, he often left artillery shells where he found them in the woods. Besides, deactivating one could be dangerous. In the 1960s, Williams' high school history teacher, a Marine and World War II vet, lost two fingers when a Parrott shell exploded as he was removing the gunpowder charge.

For years, Williams charged fellow relic hunters a fee for taking them to privately owned areas of the Cold Harbor battlefield and beyond—with a landowners' consent, of course. The armies clashed in Williams' own backyard, after all, and he knew almost every farmer and landowner, every dip and rise, every potential hot spot.

Many of his fellow relic hunters became lifelong friends. A tourist from Pennsylvania visiting the battlefield with his family taught Williams how to cast buckles, which eventually became his profession. In 1967, Williams started reproducing belt plates he had unearthed for collectors and reenactors.

An Atlanta real estate agent named Tom Dickey became one of Williams' closest relic hunting pals. Together the men scoured area battlefields—from Cold Harbor and Gaines Mill to White Oak Swamp and Malvern Hill. Dickey, who died in 1987, amassed one of the foremost collections of Civil War artillery shells. Unintended humor resulted from their hunts.

"One time he took nine shells back with him on an airplane," Williams says, smiling at the memory. "They didn't check nothing back then.

"A stewardess came up to him and asked him, 'Sir, would you mind putting that rifle up front for safekeeping?'"

"Relic hunting," Gary Williams says, "ruined me."

Dickey had also unearthed a rusty musket and bayonet during the day's hunt with his friend.

"And here he was with nine unexploded artillery shells underneath his seat," Williams says.

I chuckle and then wince at the thought of a worst-case scenario.

On another trip, Dickey bought a 15-inch Rodman shell from Williams, who had recovered the 300-plus-pounder at Dutch Gap, Virginia, near the James River. Dickey put the behemoth in a cardboard box on the floor of the back seat of his station wagon for the return trip to Georgia.

As Dickey was driving home, the shell rolled toward the front of the vehicle, pressing him awkwardly against the horn.

"And that thing was going off as he drove on down the road," Williams says.

What a hoot.

To this day, an eerie somberness blankets Cold Harbor, making it unlike any other Civil War battlefield I've walked. During my first visit years ago, the hair on my arms and back of my neck stood straight up as I navigated a hill toward the 2nd Connecticut Heavy Artillery monument—one of the few monuments on the battlefield.

In an ill-fated charge on June 1, 1864, the Heavies suffered 85 killed among more than 300 casualties. "Pray for me … am not in a fit state of mind," the regimental chaplain wrote his wife in a letter about the bloodletting.[1]

In Ulysses Grant's infamous, poorly coordinated charge on June 3, 1864, thousands of U.S. Army soldiers fell. Some historians say as many as 7,000. In the two-week engagement, which soon devolved into trench warfare, Federal casualties (12,737) vastly outnumbered the Confederates' (4,595).[2]

One dreadfully hot afternoon, I lay alone among the pines on Cold Harbor battleground maintained by the National Park Service, staring into a cloudless sky. Only a fraction of the vast battlefield is NPS property. The humidity was thick and so was the gloom. But I couldn't get my mind off birds. As scores of Union wounded and dead lay in no-man's land at Cold Harbor in early June 1864, black vultures circled above. Then the creatures descended to earth to do their horrid work.

Williams has personally confirmed tangible evidence of the carnage.

"My wife found seven bodies in a hole over in Farmer Adams' field on Turkey Hill," he says.

Williams retrieved the relics found among the bones and re-buried the bodies at the request of Marius Adams, the farmer, whose grandfather had farmed the ground in 1864.

Years ago, a local relic hunter, a longtime friend of Williams, unearthed at Cold Harbor photos of a woman and a young girl among the remains of a soldier.

"Many a poor fellow had quick interment in the trenches where he fell, and these little scars in the ground each did duty as a soldier's rude shroud," wrote a reporter who visited Cold Harbor in 1881.[3]

---

1. Winthrop Phelps letter to Lucy Phelps, June 1, 1864, Litchfield (Conn.) Historical Society collection

2. American Battlefield Trust web site

3. *Philadelphia Times*, Aug. 30, 1881

The remains of Cold Harbor dead. No other Civil War battlefield is more haunting. Library of Congress

On the foggy morning of June 3 on Turkey Hill, Grant's army briefly punctured the Confederates' line, one of its few successes that day against the well-entrenched Army of Northern Virginia. Hand-to-hand fighting broke out.

"Clubbed muskets, bayonets, and swords got in their deadly work," a Union veteran recalled.[4]

The 7th New York Heavy Artillery carried the fight to the Rebels, taking a trench and hundreds of prisoners, before an onslaught forced them back. Dozens of New Yorkers fell. Sergeant George Sanders suffered a mortal wound. Days after his death, his wife died of typhoid fever, making orphans of their children.

"Two small children are thus thrown upon a cold world, to pass through the perils of childhood and youth without the guiding and staying hand of father or mother," Sanders' hometown newspaper wrote.[5]

A sharpshooter's bullet paralyzed beloved Colonel Lewis O. Morris, who prayed for mercy as he lay dying.

---

4. *Richmond (Va.) Dispatch*, April 27, 1902

5. *Albany (N.Y.) Morning Express*, June 27, 1864

"At one o'clock his spirit departed, and, as I cannot doubt, passed into the glory of the saints in light," a pastor wrote. "When we undressed him we found his Testament in his pocket, and showing marks of use."

Upon hearing news of his death, soldiers in the regiment wept.[6]

Private Henry C. Leslie took a bullet through the hips. Sent to Washington to recuperate, he appeared on his way to recovery. Then an artery burst, and he died days later.

Comrades found Private Frank Carpenter's body on the field. He suffered a wound nearby, at the Battle of Gaines Mill, nearly two years earlier.

"Let us not talk of our sacrifices until we can emulate his example," a comrade of his wrote, "and never rest until 'Treason shall go down.'"[7]

On Adams' farm on Turkey Hill, Williams has unearthed thousands of relics—bullets, buttons, bayonets, breastplates, a 24-pound Coehorn mortar shell and the shattered leg bones of a soldier from North Carolina. (The bones were later re-buried elsewhere.)

When he was a boy, Farmer Adams and his father used mules to help fill the trench lines on Turkey Hill.

"He always said, 'I filled those trenches in and now you boys are digging them out again,'" Williams says. Adams died on June 3, 1986—the 122nd anniversary of Grant's doomed charge.

Two of Williams' finds represent the ferocity of the fighting at Cold Harbor: a Union eagle breastplate and canteen, each punctured by a bullet. Neither owner likely survived.

From a desk, Williams retrieves a ledger he kept of relic hunting finds decades ago. Williams' entries from June 12, 1969-May 29, 1972, are jaw-dropping:

28,435 Minies

303 buckles & plates

173 Confederate buttons

45 bayonets

35 cannonballs

15 I.D. tags!!

Nine pistols

---

6. Clark, Rufus W., *The Heroes of Albany*, Albany, N.Y.: S.R. Gray Publisher, 1867, Pages 220 and 222

7. New York State Military Museum and Veterans Research Center web site, Unknown Albany newspaper, 1864

"You didn't even have to know how to hunt back then," Williams says.

On another ledger appears Williams' drawing of the left half of another buckle. The rare casting included a sailing ship. He gave the relic to a friend. On another appears the outline of a .22-caliber pistol he had unearthed.

In a Burnside carbine cartridge, Williams discovered a clipping from a Baltimore newspaper of a story about a soldier killed during a Seven Days' battle near Richmond.

Teresa frequently hunted with her husband, too. In the late 1970s, she discovered at Cold Harbor a rare Louisiana state button of solid silver.

"I was just lucky to live in them days," Williams admits.

Williams disagrees with those who say relic hunters destroy history. His aim all along has been to preserve the relics and therefore the memory of the soldiers who fought. "These things have a real beauty to them," he says of the artifacts.

Williams' voice trails off. Then he reflects on the horror the relics represent, too.

"How lucky we are," Williams says, "to not be in a war like the Civil War."

Before I depart, Williams hands me a reproduction of a brass buckle worn by Robert E. Lee, who stymied Grant at Cold Harbor. What a great gift.

And then I drive north, destined for another Civil War killing field—one of the war's deadliest. I'm going to walk the ground with the great-great-granddaughter of a soldier who died there.

CHAPTER 29

Sharpsburg, Maryland

MAYHEM AND MONARCHS IN THE 40-ACRE CORNFIELD

Over breakfast at Bonnie's At The Red Byrd in Keedysville, Maryland, where I once talked Civil War with a man who billed himself as an ex-CIA agent, Laurie Buckler Mack spills a family secret.

"After college, I followed The Grateful Dead around for a year, but I hope my mother doesn't find out," she reveals decades after the adventure.

Uh-oh.

Mack is a 53-year-old, full-time licensed veterinary technician and part-time character. She lives in Annapolis, Maryland, with a rescue dog named Darcy Jane. Her best friend's children call her "Aunt Lobster" for her head of red hair, now streaked with gray. As I gobble breakfast, Mack delivers a Gatling gun-like blast of personal and family history.

"I was accepted to go to Gettysburg College," she says, "but I couldn't go there because of too much stuff"—that "stuff" being a strange vibe on campus, perhaps Civil War related.

In her first job out of college in the late 1980s, Mack worked for a woman whose direct descendant, Dr. Samuel Mudd, set John Wilkes Booth's broken left leg following his assassination of President Lincoln. A childhood friend of Mack's claimed Ambrose Burnside, the bewhiskered commander of the Union Army's Ninth Corps at Antietam, as a tangential ancestor.

In a what-a-small-world coincidence, Burnside led troops that included the 16th Connecticut—the regiment of Mack's maternal great-great-great-grandfather, 1st Lieutenant William Horton. During the Battle of Antietam on September 17, 1862, the 31-year-old married father of three suffered a mortal wound that sent his family into a downward spiral.

When Mack first read of the circumstances of Horton's death in 2022 in a book about his regiment, she was crushed.

"Ugly crying for days," she says.

After we had connected online, I pitched to Mack the idea of walking in her ancestor's footsteps at Antietam—from Snavely Ford, where Horton and the 16th Connecticut forded Antietam Creek, to the 40-Acre Cornfield, where he bled to death on the battlefield. She readily accepted.

I have an almost mystical connection with the 16th Connecticut, a diverse group that included a professor, pistol makers, sailors, farmers, machinists and a cigar maker from Suffield named Richard Jobes, who suffered a grievous bullet wound in the 40-Acre Cornfield. Jobes walked more than a half-mile to a makeshift hospital, where a harried surgeon amputated his left forearm. After the war, when the pain in the injured arm became too great, Jobes dipped the limb in cold well water.[1]

Antietam was the first battle of the war for the 16th Connecticut, whose enlisted men barely knew how to load and fire their weapons. In April 1864 in Plymouth, North Carolina, Confederates captured nearly the entire regiment. Most ended up imprisoned at Andersonville, America's saddest place. Dozens of them remain there in the national cemetery.

When we lived in Connecticut, visits to the gravesites of 16th Connecticut soldiers often filled my weekends. The memory of Horton's final resting place in Stafford Springs, near the Massachusetts border, remains embedded in my brain for two reasons: the yapping (and unchained) dogs nearby and the lieutenant's ornate, red sandstone gravestone with a sword carved in bas-relief on the front.

---

1. Jobes pension file, National Archives, Washington, D.C.

My Antietam visit with Mack falls on Father's Day, an unseasonably cool, blue-sky morning of wispy clouds and bright sunshine. The gods of battlefields smile upon us.

"This is what my father would want me to be doing on Father's Day," Mack says. Her dad, who served in the U.S. Air Force and Maryland National Guard, died several years ago.

Mack knew little about her Civil War ancestor until 2021, when her mother dropped in front of her a box of family photos and papers—including a wartime image of Horton and a copy of the sermon preached at his funeral. Since then, she has consulted with undertakers, historical society docents, vital records officers, cemetery caretakers and archivists for information about her great-great-great-grandfather. She figures it's more of a calling than an obsession.

In 1855, Horton—a descendant of *Mayflower* passengers and Revolutionary War soldiers—married Laura Orcutt, a factory operator's daughter. The couple raised three children: Jennie, Hattie and the youngest, a boy named James. Before the war, William worked as a spinner in Stafford, where the factories churned out textiles and other supplies for the Union Army. After service in the 11th Connecticut early in the war, Horton resigned and returned home. Facing accusations of cowardice, he reenlisted in the 16th Connecticut in the summer of 1862.

"I'll show you whether I am a coward or not," he vowed to a comrade.[2]

In the parking lot above Burnside Bridge—our starting point a few miles from the Red Byrd restaurant—we are joined by my friend Laura Van Alstyne Rowland. As you may recall, she is an Abraham Lincoln fanatic who owns a framed Oreo cookie with the 16th president carved in the white icing. Rowland lives with her husband, "Bear," in a late 18th-century house on Main Street in Sharpsburg.

As we wind our way toward Snavely Ford, I point to the steep, wooded bluff to our right from which a small force of Georgians fired upon the Ninth Corps. To our left, hip-deep Antietam Creek cascades over rocks and creates eddies close to the bank. We step over barbed-wire fencing to get to the ford. It's an unremarkable spot, unmarked and remote. But it's steeped in Civil War history.

---

2. Ezra Burgess to George Q. Whitney, March 22, 1909, Whitney Collection, Connecticut State Library, Hartford

On the afternoon of September 17, 1862, roughly a mile from Burnside Bridge, 16th Connecticut soldiers held their weapons and cartridge boxes high above their heads as they crossed the creek. They heard the boom of cannon and crackle and reverberation of musketry as the battle at the bridge raged.

In a nearby cut from a stream, Ninth Corps soldiers may have sheltered from Confederate fire as they marched toward a field near the undulating 40-Acre Cornfield—ground owned in 1862 by farmer named Joseph Sherrick. He supposedly had stashed $3,000 in gold in a stone wall on his property for safekeeping during the battle. I wonder if some of it is still there.

In an open field to our right, at the top of a hill, Horton and his comrades formed for their defining event of the war.

"I should have brought Hattie's ring," Mack says of the rose gold and amethyst relic of Horton's middle child. "What a crazy talisman for this moment."

In the field, Confederate artillery found its mark, wounding roughly a dozen 16th Connecticut soldiers. The concussion of a cannon shot knocked three soldiers senseless. Of the enemy gunners, a German aide to Army of the Potomac commander George McClellan said: "Boys, does Rebs is tam-med-sassy."[3]

Passing wildflowers and brush, we make our way to the knoll in the 40-Acre Cornfield where the 16th Connecticut monument stands. It's a 15-foot-high beacon of multicolored granite, dedicated by the regiment's veterans in 1894.

"We raise our kids to be kind," Rowland says, "and to think kids were killing other kids in this field."

Overhead, a huge bird circles while a stiff breeze blows. The former killing field is now a waystation for monarch butterflies. I have visited this spot—my favorite on the battlefield—dozens of times. On a ghostly gray winter morning, I stood, seemingly alone, in front of the 16th Connecticut monument. Moments later, a massive Saint Bernard with bad intentions arrived behind me to my left, sparking memories of the horror film *Cujo*

---

3. Relyea, William H., *16th Connecticut Volunteer Infantry: Sergeant William H. Relyea*, Edited by John Michael Priest, Shippensburg, Pa.: Burd Street Press, 2002, Page 25

and ruining the battlefield vibe. The dog's masters finally appeared to restrain him.

A postwar map created by a 16th Connecticut veteran indicates the spot near the monument where comrades found the bullet-riddled body of Captain Samuel Brown. I think about him every time I walk the ground. Brown was a 26-year-old teacher with "long and beautiful whiskers." When a cannonball whizzed near the captain that day, Richard Jobes said his commanding officer briefly turned pale before coolly issuing commands.[4]

Nearly 50 years after the battle, relic hunters turned up a soldier's bones in this field.[5] Mrs. B may secretly spread my ashes here when I'm gone. Please don't tell the National Park Service.

Mack has walked this ground before, too.

"I was a mess," she says of her emotional first visit in 2020.

Near 3:30 p.m. on the day of the battle, the Ninth Corps formed a line roughly a mile long in fields on the outskirts of Sharpsburg. In a field of tall corn, the 4th Rhode Island, a veteran regiment, and the 16th Connecticut anchored the extreme left.

As the 16th Connecticut advanced, they panicked under a hail of musketry mixed with artillery fire that included railroad iron and blacksmith tools.

"My Got!" said a Union cannoneer, another German, of Rebel artillery that day. "We shall have the blacksmith's shop to come next."[6]

In the cornfield, a desperate 16th Connecticut officer shouted to his colonel: "Tell us what you want us to do, and we'll try to obey you!"[7] The 16th Connecticut suffered 43 killed, 161 wounded and 204 captured or missing of more than 1,000 engaged. More than two dozen 16th Connecticut soldiers deserted.

"[I]t certainly was best for us to break and run," a 16th Connecticut veteran remembered years later, "than to stay and be killed by the hundreds."[8]

4. George Q. Whitney Collection, Connecticut State Library, Jobes' letter to Fanny Brown, Feb. 10, 1909

5. *Shepherdstown (W.Va.) Register*, Sept. 23, 1909

6. *Cleveland Daily Leader*, Oct. 1, 1862

7. *16th Connecticut Volunteer Infantry*, Page 26

8. 16th Connecticut veteran William Nott postwar diary, copy in author's collection

Laurie Mack holds a wartime photo of her ancestor, Lt. William Horton of the 16th Connecticut, near a monument to the regiment in the 40-Acre Cornfield.

In the 40-Acre Cornfield, James Brooks, an 18-year-old private from Stafford, suffered six wounds. Days after his 19th birthday weeks later, he died at a Sharpsburg church used as a U.S. Army hospital. The death of Nelson Snow, a private from Suffield, sent his brother Orlando into a deep depression. Two years later, Orlando died in Andersonville. Rufus Chamberlain, a 43-year-old sergeant from Stafford, took a bullet in the knee. Weeks later, he died in a battlefield hospital. A comrade gave his widow the bullet that killed him. Wounded Private Henry Adams lay in the field for 52 hours until soldiers rescued him. Years later, he wondered, "Why did I not die?"[9]

These are *my guys.*

Somewhere out here among the monarchs and wildflowers, Mack's great-great-great-grandfather lay grievously wounded. A comrade believed Horton could have been saved with proper care. "[Horton] was a brave

9. Ibid; for more details on the soldiers, see Banks, John, *Connecticut Yankees at Antietam,* Charleston, S.C.: The History Press, 2013

man, although he had to enlist a second time to prove it," the soldier recalled.[10]

From a plastic bag, Mack pulls the wartime image of Horton for a photograph near the 16th Connecticut monument.

"I can still see the bodies and hear the gunfire here," she says.

In the image, Horton—who sported a dark beard and hair—wears an officer's uniform with sash tied to his belt. The somber-looking soldier grasps an inscribed sword—probably the one that has disappeared into a family labyrinth. Mack seeks its return, along with Horton's wartime journal and letters another descendant unloaded years ago.

Days after the battle, the 16th Connecticut adjutant saw that the regiment's dead received a decent burial in a field behind a nearby farmhouse.

"The collection of the bodies was conducted under my own personal supervision, and after the men had reported them all picked up, I examined the whole field myself, so that I am confident none were left on the ground," he wrote.

In a separate grave marked by a crude wooden headboard, comrades buried Horton near other 16th Connecticut officers.

"If any mortal was ever rejoiced at the completion of any task," the adjutant wrote, "it was myself when this sad work was over."[11]

Mack, Rowland and I visit the burial area, inaccessible because of weeds and brush, to briefly commune with Horton's spirit. Weeks after the battle, the lieutenant's badly decomposed body was recovered, placed in a hermetically sealed lead casket and returned to Connecticut for burial.[12]

On October 8, 1862, in Stafford Springs, Connecticut, the crowd was so large at Horton's military funeral that Reverend Alexis W. Ide moved it outside and preached from the steps of the Congregational Church, "under an awning formed by the national flag."

Late in his sermon, Ide addressed Horton's 27-year-old widow, Laura.

"Your husband, and the event, you must leave in hands of the supreme Ruler of the universe," he said. "Real good from your present affliction can only be found in God."

10. Burgess to Whitney, March 22, 1909, CSL collection

11. *Hartford Courant*, Sept. 30, 1862

12. Historical Vignettes Vol. 1, Stafford, Connecticut, 275th Anniversary, 1719-1994

"I'll show you whether I am a coward or not," 16th Connecticut Lt. William Horton told a comrade.

Nearly 10 months after Antietam, another tragedy rocked the Hortons: the death of the couple's young son, James, from an unknown cause. Laura, who never remarried, died in 1903.

Before we leave the 40-Acre Cornfield and the monarchs, wildflowers and tragic stories behind, I ask Mack what she would like to convey to her ancestor.

"I want him to know we have not forgotten him," she says, "and that we are keeping his sacrifice in mind."

Who knows if Horton's spirit lingers in this beautiful, serene field.

In Gettysburg, an hour's drive north, some will tell you the spirits of soldiers are omnipresent. I'm eager to find out if they're right.

CHAPTER **30**

Gettysburg, Pennsylvania

MY FIRST GHOST WALK
AND INVESTIGATION

Near a rack of "Past Lives Matter" and "Gettysburg Ghost Mecca of the World" T-shirts, "Major Finn" barks instructions to my "Battle Cry" ghost walk tour group on Steinwehr Avenue.

"People in town are horrible drivers," the New Englander shouts while traffic crawls by. "Watch where you're walking. Follow my lantern of safety!"

On this jaunt, Major Finn and I are joined by a family of four from Western Pennsylvania—a couple with an 11-year-old girl and a 9-year-old boy dressed as a Billy Yank. Here, on Gettysburg's kitschiest stretch, tourists can buy "Yankee Hurrah" and "Rebel Yell" ice cream cones, munch on "Battlefield Fries" and purchase real battlefield relics. The atmosphere reminds me of the midway at the Texas State Fair but without the ring toss and "Guess Your Weight" guy.

Submitting to inner demons, I have booked a one-hour early evening ghost walk about town and a three-hour, late-night Xtreme Ghost Hunt investigation with Gettysburg Ghost Tours. After a long morning in Antietam's 40-Acre Cornfield, I'm weary, sore and looking like death warmed over.

Full disclosure: In dozens of visits to Gettysburg over the years, I've never spotted a ghost, captured a mysterious spirit in a photograph or purchased a "Show Me Your Orbs" T-shirt. This will be my first ghost walk and ghost hunt. I'm a ghost skeptic.

In a chance meeting on the battlefield at Devil's Den in 2008, Stewart of the Mason Dixon Paranormal Society played for me an unconvincing tape of an electronic voice phenomenon investigation at a local house.

"*Crrrrrrrrrrr.*"

Stewart heard a soldier's cry on the EVP tape. I heard static.

A well-regarded historian, a longtime local, erupted with unvarnished opinions when I asked him about Gettysburg ghost tour operators.

"Dregs of society!"

"Scammers!"

"The worst!"

"They just make up stories, embellish them."

"There are no ghosts. *Nowhere, you stupid imbeciles*!"

He calls the thousands of tourists who go on ghost tours and investigations "nutty people," which makes me squirm.

And yet ghost stories linger in Gettysburg like an ornery drunk in a bar at closing time.

An early-20ish Gettysburg barista named Whitney told me she witnessed the inexplicable while employed at The Gettysburg Hotel on the square. Lights flickered. Chairs moved. Strange footsteps echoed. Whitney is aligned with thousands of other true believers.

Google "Gettysburg Ghosts," and more than a half-million results pop up. On Facebook, the "Gettysburg Ghost Pictures" page has over 64,000 followers, more than five times the number in the "Battle of Gettysburg Discussion Group."

Ghost tours began flourishing in Gettysburg in 1980s, when there wasn't much to do in town at night. The tours proved popular, and most locals didn't seem to mind. Tourists mean money, after all, and what town wouldn't want more of that? Today there are at least a dozen ghost tour operators in Gettysburg—offering everything from a pub crawl ghost walk to a "Dark Side of Christmas" tour that seems almost sacrilegious.

In 1917, an American professor offered a possible explanation for "battlefield ghosts." He said the human body contains about 55 ounces of phosphorous, mostly in the bones. When a body deteriorates, "phosphorescent compounds are given off that might easily be mistaken by the superstitious or credulous for phantoms."[1]

Roughly 8,000 soldiers died at Gettysburg, so perhaps the professor's strange hypothesis explains those weird photos of battlefield orbs and ghost sighting stories I find online. But a retired physician gives me a succinct assessment of the professor's finding: "Bullshit."

Major Finn, whose real name is Eric Reeder, is a 61-year-old former history teacher and TV producer from Maine. A longtime reenactor, our ghost walk leader often portrays John Burns, the crotchety Gettysburger and War of 1812 veteran, who lugged his ancient musket into battle to fight alongside Union soldiers on the battle's first day.

For this evening's walk, though, Reeder portrays an oddly dressed Civil War soldier. Our tour leader sports a neatly trimmed white beard, carries a cane as a prop, and wears a scruffy brown jacket and pants and a white felt top hat. This is his chief gig now that he has retired to Gettysburg.

"I was visiting the battlefield so often, I figured I'd move here to save gas," he tells us.

Reeder is distantly related to the delightfully named Adney Boothby, a 45-year-old private in Company F of the famed 20th Maine. Led by Colonel Joshua Lawrence Chamberlain, the Mainers held the extreme left of the Union line at Little Round Top on July 2, 1863.

At the Dobbin House Tavern on Steinwehr Avenue, our first stop, Major Finn shifts into full carnival barker mode.

"See that second-floor window," Major Finn says. "A mysterious young girl sometimes lingers there." He says in July 1863 piles of amputated arms and legs formed outside the first-floor windows of the tavern—a makeshift military hospital then and a popular restaurant now.

"See that red door," Major Finn says of the tavern entryway. "That was used as an operating table and is stained with blood!"

Outside the 1950s-era Three Crowns Motor Lodge, Major Finn points to Room 105.

---

1. *The Washington Times*, July 16, 1917

I think the ghost hunt got to me.

"Some say it's haunted because Confederate dead may lie underneath the parking lot. This ground was battlefield in 1863, too."

I feel silly shooting a closeup of the Room 105 door. Then Major Finn continues his spiel.

"Bodies were exploding here," he says of Gettysburg. "They said they could smell them 30 miles away."

My fellow ghost tour walkers shift, nervously.

"There are 1,400 unaccounted for soldier burials out here," Finn says. "When they find them all, I may be out of a job." But the good major admits he doesn't think that will happen anytime soon.

Outside a bar, where our group rests, I have a brief discussion with a glassy-eyed biker smoking a cig and staring at us.

"Do you believe in ghosts?"

"Nope," he said, smiling.

At the next ghost walk tour stop, a one-story stone building on Steinwehr Avenue, I press my nose to a window. On July 1, 1863, the body of Union Maj. Gen. John Reynolds—the highest-ranking officer to die at Gettysburg—lay inside. During the war, the building served as the residence of a day laborer named George George, whose parents apparently lacked imagination. Now it's a studio where tourists can get their pictures taken. Reynolds' ghost is said to linger in George's former haunt, but I don't spot a single orb.

The walking tour becomes a dizzying blur of Major Finn stories—of a ghost carrying a flaming sword into battle near Joshua Chamberlain; of a mass grave on the Gettysburg High School football field; and of ghost-like figures marching from the national cemetery. Think *Night of the Living Dead* invading the most famous Civil War battlefield of all.

I remain a skeptic. *Damn.* Should I have booked the "Traditional Black Cat Tour" instead? According to a guide, it includes visits to dark alleys by candlelight to locations that were "active battlefields and homes of make-shift shallow graves."

Or maybe I should have grabbed a brew at the Reliance Mine Saloon off Steinwehr. I know that "Fraz"—William Frassanito, the legendary Civil War photography expert—hangs there.

Perhaps evidence of spirits will come on my three-hour Xtreme Ghost Hunt—"the most extreme ghost hunt available to the public!" according to my tour's web site. "Ghost hunt like the pros with the pros!"

Minutes before the investigation, I quiz a mid-60ish woman wearing a hoop dress about soldier spirits.

"The Sach's Covered Bridge is *extremely haunted*," the tour employee insists about my final stop. "You can play *Dixie* and *Stonewall Jackson's Way* for the soldiers. Music will get them going."

Nearby, a professional ghost investigator talks of ectoplasm, a super-natural viscous substance, with a tourist while a half-dozen others stare at their phones. Next door, the bar has closed for the night. Too bad. Real spirits and soldier spirits seem like a compelling combination.

Shortly after 9 p.m., our nine-person group of amateur ghost hunters gathers for a pre-investigation briefing behind Gettysburg Ghost Tours HQ. Our team includes the dad with the nine-year-old son dressed as a Billy Yank; a skinny, purple-haired 20-something gobbling purple ice cream from a cone; a teenager and his dad, who totes a skateboard and wears a *Rick and Morty* T-shirt and a Marvin the Martian *Looney Tunes* bandana; and an Arizona couple on vacation with their granddaughter.

Our lead investigator, a 22-year-old ex-Dairy Queen employee named Mikayla, briefs us on our adventure. Her boss is a woman who goes by "Spooky." We all get a zipped bag of ghost-hunting equipment. Mikayla warns us not to shine the Spirit Net into traffic or a fellow ghost hunter's eyes because it could cause color blindness. The device emits a dizzying spray of green light.

"And don't shine it into the woods," she says, referencing our first destination, "because a man lives back there, and he can get grumpy."

Besides a mini-flashlight, I practice with a ghost-hunting device called a Temperature Gun, a laser that emits red light. Point the ghost hunter-friendly device at a target and click the gun. Detect a significant rise or dip on the temperature gauge and you may have a spirit on your hands.

"Use it to detect ghosts," Mikayla warns, "not play doctor."

We're also issued an instrument that emits white noise. But I avoid it because Mikayla says it can cause migraine headaches and nausea. I also avoid the ghost-detecting dousing rods, mainly because of the complexity of their operation.

"They can fling over," Mikayla says, "so be careful."

Those on the Xtreme Ghost Tour get an EVP recording device and a warning: "Don't take it with you to the bathroom," Mikayla says. "Don't whisper or yell." The device is supposed to record spirit voices. In two or three months, the tour group will e-mail us results of our investigations.

I turn to the father of the nine-year-old Billy Yank.

"If my body does not return to Tennessee, please message my wife."

"What should I tell her?"

"Tell Mrs. B I love her."

We both chuckle.

I ride with Mikayla in her car to our first destination, the late 19th-century McCurdy Schoolhouse on Emmitsburg Road. In the dead of night, her car's headlights reveal familiar sites—the wartime Codori and Sherfy farmhouses and the Peach Orchard. As we leave the military park, Mikayla—who claims to be an ardent believer in ghosts and spirits—dishes on her own real-life encounter with a one.

After a late-night shift at the Dairy Queen, she was driving home on Baltimore Pike. The longtime Gettysburg resident, then almost 17, sensed

Mikayla, my ghost hunt leader, is a true believer.

something dropping into her lap. Then she spotted a figure in front of her car.

"I swear it was a soldier," says Mikayla, who thought she hit whatever it was. Then she called 9-1-1. The police arrived and searched the area but found nothing.

"One of them told me, 'Mikayla, I think you might have seen a ghost.'"

I shiver. But it's not because of the revelation. It's unseasonably chilly.

Across the road from a sketchy 1950s-era motor lodge, we park at the school and pile into the musty place. Mikayla shows us a copy of a long-ago image of former students. Perhaps their spirits lurk in the empty building, she says. A mind-boggling light spectacle breaks out as ghost hunters deploy Temperature Guns and Spirit Nets. It reminds me of my college days listening to Pink Floyd in a strangely lit room in the student union but without the weed and haze.

"Dad, can you take a picture of me on this stool?" asks the son of the *Looney Tunes* bandana guy. "I feel a lot of spirit energy on this stool."

"Will you tell us your name?" a ghost hunter asks a "spirit presence."

"Can you repeat that, please?" the hunter asks.

I'm getting a headache. Perhaps it's the mustiness.

Mikayla shows me orbs and ghostlike faces in the background of photos taken in previous schoolhouse investigations.

"You may want to go outside," she tells me. "We've discovered much more of a military presence out there."

Clumsily juggling a notebook, EVP recorder and Temperature Gun, I head out into the darkness. I feel silly pointing the red light of the laser at the ancient well next to the school. The reading on the gun dips from 62 degrees to 47. But I have no idea if there's a ghostly presence. If there is, they could be soldiers in Union Brig. Gen. John Wesley Merritt's cavalry. On July 3, 1863, they dismounted near the schoolhouse and chased after Johnny Rebs somewhere in the vicinity.

I mistakenly point my Temperature Gun into the woods, where "Grumpy Guy" lives. But nothing stirs in the area—not even the ghost of Merritt, who became West Point superintendent in 1882.

As I walk back inside the schoolhouse, the Billy Yank kid says to no one in particular: "He just said this is a death place." Perhaps Gettysburg Ghost Tour investigators can narrow down the subject on my EVP recorder.

At 10:52 p.m., we arrive at Sach's Covered Bridge, built in 1852 across Marsh Creek. On July 1, 1863, two brigades of the Union Army's First Corps crossed the bridge enroute to Gettysburg. Days later, most of the Gen. Robert E. Lee's Army of Northern Virginia retreated over it.

Almost immediately, I sense a bump in the night. But it's not what you think. It's a Rem Pod—a small, merry-go-round-like thingy—placed on the bridge to detect spirits. You can buy one online, according to Hayden, the bearded dude in his 20s who placed it there. He works for a rival paranormal operation that also conducts ghost investigations at the bridge.

"Go over to the rushing water," he tells me. "Water generates energy for the spirits."

At the far end of the bridge, I observe a bespectacled 70ish woman from Ohio named Janet holding those challenging dousing rods.

"Are you Union?" she asks while staring into the creek.

"Are you Confederate?"

Earlier, Mikayla revealed to me that a Sach's Covered Bridge spirit nicknamed "Tennessee" will smoke a cigarette if you leave one on the railing.

"Hi, Tennessee," Janet says. "Do you need another cigarette?"

A pile of cigarette butts below the railing indicates many previous ghost hunters have taken the bait. Or perhaps it's simply litter left by "Tennessee," who may be ignorant of the surgeon general's warnings about the harmful effects of nicotine.

At 12:22 a.m., we wrap up the investigation. I don't have the energy to play *Dixie* for any soldier ghosts. I'm content to await for the results of my investigation in two or three months. Mikayla hands me a certificate of participation signed by "Spooky" from the Gettysburg Paranormal Association. It's a fitting ending to my spirited evening without spirits— imagined, real or liquid.

But my time in Gettysburg is far from over. A visit to a furniture sales-man with a remarkable Civil War collection in his own personal Gettysburg museum awaits in nine hours.

CHAPTER 31

Gettysburg, Pennsylvania

A COLLECTION THAT GOT OUT OF HAND

After a night vainly searching for spirits, I pay respects on Little Round Top to the 20th Maine and Private Adney Boothby, the ancestor of "Major Finn," my Gettysburg ghost walk tour leader. In the parking lot nearby, a bus filled with smiling Australians, Brits and Germans empties for another stop on their cross-country tour.

While I drive to my own next stop, Lynyrd Skynyrd's "Sweet Home Alabama" blares from the car radio near the famous "Copse of Trees," the epicenter of the Union Army line on Cemetery Ridge during Pickett's Charge on July 3, 1863. Let's hope the Union Army spirits, lingering as they may be, aren't offended.

Soon thereafter, I park near the square and drop change into the meter for an extended stay at one of my favorite places: Ronn Palm's Museum of Civil War Images. Inside the early 19th-century, brick rowhouse on Baltimore Street, Palm—a 71-year-old furniture salesman—is holding court with two visitors.

On July 1, 1863, steps from the museum's front door, Rebels fought their way through the streets toward the Union-held high ground on Cemetery Hill. The house—believed to be the second oldest in

Gettysburg's historic district—was home during the war of a doctor who also served as minister.

Palm, who lives on the second floor, wears shorts, an open, short-sleeved checked shirt over a light-blue T-shirt and a smile. We've known each other for nearly a decade, bonding over our Western Pennsylvania roots and a shared love for original photographs of Civil War soldiers. Palm speaks "Yinzer," a language only fellow Pittsburghers like us can fully comprehend.

After the tourists depart, Palm weighs in with his own ghost and spirit stories.

"A man comes in here with his wife and spends about two hours looking at my photographs," he says. "Then he comes over to me and says, 'I have to take her on one of those ghost tours.' He figured it would be the least he could do after spending so much time here.

"The next day he comes in, shaking. Then he shows me this."

On his phone, Palm points to photos taken on Hancock Avenue on the battlefield. I'm not sure what, if anything, to make of the wispy white blobs swirling in the air.

"Another time a man comes in here and says, 'Hey, there's a man standing back there,'" says Palm, who otherwise was alone. The tourist gestured toward the glass display cases in the rear of his museum. Nothing was there, but the hair was standing up on the man's neck and arms.

I sense Palm—whom I had pegged as a ghosts and spirits skeptic—subtly attempting to reel me in.

"One time a woman came in here with something called a 'spirit meter'," he continues. Perhaps it was like the device we amateur ghost investigators deployed the previous night at the McCurdy Schoolhouse on Emmitsburg Road.

"The woman got a high reading," Palm says. "She says, 'Hey, this has never happened to me before. There's so much energy in here.'"

I don't sense spirit energy but do admire—ogle, actually—dozens of Civil War soldier photographs in the first room of the 604-square-foot museum. Bearded and mustachioed men gaze from behind brass mats, glass and old wooden frames. They are just a fraction of Palm's collection, one of the most remarkable of its kind. In all, he displays roughly 5,000 images—tintypes, ambrotypes, albumens, *cartes de visite* and more. I'd be jacked to have only a half-dozen of these photos.

Palm collects mostly Pennsylvania photographs and other Civil War artifacts and memorabilia associated with the state—swords, a wartime frock coat, muster rolls, books, documents, Grand Army of the Republic photos and the like. His collection includes oddities, too, such as the meager, crumpled remains of the 85th Pennsylvania regimental flag and spearhead, embedded with a bullet from the obscure Battle of Strawberry Plains in Virginia in July 1864. In addition to the 85th Pennsylvania, Palm's favorite regiments are the 140th Pennsylvania and the 22nd Pennsylvania and its Ringgold Battalion. Each hailed from Western Pennsylvania.

Palm grew up in Port Vue, Pennsylvania, a working-class town along the Youghiogheny River, a dozen miles southeast of Pittsburgh. As a kid, he worked in his dad's radio and TV shop, delivered the local newspaper and collected coins and baseball cards. American history enthralled Palm, the grandson of a World War I veteran. But his Civil War photography collecting didn't begin until 1970, when he visited a collector in nearby Carrick.

"What do you collect?" the man asked him.

"*Not this stuff,*" Palm scoffed.

The man had artillery shells and other Civil War artifacts scattered about the floor of his dingy basement.

Then Palm spotted a shiny object on the floor, a darkened ambrotype behind cracked glass of a standing Union officer, his name lost to history. Palm bought it for a buck seventy-five and later figured he had overspent.

"One thing led to another, and then things got out of hand," he says, smiling.

Palm keeps his first photograph in a display case behind the counter where he typically greets visitors.

"Hey, where's *my guy?*" I ask.

Palm walks me to a display case of images and artifacts from the 63rd Pennsylvania, a Western Pennsylvania regiment that saw action in the war's greatest Eastern Theater battles. At about eye level, Corporal David Mahaffey—standing ramrod straight with a revolver tucked into a holster—stares back at me from behind glass and a brass frame. He sports a kepi and a belt with a brass U.S. belt buckle, tinted gold by the photographer.

"I'm honoring these soldiers," Ronn Palm says of his vast photo collection in his Gettysburg museum.

Mahaffey was a blue-eyed, brown-haired farmer from Dorseyville, near Pittsburgh. At Gettysburg, the 63rd Pennsylvania fought north of the Peach Orchard, near the Emmitsburg Road. His name appears on the majestic Pennsylvania memorial on Cemetery Ridge. At Petersburg, Virginia, on June 16, 1864, a Rebel bullet crashed into his leg, resulting in its amputation. Mahaffey, in his mid-20s, died days later.

It's hard to read, but the corporal's name was etched into the top of the tin plate, probably by the photographer. I know this detail because the tintype belonged to me years ago. I had traded Mahaffey to another collector for a letter from 16th Connecticut Captain Newton Manross, who suffered a mortal wound at Antietam, and the envelope addressed to another Connecticut soldier who had been a patient at a hospital in Sharpsburg, Maryland. A brilliant man, Manross is one of my Civil War heroes. My collector acquaintance sold Mahaffey to Palm, who relishes acquiring almost any Pennsylvania soldier image.

Photographs of Civil War soldiers often magically find their way to Palm, who seems blessed with that magnetic field all the great collectors have.

"If it talks to me," he says of an image, "I grab it."

In more than a half-century of collecting, Palm has acquired images from antique shops, Civil War shows and auctions as well as via trades and on eBay. He opens a closet revealing large plastic bins filled with thousands of Civil War soldier photographs awaiting display.

"And I have, like, four million albumens on the walls upstairs," he says.

Palm has no formal training as a museum curator. But the display cases appear professionally presented.

"I rotate the stuff when I have the energy," he says. "All my favorite stuff is out here."

Palm bought the Gettysburg rowhouse in 1997 after realizing he couldn't display all his images at his Pittsburgh-area home. Three years later, he opened the museum. In 2020, Palm moved permanently from Western Pennsylvania to Gettysburg to keep the museum open regularly and to be closer to his guys. They are more extended family than anything else.

"Here's Pat Bane," Palm says.

He points to an image of one of the tallest soldiers in either army. Bane, who may have been as tall as 7-foot-4, served with the Ringgold Battalion, Company A. Following the war, he often was spotted wearing a stovepipe hat and an exceedingly long brass-buttoned coat.

"They called him the 'Gentle Giant of Greene County'," Palm says. "Everyone loved him."

Bane, a shingle maker, became a familiar face at veterans' reunions, especially national Grand Army of the Republic events, and made a great impression leading parades. The genial veteran reportedly contracted rheumatism during the war because of the snugness of his uniform.[1]

"Long after all that was mortal of Pat Bane has returned to the dust the kindly giant with his gentle inquiring eyes and his pleasing little boast of his great height will be remembered by young and old," a Pennsylvania newspaper wrote following the death of the lifelong bachelor in 1912.[2]

---

1. *Freeland (Pa.) Tribune*, March 17, 1898
2. *The Daily Republican*, Monongahela, Pa., March 18, 1912

The connection Palm has with Bane and the other photos in the museum—*his guys*—may best be described as metaphysical. Years ago, he was walking through a cemetery in Washington County, south of Pittsburgh, visiting the grave of another Union soldier.

"Then and I looked down," Palm says, "and I'm standing on Pat's grave."

Many images in the museum include a slip of paper that includes the soldier's name and unit. Brief details of a soldier's life—and death—reach out from time. Poignant details captivate.

"I'm honoring these soldiers," Palm says. "That's what it's all about." If he acquires an image of an unknown soldier, Palm aims to identify him.

7-foot-4 soldier Pat Bane, the "Gentle Giant of Greene County." Ronn Palm collection

"Nothing," he says, "makes you feel better."

While Palm makes coffee, I examine images.

A photographic grouping includes Sergeant Benjamin O'Bryon of the 140th Pennsylvania, his wife and their baby daughter. The photographer tinted the girl's cheeks pink. O'Bryon was a 25-year-old tanner from Uniontown. On May 14, 1864, during Ulysses Grant's Overland Campaign in Virginia, he suffered a mortal wound at Totopotomoy Creek. His daughter's baby booty, which O'Bryon carried with him while he served in the Army of the Potomac, found its way to Palm's museum, too.

On a CDV, Lt. Col. Jonas W. Lyman of the 203rd Pennsylvania posed seated while his curly-haired daughter, Libbie, stood next to him. Clad in a dress, the young girl rested her hand on Lyman's arm. On January 15, 1865, he was killed while leading an assault at Fort Fisher in North Carolina. Lyman "fell instantly with his face toward, and almost in the midst of the enemy," wrote the regimental chaplain.[3]

On October 10, 1864, John Mosby's raiders captured Private Francis Marion White of the Ringgold cavalry. "Narrowly escaped being hanged at

---

3. *Philadelphia Inquirer*, Feb. 7, 1865

the time," reads Palm's caption below the CDV in a cardboard frame. "Sent to Andersonville for 10 months and died soon after."

In the display case with the image of Mahaffey sit the blood-stained vest as well as the boots, saddle blanket, saddle bag and slouch hat of 63rd Pennsylvania Captain William Thompson, killed in action at Chancellorsville on May 3, 1863. A ragged tear through the hat—caused by a bullet—speaks to the officer's awful last moments.

Palm points to a display case of images, artifacts, and memorabilia of the Pennsylvania Bucktails—one of the war's more renowned units. He has roughly 500 images of soldiers who served with the Bucktails. "Their reenactors consider this their museum," Palm says.

Then he points to another of his favorites, Charles Taylor, a colonel in the 42nd Pennsylvania of the famed Bucktails.

"Here's the bullet that killed him," Palm says.

Apparently flattened by hitting bone, the little piece of lead sits in a small vial in the display case.

As Taylor moved behind a tree near The Wheatfield at Gettysburg on July 2, 1863, the Rebel round crashed into his chest, dropping the 23-year-old into the arms of a lieutenant.

Near the bullet, 42nd Pennsylvania colonel Hugh McNeil—a Pennsylvania Bucktail renowned for his marksmanship—gazes from a CDV. A bucktail rests across the bill of his kepi. Early in the war, the talisman became the unit's symbol. A story of McNeil's marksmanship, perhaps apocryphal, gained steam after the Battle of South Mountain in Maryland on September 14, 1862. The Bucktails were exchanging fire with Confederates protected behind a series of large, craggy rocks.

"Wait a minute," said McNeil. "I will try my hand. There is nothing like killing two birds with one stone." The 32-year-old colonel fired a bullet that ricocheted off a rock.

"All is right now," McNeil shouted. "Charge the rascals!"

Then, after the Bucktails had driven away the Rebels, McNeil examined his marksmanship. Two dead Rebels lay near the rocks, each with a head wound. McNeil pocketed the deadly bullet that lay beside them.[4] Two nights later, the colonel himself lay dead in the East Woods at Antietam.

---

4. *The Daily Pittsburgh Gazette*, Dec. 8, 1862

"All his men loved him," Palm says.

I ask Palm about his deep connection to his guys.

"Do you think all this was just meant to be?"

"Honestly …"

He pauses and briefly looks to the floor.

"Yes."

In a little more than two hours, I have absorbed only a fraction of Palm's collection. Pangs of guilt creep over me. Should I stay another hour? But I have a 10-hour drive back to Mrs. B in Tennessee. Alas, I must go.

"You should come back when you have more time," says Palm. He seems almost wistful, like another photo of Pat Bane—the "Gentle Giant of Greene County"—slipped away from him at an auction.

And so I leave behind the great collector—alone with his guys, the spirits and the memories of battlefields and campfires long ago.

As I drive home to Tennessee, the New Market Heights battlefield and unfinished business there remain on my mind. Weeks later, I'm rambling again to Virginia.

CHAPTER 32

Trevilians, Virginia

WHERE CUSTER LOST HIS UNDERWEAR AND LOVE LETTERS

After an overnight stay in Staunton, a Virginia town in the Shenandoah Valley looted and burned by U.S. Army raiders in 1864, I'm back on the road. My ultimate destination is Richmond, but 60 miles northwest of the capital, a roadside sign along the interstate grabs my attention: "Trevilian Station." I vaguely remember it as the place where George Armstrong Custer, "The Boy General," suffered an embarrassing defeat.

I take the exit, driving twisting rural roads for 15 miles before reaching the battlefield. In unincorporated Trevilians, *another* roadside sign—this one for a Civil War museum—ricochets me to the Netherland Tavern, a replica of the wartime inn that once stood nearby.

Under a canopy of oaks stand a man and woman preparing to manhandle two bed frames, a crib and two mattresses inside the tavern. The sweaty man wears camo shorts and a Civil War Trust/The History Channel T-shirt. With his full, white beard, he bears a passing resemblance to Santa Claus.

It's only 10:45, but the temperature already is soaring into the 90s. I feel like the goofy pilot in *Airplane,* sweat gushing from my every pore. This is my first visit to the battlefield.

270

"Hi, where can I find the museum?" I ask the man. "I saw the sign down the road and …"

"Oh, that's an old sign," he scoffs. Then he extends his hand.

"I'm Ed Crebbs."

He introduces me to his wife, Charlaine. She wears jeans shorts and a "I'm Not 71. I'm Sweet 16 With 55 Years of Experience" T-shirt. Both are 72 and retired. The couple have been married 51 years.

Ed Crebbs speaks what I call "rural Virginian," a dialect not nearly as pronounced as a stereotypical white Southerner's. Charlaine is a native of Winnipeg, Manitoba, and still has a hint of a Canadian accent. They live six miles down the road in Boswell's Tavern, population about 60.

"Don't forget we have Ms. Holley's convenience store, too," says Ed, who then dishes on family history.

Crebbs' great-grandfather, John Calvin Crebbs, served in the 23rd Virginia's Company D—the "Louisa Grays." In late May 1864, the Union Army captured Private Crebbs at Spotsylvania Court House. He spent the rest of the war in a POW camp. Charlaine is a distant relative of the melodiously named Pierre Gustave Toutant-Beauregard, the Rebel general of Louisiana Creole descent.

As it turns out, the small museum closed years ago. The replica Netherland Tavern, built near the trace of the wartime road, serves as a special events building for the Trevilian Station Battlefield Foundation, a local preservation organization. Ed and Charlaine are longtime members of its board. The original tavern was a battlefield landmark until it was razed in the 1950s.

While we stand in the shade of trees, Ed raises my Battle of Trevilian Station IQ.

"Biggest cavalry battle of the war," he proclaims about the fighting on June 11-12, 1864.

"Now wasn't that Brandy Station in June 1863?" I ask.

"Trevilian Station was the largest *all-cavalry* battle of the war," Charlaine interjects.

In early June 1864, Ulysses Grant—bogged down in a bloody stalemate at Cold Harbor—aimed to distract the Rebels from his movement south toward Richmond. He ordered "Fightin' Phil" Sheridan's cavalry westward to destroy railroads in the Shenandoah Valley and to link up with another Union army.

Early on the morning of June 11, Sheridan and Custer clashed with Confederate cavalry under Wade Hampton, Fitzhugh Lee and Stephen Rosser near Trevilian Station, a stop on the Virginia Central Railroad line.

By 1864, newspaper readers across the North and South had become familiar with the exploits of the brash, 24-year-old Custer. Rosser knew him well—they had roomed together at West Point. He called Custer "Fanny" because of his curly blonde hair. Some called him "Cinnamon" because he scented his locks with cinnamon oil.

In all, more than 16,000 soldiers—9,200 Yankees, nearly 7,000 Rebels—fought in fields and woods surrounding the house of Charles Trevilian. The hamlet was named for his family, who had lived in the area for decades.

Prior to the battle, Hampton—a South Carolinian and one of the South's largest slaveholders—slept on a carpenter's bench in front of Netherland Tavern.

"His wagon train and horses were right over there," says Ed, pointing 200 yards away to the south, beyond the railroad track. That's the old Louisa Courthouse Road, present-day Louisa Road. The modern railroad track largely follows the wartime line.

About three miles over the rise to the north surged 7,000 U.S. Army cavalrymen, four abreast, down the narrow Fredericksburg-Charlottesville Stage Road (Oakland Road/State Route 613 today).

"Just *imagine* that scene," Ed says.

Approaching from the east, Custer briefly captured Hampton's lightly guarded supply train and hundreds of prisoners. Then the Rebels counterattacked, eventually surrounding Custer's Michigan Brigade.

"There had been a constant din and roar of cannon and musketry and of bursting of shells from six in the morning til noon, and no one could tell Custer's guns from those of the enemy," a New York newspaper correspondent wrote of the fighting.[1]

In the chaotic battle, the Michigan Brigade suffered nearly 400 casualties—including Custer's guidon bearer, who, after suffering a mortal

---

1. *New York Daily Herald*, June 21, 1864

For nearly 30 years, Charlaine and Ed Crebbs have taken care of the Charles Trevilian House – George Custer's battle HQ.

wound, handed the brigade flag to his commander. The quick-thinking Custer stuffed the treasured flag into his shirt.

"The Boy General" seemed to be everywhere.

While Custer was carrying a mortally wounded Michigan Brigade soldier out of harm's way, a sharpshooter took aim at the general. A spent bullet stunned and badly bruised the general.

"Where in hell is the rear?" Custer reportedly said while making his escape.[2]

2. Lee, William O., *Personal And Historical Sketches And Facial History of and by Members of the Seventh Regiment Michigan Volunteer Cavalry*, Detroit: The Ralston-Stroup Printing Co., 1902, Page 230

In the melee, Rebels under Fitzhugh Lee captured Custer's headquarters wagon and nearly all his personal possessions. That included Custer's underwear, field desk, ornate Tiffany & Co. presentation sword, the commission as general that he had received only days earlier, the dress uniform from his wedding and his favorite stallion, Clift. The Rebels even captured Custer's servant, a 20ish Black woman named Eliza, whom the general's cavalrymen called "The Queen of Sheba."

In a leather writing pouch in his HQ wagon, Custer kept a large envelope with locks of his famous blonde hair. He intended to send them to Libbie, his beautiful 22-year-old wife of four months. But the Rebels got the envelope and hair, too. They'd probably be amazed today that Custer's last strands of hair sold at auction in 2018 for $12,500.

But the loss of his underwear, horse, sword and the rest were hardly the worst news for Custer.

To the general's great embarrassment, the Rebels also snatched the intimate love letters he had received from Libbie. They became popular reading material among Confederate soldiers and other Southern citizens.

"I send you a thousand kisses," Libbie wrote in one of them. Dozens of "O's"—Libbie's symbol for kisses—appeared on the bottom and sides of that correspondence.[3]

Richmond newspapers eagerly threw shade Custer's way.

"His letters show a depravity in Northern society beyond anything our people could imagine," wrote a *Richmond Examiner* correspondent.[4]

Thank God most of my texts to Mrs. B are tame by comparison.

"I regret the loss of your letters more than all else," Custer wrote to Libbie days later. "I enjoyed every word you wrote, but do not relish the idea of others amusing themselves with them, particularly as some of the expressions employed."[5]

Near the end of the war, a Union officer recovered a cache of the love letters from the home of a Virginia doctor and returned them to Custer. Nearly the entire contents of the general's HQ wagon—including the

---

3. Transcript of Wilmon Blackmar diary, Cisco's Gallery in Coeur d'Alene, Idaho

4. *Richmond Examiner*, July 1, 1864

5. Custer, George A., *The Custer Story: The Life and Intimate Letters of General George A. Custer and His Wife Elizabeth*, Edited by Marguerite Merrington, New York, The Devin-Adair Co., 1950, Page 105

ornate presentation sword in its original rosewood box—are in a gallery in Idaho. The whereabouts of the underwear and risqué love letters, however, are unknown.

After "The Boy General" escaped from peril at Trevilian Station, Sheridan asked him: "Did they get your headquarters flag, general?"

"Not by a damned shot," shouted "The Boy General," who then revealed the flag from beneath his coat. "There it is!"[6]

The next day, following more fighting, Sheridan withdrew.

Historians bill Custer's narrow escape at Trevilian Station as his "First Last Stand." Twelve years later, at Little Big Horn in Montana Territory, he made his "Last Stand."

Charlaine, no fan of the "The Boy General," calls him "arrogant." Ed calls him impulsive but a commander who would lead by example. I think the man is endlessly fascinating but wish his love letters had turned up somewhere.

The Battle of Trevilian Station resulted in roughly 600 Confederate and 900 U.S. Army dead. Some may remain buried in the woods near the Netherland Tavern site, Ed tells me.

Near the Virginia Central track, Custer made his headquarters in the front yard of Charles Trevilian's two-story frame house. With a family member ailing upstairs, Trevilian persuaded the general and his staff to remain outside.

"Would you like to see it?" Charlaine asks me about the historic house.

Well, of course. But first there's work to do. Despite a lack of serious manual labor experience, I help Ed and Charlaine haul the bed frames and mattresses into the second floor of the tavern. Afterward, sweat soaking my shorts and T-shirt, I'm whipped.

"You don't know what hard work is until you spend a day in a hay field," says Ed.

A quarter mile down the road, behind a convenience store on Route 33, stands the Trevilian house—a circa-1840s "two-over-two" with a postwar addition. It's owned by the foundation. A small outbuilding in the front yard is believed to have served as the village post office. In April 1861, John Calvin Crebbs—Ed's great-grandfather—and other county residents cast their votes for secession in the humble structure.

---

6. *The National Tribune*, Jan. 5, 1888

Inside the house, out of the brutal afternoon sun, I plop myself next to Ed on a Civil War-period couch. The foundation purchased it and other furnishings for the house at an auction of stuff used on *Mercy Street*—the public television Civil War series about the workings at the Mansion House Hospital in Alexandria, Virginia.

Other house furnishings, including a bookcase, belonged to Private Crebbs and his wife—Ed's great-grandmother. In the corner stands a piano from the house Grant slept in the night before Lee surrendered at Appomattox Court House. But the 500-pound instrument needs refurbishing.

"It would cost us $15,000," Charlaine says.

"I regret the loss of your letters more than all else," George Custer wrote to his wife Libbie days after the capture of the risqué correspondence.* Library of Congress

Like most small battlefield preservation organizations, the Trevilian Station Battlefield Foundation isn't blessed with a bottomless bank account, so the piano and its broken key may never be repaired. But the organization, along with the American Battlefield Trust, can revel in the fact it has preserved more than 2,000 acres of Trevilian Station battlefield.

For nearly 30 years, Ed and Charlaine have taken care of the Trevilian house. She tidies the inside and does yardwork. He tends to the flower beds and mows the lawn, among other chores.

"If the grass looks like crap," Ed says, "who'd want to stop here?"

Every Thursday morning and occasional Sundays, the Crebbs place two Confederate flags—the first national flag and the Bonnie Blue flag—out front. Then they add a flutter flag indicating the house is open.

"Then," says Ed, "we sit and wait and hope someone comes in."

But visitation rarely tops two or three people a month. The Crebbs remind me of Sisyphus, the figure in Greek mythology who pushed a huge stone to the top of a hill, only to have it roll back again. Still, they seem pleased with the occasional success.

"Every once in a while we get a teen," says Charlaine, "and that makes it worth it."

Perhaps the spirits of Custer, "The Queen of Sheba" and other supernatural forces keep the curious at bay.

While we sit in a back room of the Trevilian house, the couple tell spirited tales—of apparitions and a trail of fire from a bullet appearing in battlefield photographs; of strange footsteps in the night at the house; and of forks and teaspoons mysteriously disappearing.

"Last weekend in the Netherland Tavern two ghost investigators heard a boom," says Ed. "They pointed to where it came from, and it was exactly where Fitzhugh Lee's artillery was."

I have flashbacks to my own unsuccessful ghost "investigation" at Sach's Covered Bridge in Gettysburg, where a soldier spirit named "Tennessee" supposedly smokes lit cigs left by visitors.

"Are you a ghost believer?" I ask Ed.

"Oh, I'm beginning to be," he insists.

Behind the Trevilian House, Ed says spirit seekers supposedly determined the location of a soldier's grave.

"They did their thing looking with the divining rods. The rods went like this."

Ed puts his thumbs together and points his index fingers toward the floor.

Maybe they discovered the grave of 1st U.S. Cavalry Lt. John H. Nichols, killed instantly by a bullet from an Enfield on June 12, 1864. Comrades buried him in Charles Trevilian's backyard. The leader of the burial detail left a sheet of paper with details for the soldier's relatives, in case they wanted to reclaim the body.[7]

7. Wittenberg, Eric J., *Glory Enough For All: Sheridan's Second Raid and the Battle of Trevilian Station*, Washington, D.C.: Brassey's, 2002, Page 188

But no tombstone is believed to have ever marked Nichols' grave, wherever it may be in the backyard. Ed keeps the grass a little higher on the spot discovered by the spirit seekers. Someday he may mark it more formally.

"You know," Ed says, "we used to have a 'witness tree' here."

I snap to attention whenever those magic words are spoken. Over the years, several hunks of witness wood have found places of honor in our garage.

"Close to three-quarters of a witness tree was hanging over this house," Ed says.

Alas, the ancient tree was cut down, but remnants of its stump remain.

"Do you want to see it?" Ed asks.

Out back, I grab a loose chunk for the road.

I call Mrs. B with the breaking news, which she receives with all the glee of Jefferson Davis learning of the fall of Richmond. I tell her about my next stop, a visit to earthworks in tick-infested woods.

Civil War Mission Control sighs, but I can't wait.

CHAPTER 33

Henrico, Virginia

MESSY HISTORY

After spending a sleepless Saturday night in a sketchy hotel in Richmond, I drive surprisingly uncongested highways to the New Market Heights battlefield, where U.S. Colored Troops made history.

My interest in the battlefield stems from a meeting at nearby Fort Harrison weeks earlier with Damon Radcliffe, the great-great-grandson of Edward Ratcliff. A former slave, Edward served in the 38th U.S. Colored Troops and earned one of the 14 Medals of Honor awarded to Black soldiers for bravery at New Market Heights. Damon and I couldn't walk the battlefield that day, but I vowed to return. My mantra: *If you want to understand a battle, you must walk the ground.*

Promptly at 8:30, I arrive at the already-crowded Four Mile Creek Park parking lot, located behind a snake-rail fence astride New Market Road. All my essentials are accounted for before a battlefield walk deep into the woods: bug spray, long pants, hiking boots, water, snacks, a cellphone and backpack and curiosity.

Days earlier, Tim Talbott—my New Market Heights guide—had messaged me a warning: "It's supposed to be as hot as blue blazes." His forecast proves spot-on. Virginia in late July is hell with the lid off. But I figure Talbott—the 52-year-old Central Virginia Battlefields Trust chief administrative officer—won't mind.

"It's always an honor to be on that ground," he messaged me in a follow-up to his weather report.

In the parking lot in Henrico, ten miles southeast of downtown Richmond, Talbott and I exchange pleasantries. This is our first meeting in person, although we've made dozens of Civil War-related connections online. Talbott wears blue jeans, an olive ballcap with a Central Virginia Battlefields Trust logo and a maroon T-shirt. Strands of gray appear in the soft-spoken Tennessee native's black goatee. He lives in Fredericksburg, Virginia, a 75-mile drive north on beastly Interstate 95.

Talbott has secured permission from Henrico County for us to walk core New Market Heights battlefield. The county owns the most important swath of the battlefield, now blanketed by a forest of pine, holly, gum and oak.

Our battlefield walk begins at a large garbage dumpster, behind a Dairy Queen on the opposite side of New Market Road. Three feral cats—two black, one gray—scatter as we walk toward them and disappear into the woods.

New Market Heights, stiff-armed in the history books, is Talbott's favorite battlefield. But armchair historians often confuse it with the Battle of New Market, fought in the Shenandoah Valley in mid-May 1864. Talbott's interest in the battle stems from a talk given by a professional historian nearly 20 years ago.

"The way he told the story made it come alive," he says while brushing away pine branches along our narrow path through the woods.

Fifteen minutes into our walk, we reach a section of woods where the earth undulates like a haphazardly tossed brown blanket. We have arrived at the remains of earthworks created by the famed Texas Brigade, veterans of Antietam, Gettysburg and other major battles in the Eastern Theater.

"Used to be chest high," Talbott says of defenses, now only as tall as three feet in places.

Piles of brown leaves, as well as gnarly tree roots, scattered broken twigs, tree branches and limbs, carpet the forest floor. Mayflies make pests of themselves while cicadas buzz and click. About a half-mile away, traffic hums on six-lane Interstate 295, which slices through the battlefield like a bayonet through the heart.

"Unbelievable bravery," Tim Talbott says of the USCT, who advanced under fire of Texas Brigade soldiers from behind these earthworks.

On the bleak, foggy morning of September 29, 1864, Black soldiers sought revenge and potentially glory. With one great push by the Union Army, USCT soldiers could soon be marching into the capital of the Confederacy with their white comrades in the Army of the James.

The USCT endured the racism from many of their own Union Army white comrades, who wondered: *Will these men fight?*

Behind earthworks, the Texas Brigade, some 2,000 strong, fired thousands of rounds into the oncoming USCT soldiers they despised. Meanwhile, Rebel artillery, positioned at opposite ends of the heights behind the brigade, poured iron into the USCT.

Fifty to 75 yards in front of their earthworks, the Rebels had placed abatis—sharpened tree branches—and wooden *chevaux de frise.* Gaps in the defenses funneled the Black soldiers into a kill zone.

"The Texans," a Georgia officer wrote, "killed niggers galore."[1]

Confederate soldiers occasionally advanced beyond their earthworks to strip the dead of shoes, weapons and ammunition. They murdered at least one captured USCT soldier behind their lines.[2]

Talbott and I venture deeper into the woods, to get a USCT soldier's perspective of the battlefield.

Perspiration pours down my arm, soaking my reporter's notebook and blurring my scribbled words. I've never sweated so much on a battlefield—even in Resaca, Georgia, during a reenactment on a blistering mid-May afternoon.

Soon, the drone of interstate traffic becomes a memory. The ground slopes gently up toward the Texas Brigade's earthworks, which stretched for roughly three-quarters of a mile. But the tree-covered landscape—largely open ground in 1864—makes New Market Heights mostly a battlefield of the mind.

"Our men were falling by the scores," Colonel Alonzo Draper recalled of the fighting here.[3]

---

1. Price, James S, *The Battle of New Market Heights*, Charleston, S.C.: The History Press, 2011, Page 72

2. Robert Davis pension application for son Pvt. Benjamin Davis, 6th USCI, National Archives and Records Administration, Washington, D.C.

3. *Official Records*, Vol. 42, Part 1, Page 819

To create a path through the woods, Talbott uses a long stick to swat away holly branches and spider webs. Neither of us wants to take home a blood-sucking tick as a memory of this experience.

"Is this remote enough for you?" Talbott asks.

Eighty yards or so beyond Rebel earthworks, we stop at the edge of a 50-acre rock quarry filled with water—a nasty 20th-century scar on hallowed ground.

"A friend of mine jokes that you could only give kayak tours here now," Talbott says.

In Talbott's perfect world, the quarry would be emptied and filled in. The battlefield where hundreds of Black soldiers and their white officers shed blood would be restored to its 1864 appearance and interpreted. Soldiers such as Corporal Miles James of the 36th USCT, among the 14 Medal of Honor recipients, would be at least as well-known as Benjamin Butler—the Army of the James general who commanded them.

Born in Princess Anne County, Virginia, James had enlisted in Norfolk in November 1863. A farmer, he probably was enslaved before the war. He stood 5-foot-7 with black eyes and hair.

Within 30 yards of Texas Brigade defenses, a bullet burrowed into James' upper left arm, shattering bone. But the corporal continued to load and fire his weapon with his good arm, urging on comrades as the battle swirled. James endured battlefield surgery to remove the useless limb. Later, the corporal received treatment at Fort Monroe, 75 miles east on the Virginia coast, and a promotion to sergeant.

Despite losing an arm—a golden ticket out of the service if he wanted it—James refused to leave the army. In February 1865, Draper—the colonel who commanded James' brigade at New Market Heights—wrote Fort Monroe's chief surgeon:

> *He is one of the bravest men I ever saw; and is in every respect a model soldier. He is worth more with his single arm, than half a dozen ordinary men.*[4]

---

4. Miles James' Compiled Military Service Record, National Archives, Washington, D.C.

James served in the U.S. Army until a disability discharge in October 1865. Hundreds of other Black soldiers like him, nearly all of them former slaves, fought as well as James at New Market Heights.

"Unbelievable bravery," Talbott says of the USCT.

Hollywood made *Glory*, the 1989 movie about the valor of Black soldiers at the U.S. Army's defeat at Fort Wagner in South Carolina in 1863. But how could movie makers overlook New Market Heights? *Fourteen* of the 25 Black Medal of Honor recipients in the Civil War fought in the U.S. Army's dramatic showdown,

Powhatan Beaty was among 14 USCT soldiers to earn a Medal of Honor at the Battle of New Market Heights. Library of Congress

virtually in the Confederate capital's shadow.[5]

One of them, First Sergeant Powhatan Beaty of the 5th USCT, had been born into slavery in Richmond. After retrieving his unit's fallen flag, Beaty rallied soldiers in his regiment after its officers had been killed or wounded. After the war, he became a Shakespearean actor.

"The flag stood glamorous in his eyes," wrote a reporter years after Beaty's death in 1916. "It was the banner of the Lord leading his children unto the Promised Land."[6]

At the height of the battle, James Gardiner of the 36th USCT raced ahead of his comrades and shot a Confederate officer standing atop the Texas Brigade's earthworks. Then the 20-year-old ran his bayonet through the man. After the war, following disciplinary issues in the army, he became a Catholic missionary. Gardiner died in 1905, on the battle's 41st anniversary.

While the attack faltered, 5th USCT Sergeants Robert Pinn and Edward Ratcliff—Damon Radcliffe's great-great-grandfather—steadied their

---

5. Congressional Medal of Honor Society

6. *The Cincinnati Post*, July 9, 1930

comrades. Pinn, who also earned a Medal of Honor, became a lawyer after the war. In 1888 in Massillon, Ohio, his former Union comrades elected him the commander of the Grand Army of the Republic post "by a handsome majority."[7]

At Four Mile Creek, which snakes its way through the battlefield before spilling into the James River, Talbott and I talk about the white officers on horseback who became prime targets of the Rebels.

"This is where the Rebels thought the USCT would become nothing but rabble after the officers fell," Talbott says. The creek itself became a devilish impediment to USCT soldiers under withering fire.

While we stand creekside, I think of a poor soldier named Emanuel Patterson of the 6th USCT, the married father of a young daughter. On the morning of the battle, he had complained of feeling ill. A white captain escorted Patterson to an army doctor, who judged him well enough to fight. As the fighting swirled, perhaps near where Talbott and I stand, the white officer spotted Patterson suffering from a gruesome wound.

"One of the most terrible spectacles I ever beheld," the officer recalled years later. "He was shot through the abdomen, so that his bowels all gushed out, forming a mass larger than my hat, which he was holding up with his clasped hands, to keep them from falling at his feet. Then, and a hundred times since, I wished I had taken the responsibility of saying to him that he could remain in the rear."[8]

At creekside, I learn more about Talbott, too.

He grew up in Madison, Indiana, a stop on the Underground Railroad—the network escaped slaves used to flee to free states and Canada. At his 1,000-student high school, he played football ("not very well") and grew to enjoy rap and hip-hop—which some of his white peers thought strange.

Talbott's high school history teacher—"a 1960s hippie"—exposed him to "all the cultural stuff," including the Civil Rights era and two of its leading personalities, Malcolm X and Martin Luther King. For the past 30 years, he has immersed himself in the experiences of Black people during the Civil War.

On his phone, Talbott displays wallpaper of Frederick Douglass—the famous Black orator, abolitionist, writer and reformer. The copy of the

7. *The Summit County Beacon*, Akron, Ohio, May 16, 1888
8. *The Jeffersonian-Democrat*, Brookville, Pa., May 5, 1898

painting on his maroon T-shirt, now drenched with sweat, is of a one-legged USCT soldier on crutches. Talbott dreams of a monument at Four Mile Creek Park to honor the USCT, who forced the Texas Brigade to fall back to a secondary line.

As we walk through the Virginia forest, Talbott and I wonder why this battle—and this battlefield—have been consigned to the shadows of history. *Racism? Indifference? Ignorance?* In the late 1980s and early 1990s, an effort failed by a Black military history group to have the battlefield named a national historic landmark.

The American Battlefield Trust and other preservation groups have saved hundreds of acres of battlefield. But much has been lost forever because of modern development.

Two hours after our walk began, sweaty and dirty, we leave the woods and September 1864 behind. On a pathway along New Market Road to the Four Mile Creek Park parking lot, Talbott and I talk about the battle, preservation and Civil War memory.

"Many people say they love history, but what they really love is nostalgia," he says. "I love messy history. That's where the good stuff is."

Messy history—that's a perfect encapsulation of the Battle of New Market Heights.

More messy history may be found 400 miles to the southeast, in the mountains of western North Carolina, where Rebel soldiers committed one of the worst atrocities of the war.

CHAPTER 34

Marshall, North Carolina

FOUR HOURS IN 'BLOODY MADISON'

As I pull into Marshall, North Carolina, The Grateful Dead blaring on my car radio, I have no idea what to expect. The day before, a Facebook messenger told me of this hippie town's tragic connection to the Civil War: a massacre perpetrated nearby by Rebel soldiers in 1863.

Mrs. B is 20 miles south in Asheville, probably tapping her foot or watching the clock. We're supposed to be on vacation. But I've managed to talk her into giving me four hours–*and only four hours*–to explore the area and find out more.

I know virtually nothing about this obscure tragedy.

So at the very least, I want to see the historical tablet that marks the massacre site. I hear it stands somewhere deep in these rugged southern Appalachians.

Marshall is a place where you can enjoy funky art galleries, bluegrass, a stay in a former county jail-turned-boutique hotel and more than just a whiff of weed (still illegal in the state) if you are inclined. The Dead's Jerry Garcia—R.I.P.—would have loved this place.

Outside a coffee shop, across the street from the early 20th-century Madison County Courthouse, I introduce myself to a bearded dude drinking a Colombian and minding his own business. It's Shane Elliott. He's a

On the main street in Marshall, I enjoyed a visit with Shane Elliott – an "old, anarchist, ornery, hillbilly guy" – and his daughter, Zetta.

49-year-old architectural designer hanging with his two-year-old daughter, Zetta. Half the enjoyment on my Civil War road trips is meeting characters like him.

"I'm just an old, anarchist, ornery, hillbilly guy," he tells me.

Elliott lives in a tiny house on wheels in the hills with his wife, Meg, a former teacher turned "domestic engineer." She's also a clogger for the Green Grass Cloggers.

"They're legendary," he says.

Elliott and I bond over our love for history and conversation. He is a Tennessee native with ancestors who served on both sides during the Civil War. The Yankees captured a Rebel ancestor of his, he tells me, in Mississippi at the Battle of the Big Black River in late-spring 1863.

"Another one switched sides like three times," Elliott says with a laugh.

The Big Black River reference makes me smile, because that's where Sid Champion V—my Champion Hill battlefield tour guide—pointed out an alligator in the muddy water to a tourist, who immediately ran to her car and locked herself in.

Elliott doesn't know much about the Shelton Laurel Massacre or where the historical marker is. He points to the hardware store down the street and says, "Go talk with Kathy."

Decades ago, I'm told, Marshall was nothing much more than a grocery store, a funeral home, two florists and a guy who swept the street with a push broom. But rich hippies and other transplants have changed the character of Marshall and the rest of Madison County. For the better, mostly.

The natural beauty of the county is sublime. "The Switzerland of America," a 19th-century reporter wrote.[1] "Five hundred square miles of ear-popping drives and breathtaking views," a later visitor wrote.[2] But its past is like a trip along its often-treacherous, serpentine roads in the dead of a wintry night.

More than 100 years ago, Madison Country earned a reputation as a place where disputes resulted in violence—often with firearms. On a public road in 1905, two young men shot and killed each other after an argument over the killing of turkeys.[3] In the woods and hollers, moonshiners plied their illegal trade, and woe to any uninvited guests. After he had happened upon a corn whiskey enterprise in 1918, locals forced a government man to ford a creek on his hands and knees and eat raw pumpkin.[4]

Poverty and political corruption wracked the southern Appalachians for decades. And an inherent distrust of outsiders—often justified—permeated Marshall and Madison County, too. So has prejudice. Few African Americans live here. Only a decade ago, a Black woman and her white husband left town after harassment by a neighbor, who flew huge Confederate flags facing their property.

1. *Memphis (Tenn.) Bulletin*, July 15, 1863

2. Pinsky, Mark I., *Met Her on The Mountain*, Lexington, Ky.: The University Press of Kentucky, 2022, Page 8

3. *Baltimore Sun*, July 12, 1905

4. *Asheville (N.C.) Citizen Times*, Nov. 10, 1918

During the war, the town of Marshall was staunchly secessionist. On May 13, 1861, citizens gathered to elect a delegate to the Secession Convention in Raleigh. Some were liquored up. A fight broke out. The sheriff, a secessionist, shot and wounded a Union man. The man's father produced a double-barreled shotgun and blasted the lawman into eternity.[5] This was only the beginning. It got so bad the county became known as "Bloody Madison."

Throughout the war, the pall of death hovered over "Bloody Madison" like the smoke that drifts up from the shanties and cabins that dot its heavily timbered hillsides and valleys. Madison County, population about 6,000 in 1860, was toxic stew of secessionists, Unionists and people who didn't give a damn about either. Fighting often broke out.

At the hardware store, Kathy greets me. She is the proprietor—a sweet, 60ish lady wearing a plaid, checked shirt, blue jeans and a tan ballcap. She tells me the store has been in her family for decades.

"Can you tell me where I can find the historical marker about the 1863 massacre?" I ask.

Kathy pulls out a map and a magnifying glass, shows me Route 208, and points to where I should go.

"Is there anyone else here who can tell me about the massacre?"

"Well there's AJ, he's our historian, but he's making tomato juice."

An expert canner, AJ comes from a family of 14.

"And when you come from a family of 14 around here, you learn to do three things—farm, can, and square dance," Kathy says.

A hardware store customer named Wilson, a late 50ish man with an impressive, braided gray goatee, overhears our conversation.

"Don't go up in the hollers unless you're asked," he warns. "People who live here don't even do it. If you go, be wary."

"Meth?"

"Weed," he tells me.

At the liberal-leaning bookstore across the street, I admire the quotations from famous people taped to the front window. But a sign at the entrance causes me to pause: "Warning: No Stupid People Beyond This Point."

5. *New Bern (N.C.) Daily Progress*, May 27, 1861 | "Letters from North Carolina to Andrew Johnson," *The North Carolina Historical Review* Vol. 29, No. 2, April 1952, Pages 259-268

I go in anyway.

Inside, I have a brief discussion about the massacre with Jamey, the 60-something owner who suggests I visit with a woman at the department store across the street. I feel like one of those little orbs in the old Pac-Man video game, bouncing from one place to the next.

Can anyone here give me more details about the massacre?

Like Wilson, Jamey issues a warning: "You can't rely on GPS up in the mountains."

At the family-owned department store, I introduce myself to Georgette and my stomach to a fried apple pie for sale at the front counter (four bucks). She seems wary of the outsider asking a flurry of questions about the town and its history. After small talk, Georgette reveals that her husband is a direct descendant of a victim of the massacre. But he's unavailable.

"Have you seen the house across the street?" she asks. "That's where it all started."

Finally.

Across the main street stands an impressive two-story, painted blue with red shutters. Five well-worn stone steps lead to an expansive porch, a duplicate of the one above. In the early 1860s, Confederate Colonel Lawrence Allen and his family called it home. It's a private residence today. A historical marker out front explains the county's divided loyalties during the war.

In early January 1863, fifty-some Unionists—believed to be mostly Federal soldiers on leave—ransacked Marshall and raided the town's salt repository. Salt, which sold for $75 to $100 a sack, served as a life-sustaining commodity for curing of meats in the winter.[6]

The Unionists targeted Colonel Allen's house while he was soldiering somewhere in Tennessee. The marauders threatened his wife, who was caring for their three children, then suffering from scarlet fever. Two of them subsequently died.

Secessionists called the raiders "thieves," "robbers," "tories," "villains," and "bushwhackers." Intent on bringing the culprits to justice, roughly 200 soldiers in Allen's 64th North Carolina went looking for them. They

---

6. *Memphis (Tenn.) Bulletin*, July 15, 1863

marched to the isolated Shelton Laurel Valley, 16 miles north, where sentiment ran in favor of the Union.

The Shelton Laurel Valley was near the mountainous border shared with Tennessee. It was sparsely populated, but the "Laurelites" were close knit. They didn't own slaves and had little in common with the planters in the rest of the state. Many descended from Sheltons, who had settled in the area in the late 18th century and fought for the country during the Revolutionary War. During the Civil War, some joined the Union Army. Others avoided conscription, often violently, by the Confederate Army. Laurelites, I figure, mostly wanted to be left the hell alone. But that was not to be their fate in 1863.

After a brief stop at Allen's house, I drive toward that faraway historical sign, past Walnut, population 500 if you count the dogs, cats and guns.

I coast on switchbacks, hairpins and steep downhills through the Appalachians, which tower above me below a deep-blue sky. I stop in Hot Springs, population 600, to grab lunch. The Appalachian Trail—denoted by an intertwined "A" and "T" on the sidewalk—cuts through the heart of town. Like other communities in the southern Appalachians, Hot Springs had its own brushes with war.

A hotel proprietor—a woman named Carrie—set the bridge over the French Broad River aflame to prevent Union soldiers from entering town. They came anyway. One Union unit even set up a recruiting station on resort grounds.

Back on Route 208 as it winds through the Appalachians, I finally discover my quarry on the other side of a bridge—just where was told it would be.

"Thirteen men and boys suspected of Unionism were killed by Confederate soldiers in early 1863."

In the summer afternoon's sunlight, the fast-moving Laurel River shimmers against a backdrop of deep-green, forested mountainsides. I stop to take in the awe-inspiring vista. To my left, the curvy road continues up through the mountains to Tennessee.

The graves of the Unionists, the historical sign says, are on a side road off Route 208. The massacre site, I am told, is nearby, on private property.

"Don't go anywhere here unless you are invited."

My quarry, a historical sign for a little-known Civil War tragedy.

The words of warning loop in my head. Should I go?

I can't go. I'm out of time. I have another deadline to meet, the one I agreed to with Mrs. B. My presence is required at my own vacation.

Later, I peel back the layers of this horrific story. But the full story of the massacre will probably remain a mystery, like an Appalachian holler enveloped in morning fog.

On wintry day in mid-January 1863, seeking information on the Marshall raiders, Confederates commanded by Lt. Col. James Keith rode into the Shelton Laurel Valley and terrorized the Laurelites. As the story goes, they tortured two elderly women, putting ropes around their necks and whipping them with hickory rods until they bled. The Rebels tied another woman to a tree in the snow while her infant lay in the doorway of a cabin. Making light of it all, officers forced two women from the Shelton family to sing a "few national airs."[7]

---

7. *Memphis (Tenn.) Bulletin,* July 15, 1863

Keith's soldiers rounded up 15 men and boys. They put them all in a cabin. No one knows for sure whether any were among the Marshall raiders. Two escaped.

The next morning, the men and boys were taken from the cabin under guard on the pretense of going to Knoxville, Tennessee for trial. At a clearing near a stream, they were ordered to halt. An execution squad formed.

"For God's sake, men, you are not going to shoot us?" the eldest captive reportedly said. "If you are going to murder us, give us at least time to pray."

Five captives were told to kneel. A deadly volley echoed in the valley.

Five more captives knelt. Another volley echoed. Davey Shelton, 12 or 13, fell. But his wounds weren't fatal. The boy, bleeding from both arms, begged for his life. He was dragged away and finished off with Rebel lead.

Another volley echoed, and three more fell, dead.

In all, 13 were executed, including seven Sheltons. They were dumped together in a crude grave that their kin discovered the next day, lightly covered with earth. Hogs had already rooted out the grave and eaten the head of a victim.[8]

Did Keith—Colonel Allen's cousin—order the executions, as many believe? Or was it someone else? One account said Keith had threatened his soldiers with death if they didn't shoot the captives. Neither the lieutenant colonel, who lived out his days in Arkansas, nor anyone else faced justice for the war crime.

Word of the massacre and torture of civilians slowly seeped from the Shelton Laurel Valley. Union-leaning newspapers expressed outrage. "And the men who did this were called soldiers!" one fumed.[9] Even Confederate newspapers in North Carolina newspapers decried the butchery.

For decades afterward, the war—and the massacre—burrowed into the soul of polarized southern Appalachians of western Carolina. Every so often, animosity reared its ugly head, like an angry serpent.

"This feeling is one of the relics of the war," wrote a letter writer to a New York newspaper, "when two great parties were mortal enemies and

---

8. *Memphis (Tenn.) Bulletin*, July 15, 1863

9. *New York Times*, July 24, 1863

those who were loyal to the Government had to defend their opinions with their rifles."[10]

Roughly eight miles down that side road off Route 208, a stone chimney marks all that's left of the cabin where Confederate soldiers held the doomed Laurelites. The victims rest today, I'm told, on private property near the massacre site in a small cemetery on a hogback ridge.

Someday I'll return to these beautiful, and mysterious, western North Carolina mountains. For now, though, I'm pondering familiar ground.

10. *New York-Tribune*, Nov. 25, 1900

CHAPTER 35

Sharpsburg, Maryland

THE SHADOW KING

As I walk toward historic Dunker Church on the Antietam battlefield on a raw, rainy morning, a man bounds toward me on my left. He wears a floppy green hat, light-blue jeans, a dark-blue Columbia jacket and white Fila tennis shoes. Gray streaks his bushy eyebrows. Ruby-red tinges his cheeks.

"Are you John Banks?" he asks.

The man is almost gleeful, as if he had just kicked up a .69-caliber Minié ball in the grass.

"Yes, I am."

"Didn't we once drink a beer at the Holiday Inn in Gettysburg a few years ago?"

"I think you have the wrong John Banks," I tell him, chuckling. We had never met in person before.

"Oh, man, I'm sorry. And come to think of it, you don't really look like the John I was thinking about anyway."

We both laugh.

I know the man from his Civil War Facebook page and word of mouth. He's Robert J. Kalasky—you can call him Bob. A friend of Kalasky's calls him "The Shadow King." In 2012, he authored *Shadows of Antietam*. It's a book in which Kalasky analyzes, in exhaustive detail, the shadows in famous photographs taken by Alexander Gardner and his assistant days after the Battle of Antietam on September 17, 1862.

Kalasky, from Youngstown, Ohio, is a married father of three daughters. He's a 63-year-old longtime cigarette smoker, full-time massage therapist and part-time eccentric. For the past quarter-century, three times a year, he has traveled to Antietam to unlock the secrets of Gardner's images.

"*Exactly* 242 miles," he says of the distance from home to the battlefield, followed by a staccato burst of slow chuckles. "Three and a half hours."

On many of the trips to the battlefield, a mannequin head named "Dead Fred" accompanied Kalasky. "The Shadow King" sometimes used it on the battlefield to simulate the heads of dead soldiers in Gardner's photos. He eventually turned to live reenactors as superior substitutes for "Dead Fred."

In Kalasky's own head, a set of three-digit numbers resonate like chimes of a grandfather clock: "505," "550," "553," "563," "566," and more. These are the catalog numbers that Gardner assigned to the Antietam photographs and etched onto his glass-plate photographs.

While a gray sky spits droplets of rain, I walk with Kalasky and roughly 80 photo devotees at The Center for Civil War Photography's annual Image of War seminar. Our group is a unique subset of history lovers. We're known to parse the locations of boulders, rocks and tree lines on a landscape—anything to determine how, where and when a Civil War-era photographer documented history.

The high priest of historic Civil War photography analysis is William Frassanito, an iconoclastic former U.S. Army intelligence analyst who lives in Gettysburg. In the 1970s, decades before digital photography and the Internet, "Fraz" used a magnifying glass and exhaustive research to reveal previously undetected details in Civil War images of battlefields and other landscapes. He tied the historical photographs to the scenes where they had been taken.

With the publication of his photography-based books on Gettysburg, Antietam and the Overland Campaign in Virginia, Frassanito spawned thousands of fellow analysts to worship at the high priest's altar. For me and thousands of others, Frassanito's work was a revelation, like solving the mysteries of the Zapruder film of the Kennedy assassination. He demonstrated that historic images aren't simply photos but documents ripe for further exploration and interpretation.

"The Shadow King" is one of Frassanito's greatest spawn.

Kalasky has built upon the ground-breaking work of our high priest.

We devotees walk in a long line down battlefield roads and through fields, like a trail of ants marching to an open picnic basket. Today we're exploring the sites where Gardner took his images—the ultimate history high for many of us.

In September 1862, the Scottish-born photographer was employed by Mathew Brady, the most famous Civil War photographer of all. As Gardner and his assistant, James Gibson, rode about Antietam battlefield in their wagon, they found a hellish tableaux. In brutal heat, hundreds of blackened and maggot-covered corpses littered the ground, nearly all Confederate soldiers. U.S. Army soldiers already had buried most of their own first.

A noxious odor of decomposing bodies of humans and horses drifted over fields and woodlots. "From whatever point a breath of wind proceeded," a reporter wrote, "a fresh effluvium assailed the senses."[1]

In the near distance is the old Samuel Mumma farm. In the far distance is Bloody Lane, where the Rebels fought the Irish Brigade amid the cacophony of musket and artillery fire and the blinding haze of gun smoke. On the horizon looms Red Hill, site of a Union signal station during the battle, with South Mountain behind it.

For more than 150 years, no one knew the location of one of Gardner's more notable images—a cluster of four Union dead. It is one of 20 photos he made of the Antietam dead—all taken with his cumbersome stereoscopic camera.

Kalasky calls the photograph "550"—its catalog number.

In the image, one soldier has what seems to be an axe protruding from his back, perhaps used to move his body. It's a horrifying photo—one of roughly 100 of the fallen taken during the Civil War and one of the few showing Union dead.

_____

1.   *The Buffalo Commercial*, Sept. 26, 1862

Robert Kalasky stands with a huge enlargement of "550" where Alexander Gardner shot the image in 1862.

"Group of Irish Brigade, As They Lay on the Battle-field of Antietam, Sept. 19, 1862," Gardner labeled the image.

With no formal training as a forensic photographer, Kalasky went about the painstaking work of attempting to identify the location of "550." For more than a decade, he explored every cornfield location on the battlefield in 1862, eliminating ones that didn't fit the puzzle.

On a warm morning in 2006, dew clinging to the grass, Kalasky noticed something that convinced him beyond a shadow of a doubt he had found the place where Gardner photographed 550.

Gardner's image shows a cornfield about 250 feet behind the bodies with a gap in the middle of the growing corn. That day, the field once again had been planted with corn, and Kalasky noticed the same gap in the field seen in Gardner's photo. It was caused by a distinctive natural wash that ran through the cornfield, then and now.

Kalasky's finding was met with skepticism, including from "Fraz" himself, because Red Hill is a prominent background feature at this location and yet it doesn't appear in Gardner's photo.

But during the years of his research on the battlefield, Kalasky noticed how Red Hill often could not be seen in the morning, hidden behind the early mist.

Based on his studies of the illumination of the photo and the shadows visible on the bodies of the fallen—and on his posers—Kalasky determined that Gardner had created the image at 9:25 a.m.

For "The Shadow King," the discovery of the location of 550 was a eureka moment.

"Oh, I did a happy dance," he says.

At the seminar, our group has gathered in a grassy field where Gardner created 550. Kalasky stands before the devotees, who form a rough semi-circle. He talks about his research into the photograph. His book, *Shadows of Antietam*, was published in 2012 by scholarly publishing house Kent State University Press. Yet a decade later, Kalasky is still on the fringes of the Civil War world. The seminar is something of a coming-out party for him. "The Shadow King" has never talked about his work before so large a group on the field. He's nervous.

"Speak louder!" someone shouts.

Over his head, Bob Zeller, the co-founder and longtime president of The Center For Civil War Photography, holds a huge enlargement of 550. The blowup is an anaglyph, a stereoscopic photograph with the two images superimposed and printed in different colors. When viewed with the 3-D glasses with the red and blue lenses, the effect is stunning. A shocking image of death during the Civil War comes to life in the 21st century at the very spot where it was created.

To finance the many trips that unlocked the secrets of 550 and other Antietam images by Gardner, Kalasky called upon his powers of persuasion. More than two decades ago, as he began his research, Kalasky befriended Lilli Wilson, a 50ish woman who lived with her husband, Craig, in a TLC-needy, postwar house astride the Hagerstown Pike across from the West Woods. She let Kalasky use her place as his home base and campground.[2]

On Lil's farm, soldiers shot, screamed, bled, agonized, prayed, surged, swore and died. It was perhaps the mostly hotly contested ground of the Civil War—the epicenter of the battlefield, some say.

The farm and battlefield entranced Kalasky.

"Spiritual," he calls Antietam, where the armies suffered nearly 24,000 casualties in all—the bloodiest single day in American history.

Near Lil's barn, Kalasky slept on an inflatable bed in a tent. To stay warm in cold weather, he plugged a 50-foot extension cord into an outside outlet to provide the power for his electric blanket. Once he stayed at Lil's place for six days. His average stay was two or three days.

By day, "The Shadow King," would walk the battlefield. He'd figure angles of the sun, ponder association theory, visit locations to test hypotheses and persuade reenactors and others who happened by to pose on the battlefield for him.

"The Shadow King" was obsessed with discovering the time of day when Gardner shot his images, something no one else had done—not even "Fraz." He had determined that Gardner had taken most of the photos of the dead September 20, 1862, three days after the battle, but could only estimate the time.

---

2. In 2015, the American Battlefield Trust purchased the Wilsons' farm. Subsequently, the house and barn were torn down.

***Alexander Gardner's (in)famous image of Confederate dead in Bloody Lane at
Antietam.*** Library of Congress

"If I can figure out time, then I can figure out Gardner's route across the
battlefield," Kalasky thought.

Brad Wyand, a local man who portrayed a soldier in the 1st Tennessee,
became one of Kalasky's go-to posers. They often rode together over the
battlefield in Kalasky's purple van, nicknamed "The Barney Mobile."

"I just thought he was another eccentric nut working on a book that
would never get published," says Wyand.

Once he grasped what Kalasky aimed to achieve, Wyand threw himself
into posing. As he lay on hallowed ground, "The Shadow King" made him
contort at odd angles to simulate rigor mortis. Even on a hot day, Wyand
got the chills while posing on the battlefield.

"I felt very unwelcome," he says about his strange experience.

Kalasky's posers even included an Australian, the late Bob Stevenson,
who became obsessed with the battle and made the long trip from Australia
to Antietam about once a year. Stevenson liked to hang out with Kalasky

and served as a stand-in for the dead of Antietam when reenactors weren't available.

A park ranger didn't appreciate Kalasky's devotion to replicating Gardner's historic photographs on the very battlefield where they were taken, but "The Shadow King" persevered.

With Lil's permission, Kalasky would hunt for battle relics after dark on her property with his friend from New York, a rock guitarist named Chuck Morrongiello. They turned up hundreds of artifacts—bullets, artillery shell fragments and more. Chuck served as a poser, too.

At night, the battlefield morphed into an otherworldly scene.

Deer pranced. Other animals howled and cried.

One evening a tornado hit by Red Hill, about a mile away. That night, Kalasky slept in his vehicle.

A couple days later, a fog bank apparently with a mind of its own rolled out of the East Woods—the same woods Union Gen. Edwin Sumner's Second Corps advanced from on the morning of the battle.

"It parted around us, moved right past us," says Kalasky, who was on the battlefield with reenactors. "Then came another fog bank, and it did the same thing. And then another one."

Like a dog after hearing a shrill whistle, I stare at "The Shadow King," my brow furrowed and head tilted.

"I have 21 witnesses to this," he says, followed by low, staccato chuckles.

While on the farm another night, Lil's daughter told Kalasky about the ghost of a horse that supposedly gallops about the battlefield looking for its rider.

At about 3 or 4 that morning, unable to sleep, Kalasky heard strange sounds.

Clop, clop, clop.

Could it be?

"The whole time I was freaking out," Kalasky says, laughing.

He went to investigate along the Hagerstown Pike. In the distance, a car slowly made its way toward him. Its bright lights cast an eerie glow in the inky blackness.

"Have you seen a horse come down this way?" a man asked Kalasky.

Robert Kalasky—"The Shadow King"—poses in Bloody Lane where
Confederate dead lay in 1862.

A real horse had escaped from the farm of the man's neighbor.

On a battlefield trail near the Samuel Mumma farm with our group, Kalasky briefly stops. In the distance, across an electrified fence, a cow rests on the ground near a slight ridge. An orchard stood on the site in 1862.

Kalasky believes this ground could be the site of Gardner's image of four Confederate dead, plate 572. The exact location of the photo has eluded historians and us devotees alike. But Kalasky's presumed location corresponds with Gardner's movements on September 20, 1862—that's the "association theory" Kalasky often mentions as we walk the field.

"This tapestry always changes out here," "The Shadow King" says of the battlefield. "Sometimes I think I got something and then it doesn't pan out. It's a never-ending process."

Slowly, we devotees march toward our final destination, Bloody Lane. As we reach the lip of the old farm road, Kalasky had hoped for sun to demonstrate one of his greatest finds, but a leaden sky keeps it under wraps.

"Maybe someone can pull a car up here for illumination," he says. "Or you could just use your imagination."

On the afternoon of September 19, 1862, two days after the battle, dozens of Confederate dead still lay in this humble sunken lane. Gardner photographed the scene as a Union burial crew went about its grisly work. He trained his camera on the ditch. Bodies of Rebel soldiers lay intermixed with the debris of war.

As he stood behind his tripod and removed the lens cap on his stereo camera, the sun cast Gardner's own bulky shadow and those of two of the tripod legs on the lip of the south bank of the lane, just above the head of a fallen Rebel.

Kalasky made this discovery when he cast a similar shadow in his own recreations of 565. He also determined that 565 was the first ever made of dead American soldiers. It was another eureka moment.

"Shadows are a guaranteed thumbprint," Kalasky says.

"As far as I am concerned, this is Bob's greatest discovery," Zeller, The Center For Civil War Photography president, tells the group about the Gardner shadow.

Devotees nod in agreement. Some wear their 3-D glasses to view an enlargement of an anaglyph of 565.

Then Kalasky lies in the lane to demonstrate the position of fallen Confederate Charles Tew, a North Carolina colonel.

Mrs. B and mostly everyone else might find this behavior somewhat odd. No one among our unique subset considers it remotely so.

"This is the first time I ever done this in front of a group like this," Kalasky says from his prone position in the gravel of Bloody Lane.

Tew was bald, and so it appears was the unfortunate soldier in Gardner's photo.

Devotees squint to see a colorized closeup of the dead man's face held by another member of our unique subset.

"See that shadow near his right eye?" Kalasky says of the soldier. To "The Shadow King," it's a revealing clue.

Minutes later, as the sky darkens and a storm threatens, Kalasky concludes his talk. On a history high, appreciative devotees clap and smile.

"Fraz," our high priest, has downplayed his work, but Kalasky has made an impression. He seems content.

On this afternoon at least, "The Shadow King" reigns supreme.

CHAPTER 36

LESSONS LEARNED

Early the next morning, still energized by a day with "The Shadow King," I slowly cruise Antietam battlefield roads before heading home to Tennessee. It's my ritual after every visit to this hallowed ground. Each pass of a farm field, woodlot, historic house and monument evokes a name and a memory.

Along Cornfield Avenue, near the East Woods, I think of a private from Massachusetts named Samuel Gould. A world traveler and bright light, he fell in the bloody maelstrom of Antietam. Forever 19, Gould still stares at me from a picture frame on the wall of my home office.

After making a left near a cornfield, I navigate a bend by Samuel Mumma's farmhouse and turn left again. On a knoll in the near distance appears the 14th Connecticut monument, a beautiful beacon of white granite.

On William Roulette's farm nearby, amid broken cornstalks and ground-hog holes, Confederate lead sliced through the side of 14th Connecticut lieutenant George Crosby. Nearly a month later, the 19-year-old officer died at the home of his parents back in Connecticut.

At Roulette's place toiled a freed slave named Nancy Campbell, who lived on the farm. In the 1850s, her master set her value at $250, the price then of a good horse.[1]

---

1. *Cracker Barrel Magazine*, "Civil War Footsteps: Former Slave From Tilghmanton Area Finds Freedom," Richard Clem, Feb.-March 2005. Last Will and Testament of Andrew Miller, her former owner, Register of Wills Office in the Washington County (Md.) Court House

A steady drizzle blurs my windshield. A few tears cloud my eyes. Leaving this place—1862 under a bubble—is hard for me.

Near Bloody Lane, where Bob Kalasky lay in the gravel the day before, I linger for a few moments. No other living soul is around. Overhead I look for a bird or two—a sign that spirits may be aware of my presence. But I see only interminable, gloomy gray.

On this road trip of a lifetime, I have traveled thousands of miles—from Vicksburg to Philadelphia and points in between. I mentally review a partial road trip scorecard.

Meals at The Red Byrd in Keedysville, Maryland: Countless. Roadkill spotted: Dozens. Battlefields visited: 16. Large bags of red licorice consumed: 10.

Forts visited: four. Tick-infested woods walked: three. Hypnosis sessions: one. Oreo cookies encountered with a presidential profile carved into the icing: one. Wild boars met named Louie: one. CIA agents shared breakfast with: zero.

So, what have I learned?

For one, I learned Trevilian Station, Thompson's Station, Perryville, Resaca and all the other out-of-the-way places I visited are as awe-inspiring and sad as Gettysburg and Antietam.

And I learned how *deeply* people still care about them.

At the "Hill of Death," far into the woods on the Champion Hill battlefield in Mississippi, I could see it in the eyes of Sid Champion V, my psychotic connection.

"I could come up here and it could be 98 degrees," he told me from a seat on a bench amid the cedars, "but it's OK. It's *my place… it's my place.*"

On a farm in rural Virginia, the heart of the Cumberland Church battlefield, I could see it in Dirk Warner's eyes, too.

"I'm going to be buried here by those redbud trees," the farmer declared, gesturing toward the far distance.

I learned that battlefields, forts and historic houses are like photos of snowflakes—every time you see one, you see something new and different. And when they get bulldozed for a parking lot, residential development or a highway, I feel the same way the day our dog died.

At the national cemetery in Andersonville, Georgia, I learned how much a heart can ache walking among the thousands of gravestones spaced only inches apart. I wonder what the soldiers buried beneath them might have become.

In Andersonville, Gettysburg and elsewhere, I learned that people really do believe in ghosts.

"Oh, honey, there are spirits here everywhere," Cynthia StormCaller, Andersonville's quasi tourism director, told me.

On her cellphone, StormCaller showed me a photo that included a mysterious woman in a long-sleeve top and long period dress. A ghost? Who knows?

Nancy Garrison, owner of a small collectibles shop near the railroad track in Andersonville, invited me to see some of them for myself.

"You know, you ought to come back here in August, when the ghosts come around," she said without even the hint of a twinkle in her eye.

At the New Market Heights battlefield, where U.S. Colored Troops fought so bravely in late September 1864, I learned we've largely ignored an important part of our past. I knew virtually nothing about those men and what they had accomplished before my visit to the battlefield.

Why doesn't a monument stand to honor the 14 Black soldiers who earned the Medal of Honor at New Market Heights?

What other experiences of African Americans during the Civil War remain hidden in the shadows of history?

On a drizzly morning in the parking lot near the Antietam battlefield visitors center, I learned a historical cookie might crumble.

"It's sick, my Lincoln cookie," said Laura Van Alstyne Rowland.

"What?!" I said, feigning disbelief.

"Mold," said The Oreo Cookie Lady.

Blame our 85-mile trip with the cookie from Sharpsburg, Maryland to Harpers Ferry, West Virginia and beyond on the trail of her beloved Abraham Lincoln. The cookie, which doesn't get outside much, must have been affected by the chill during our travels on a frosty spring day.

In Marion, Arkansas, I learned from a local judge that Tacker's Shake Shack serves a Sultana burger—"overloaded like the real *Sultana*," according to Loretta, the proprietor.

In February 2023, Mrs. B and I split one of the behemoths with her sister and her husband, 30-dollar price be damned.

And I learned again about the fragility of life. Months after my visit to Marion, Rosalind O'Neal—the beloved Sultana museum manager and goodwill ambassador—died at 79. She loved her museum—the photographs and artifacts and, most of all, the stories.

"We've had people come here from all 50 states and 14 countries," the raspy-voiced O'Neal told me proudly.

Roz said she wanted to put a little model horse on the deck of the huge model of the doomed steamboat in the museum. Too bad she never got the chance.

I also learned we need another dog, maybe one that chases groundhogs, just like Finn at that Confederate wedding mansion in Columbia, Tennessee.

And I learned long-haul trucker must be in my DNA. No road trip fazes me, no matter the length. Fuel me up with a mug of coffee, give me a large bag of red licorice, point me to a Civil War battlefield or home, and I'm good.

Nearly 12 hours after my departure from Antietam, the bright lights of downtown Nashville appear on the horizon against a charcoal-black sky.

Bleary-eyed and eager to get home, I think of my momma, Sweet Peggy. In heaven she's probably making tiny roast beef sandwiches for my dad, "Big Johnny." With his long-ago gift of three genuine Civil War bullets purchased in Gettysburg—those three little demons—he unknowingly started me on this long road decades ago.

I think, too, of my Civil War poppa, Richard Clem.

In e-mails peppered with references to the Lord, he often offers comforting words: "Take care, my friend, while you keep history alive."

In Nashville, I pass the exit for Peach Orchard Hill, where angry Rebels eagerly cut down USCT struggling through the mud and muck on a bleak December day in 1864. That hallowed ground long ago became a residential neighborhood.

Sheesh.

It breaks my heart.

Nearly out of gas, I finally make it back to Mrs. B, Civil War Mission Control.

This road trip of a lifetime is over.

But I am already planning another one.

Let's keep history alive.

BIBLIOGRAPHY

ARCHIVES

"Confederate Spies Hung Near Ft. Granger," by Park Marshall (1855-1946), unpublished, Williamson County (Tenn.) Archives.

Francis Lawton Mobley Papers, Atlanta History Center, ahc.MSS1008

George Q. Whitney Collection, Connecticut State Library, 16th Connecticut veteran Richard Jobes' letter to Fanny Brown, Feb. 10, 1909

John Peter Baird file, Indiana State Archives, Indianapolis

Judson L. Austin Papers 1862-1865, Bentley Historical Library, University of Michigan

BOOKS

Bates, Samuel P., *History of the Pennsylvania Volunteers, 1861-1865*, Harrisburg, Pa.: 1868-1871

Berry, Chester D., *Loss of the Sultana and Reminiscences of Survivors*, Lansing, Mich.: Darius D. Thorp, 1892, Pages 191-92

Brant, Jefferson, *History of the Eighty-Fifth Indiana Volunteer Infantry*, Bloomington, Ind.: Cravens Bros. Printers and Binders, 1902

Brents, John A., *The Patriots and Guerrillas of East Tennessee*, New York: Henry Dexter Publisher's Agent, 1863

Brown, Edmund Randolph, *The Twenty-seventh Indiana Volunteer Infantry in the War of the Rebellion, 1861 to 1865*, Monticello, Ind., 1899

Butler, Benjamin F., *Autobiography and Personal Reminiscences of Major-General Benj. F. Butler*, Boston: A.M. Thayer & Co., 1892

Cannon, James P.; Crowson, Noel; Brogden, John V., *Bloody Banners and Barefoot Boys: A History of the 27th Regiment Alabama Infantry,* Shippensburg, Pa.: White Mane Publisher, 1997

Carpenter, George N., *History of the Eighth Regiment Vermont Volunteers 1861-1865,* Boston: Press of Deland & Barta, 1886

Clark, Rufus W., *The Heroes of Albany*, Albany, N.Y.: S.R. Gray Publisher, 1867

Crummer, Wilbur Fisk, *With Grant at Fort Donelson, Shiloh and Vicksburg*, Oak Park, Ill.: E.C. Crummer & Co., 1915

Custer, George A., *The Custer Story: The Life and Intimate Letters of General George A. Custer and His Wife Elizabeth,* Edited by Marguerite Merrington, New York: The Devin-Adair Co., 1950

Denison, Frederic, *Shot and Shell: The Third Rhode Island Heavy Artillery in the Rebellion*, Providence, R.I.: Third Rhode Island Heavy Artillery Veterans Association, 1879

Diary And Letters of Rutherford Birchard Hayes, Volume 2, 1865-1881, Edited by Charles Richard Williams, The Ohio State Archaeological and Historical Society, 1924

Donaldson, Francis Adams, *Inside the Army of the Potomac: The Civil War Experience of Captain Francis Adams Donaldson*, ed. J. Gregory Acken, Mechanicsburg, Pa: Stackpole Books, 1998

Drake, Edwin L., *The Annals of the Army of Tennessee, and Early Western history, Including a Chronological Summary of Battles and Engagements in the Western Armies of the Confederacy,* Nashville, Tenn.: A.D. Haynes, 1878

Dromgoole, Will Allen, *The Sunny Side of the Cumberland*, Philadelphia: J.B. Lippincott Company, 1886

Flood, Charles Bracelen, *Lee: The Last Years*, New York: Houghton Mifflin, 1981

Fout, Frederick, *The Darkest Days of the Civil War, 1864 and 1865*, English translation of Fout's 1902 *Die Schwersten Tage des Bürgerkriegs*, 1864-1865

Fox, William, *Regimental Losses in the American Civil War, 1861-1865*, Albany, N.Y.: Albany Publishing Co., 1889

Frye, Dennis, *Harpers Ferry Under Fire*, Virginia Beach, Va.: The Donning Company Publishers, 2012

Grant, Ulysses S., *Personal Memoirs of U.S. Grant, Vol. 1*, New York: Charles L. Webster & Co., 1885

History of the Corn Exchange Regiment, 118th Pennsylvania Volunteers, from their first engagement at Antietam to Appomattox, Compiled by John L. Smith., Philadelphia: J.L. Smith Publishers, 1888

Jackson, Mary Anna, *Life and Letters of General Thomas J. Jackson*, New York: Harper & Brothers, 1892, Page 247

Kellogg, Robert H., *Life and Death in Rebel Prisons*, Hartford, Conn.: L. Stebbins, 1865

Lee, William O., *Personal And Historical Sketches And Facial History of and by Members of the Seventh Regiment Michigan Volunteer Cavalry*, Detroit: The Ralston-Stroup Printing Co., 1902

Livermore, Thomas, *Number & Losses in the Civil War in America: 1861-65*, Boston and New York: Houghton, Mifflin & Co, 1900

Longstreet, James, *From Manassas to Appomattox*, Philadelphia: J.B. Lippincott Co., 1896

McCormick, Mike, *Terre Haute: Queen City of the Wabash*, Charleston, S.C.: Arcadia Publishing, 2005

McKnight, Brian D., *Confederate Outlaw: Champ Ferguson and the Civil War in Appalachia*, LSU Press, 2011

Miller, Delavan S., *Drum Taps in Dixie; Memories of a Drummer Boy, 1861-1865,* Watertown, N.Y.: Hungerford-Holbrook Co., 1905

Montgomery, Frank A., *Reminisces of a Mississippian in Peace and War*, Cincinnati: The Robert Clarke Company Press, 1901

Moore, Frank, *Women of The War, Their Heroism and Self-Sacrifice*, Hartford: S.S. Scranton & Co., 1866

Muffly, Joseph Wendel, *The Story of Our Regiment: A History of the 148th Pennsylvania Vol,* Des Moines, Iowa: The Kenyon Printing and Manufacturing Co., 1904

My Dear Wife—Letters To Matilda, The Civil War Letters of Sid and Matilda Champion of Champion Hill, edited by Rebecca Blackwell Drake and Margie Riddle Bearss, self-published, 2005

Narrative of Privations and Sufferings of United States Officers and Soldiers While Prisoners of War in the Hands of the Rebel Authorities, U.S. Sanitary Commission, Philadelphia: King & Baird Press, 1864

Old Homes And Buildings in Amelia County, Virginia, Volume 1, compiled and published by Mary Armstrong Jefferson, Amelia, Va., 1964

Pinsky, Mark I., *Met Her on The Mountain*, Lexington, Ky.: The University Press of Kentucky, 2022

Polk, Mary Branch, *Memoirs of a Southern Woman "Within the Lines," and a Genealogical Record.* Chicago: The Joseph G. Branch Publishing Co., 1912

Price, James S, *The Battle of New Market Heights*, Charleston, S.C.: The History Press, 2011

Prison diary, of Michael Dougherty, late Co. B, 13th., Pa., Cavalry, Bristol, Pa.: C.A. Dougherty Printer, 1908

Reilly, Oliver T., *The Battlefield of Antietam*, Hagerstown, Md., self-published, 1906

Relyea, William H., *16th Connecticut Volunteer Infantry: Sergeant William H. Relyea*, Edited by John Michael Priest, Shippensburg, Pa., Burd Street Press, 2002

Scott, Kate M., *History of the One Hundred and Fifth Regiment of Pennsylvania Volunteers,* Philadelphia: New-World Publishing Co., 1877

Smith, Timothy B., *Champion Hill, Decisive Battle For Vicksburg*, New York: Savas Beatie LLC, 2004

Spence, John C.H., *A Diary of the Civil War,* Murfreesboro, Tenn.: Rutherford County Historical Society, 1993

The Bravest 500 of '61, Their Noble Deeds Described by Themselves, compiled by Theo F. Rodenbough, New York: G.W. Dillingham Publishers, 1891

The Civil War Journals of John Mead Gould, 1861-1866, Edited by William B.
   Jordan, Baltimore, Md.: Butternut & Blue
The Diary of James K. Polk during his Presidency, 1845 to 1849, edited and anno-
   tated by Milo Milton Quaife, Chicago: A.C. McClurg & Co., 1910, Page 419
United States War Department. *The War of the Rebellion: A Compilation of the
   Official Records of the Union and Confederate Armies.* Washington, 1894
Vaill, Theodore, *History of the Second Connecticut Volunteer Heavy Artillery*,
   Winsted, Conn.: Winsted Printing Company, 1868
Wayland, John W., *A Scenic and Historical Guide to the Shenandoah Valley*,
   Dayton, Va.: Shenandoah Press, 1923
White, Emma Siggins, *Genealogy of the descendants of John Walker of Wigton,
   Scotland*, Kansas City, Mo.: Tiernan-Dart Printing Co., 1902
Wittenberg, Eric J., *Glory Enough For All, Sheridan's Second Raid and the Battle
   of Trevilian Station*, Washington, D.C.: Brassey's, 2002
Zimmerman, Mark, *Fortress Nashville: Pioneers, Engineers, Mechanics,
   Contrabands & Colored Troops*, Nashville: Zimco Publications LLC, 2022

CIVIL WAR PENSION FILES AND SERVICE RECORDS (National Archives, Washington, D.C.)
1st Maine Heavy Artillery Corporal George McKechnie
2nd New York Heavy Artillery privates John Davis, Edward Lindsey, Michael
   Connell
5th Minnesota privates Patrick Byrnes, Lysias Raymong
16th Connecticut Private Emerson Nichols
105th Pennsylvania privates John Shivler, Luther Calkins
36th USCT Miles James compiled services
Robert Davis pension application for son Pvt. Benjamin Davis, 6th USCT

CD-ROM
Nelson, John H, "As Grain Falls Before The Reaper: The Federal Hospital Sites
   And Identified Federal Casualties at Antietam," Privately published CD,
   Hagerstown, Md., 2004

DIARIES
2nd Connecticut Heavy Artillery Lt. Michael Kelly diary, Connecticut Historical
   Society collection, Hartford, Conn.
5th Minnesota officer Thomas Parke Gere's wartime diary (typewritten copy),
   Minnesota Historical Society (Battle of Nashville text courtesy Tim Bode, 5th
   Minnesota Research Group on Facebook)

16th Connecticut veteran William Nott's postwar diary, copy in author's collection
49th Ohio Sgt. Jonathan Rapp diary, Taylor Agan collection
115th Ohio soldier John Clark Ely diary, Andersonville (Ga.) National Historic Site
Union officer Wilmon Blackmar diary transcript, Cisco's Gallery in Coeur
    d'Alene, Idaho

DIARIES VIA CHAMPION HILL BATTLEFIELD WEB SITE (battleofchampionhill.org)

20th Ohio private Osborn H. Oldroyd
Wesley Olin Connor, CSA Cherokee Artillery. The original manuscript was
    donated to the Hargrett Special Collections Library at the University of Georgia
    by Margaret Wright Hollingsworth

DIARIES VIA SPARED & SHARED WEB SITE

100th Pennsylvania soldier Christopher Columbus Lobinger 1862 diary
Confederate Brig. Gen. Claudius Wistar Sears, entry for Dec. 7, 1864

JOURNALS

North Carolina Historical Review, April 1952

LETTERS

28th Iowa Corporal John David Myers to Frances (Nickerson) Myers, May 15,
    1863, published on Spared & Shared 18, on March 22, 2019
2nd Connecticut Heavy Artillery Chaplain Winthrop Phelps letter to Lucy Phelps,
    June 1, 1864, Litchfield (Conn.) Historical Society collection
29th Maine Maj. George Nye letter to wife Charlotte Nye, Oct. 19, 1864, and 29th
    Maine Private Uranus Stacy letter to his mother, Oct. 4 and 22, 1864, Nicholas
    Picerno collection
Horace Maynard, Attorney General for State of Tennessee, to Major General
    William Rosecrans, June 12, 1863, from John Baird's Military File, National
    Archives

MAGAZINES

Confederate Veteran, June 1900, Vol. 8, No. 6
Cracker Barrel Magazine
Danker, Donald F., "Imprisoned at Andersonville: The Diary of Albert Harry
    Shatzel, May 5, 1864—September 12, 1864," *Nebraska History*, 1957

NEWSPAPERS | WIRE SERVICES

Akron (Ohio) Beacon Journal
Albany (N.Y.) Morning Express
Alton (Ill.) Evening Telegraph
Arkansas Democrat
Asheville (N.C.) Citizen Times
Baltimore Sun
Belmont (Ohio) Chronicle
Buffalo Advocate
Buffalo Commercial
Burlington (Iowa) Weekly Hawk-eye
Charleston Daily Courier
Cincinnati Daily Press
Cincinnati Post
Cleveland Daily Leader
Commercial Appeal, Memphis, Tenn.
Courier-Journal, Louisville, Ky
Farmville (Va.) Herald
Fort Wayne (Ind.) Journal-Gazette
Freeland (Pa.) Tribune
Gettysburg Times
Harper's Weekly
Hagerstown (Md.) Daily Mail
Hartford Courant
Herald of Freedom & Torch Light, Hagerstown, Md.
Herald and Mail, Columbia, Tenn.
Hillsdale Standard, Hillsdale, Mich.
Indianapolis Journal
Kansas City Gazette
Louisville Daily Journal
Memphis Argus
Memphis Bulletin
Memphis Daily Appeal
Muscatine (Iowa) Journal
Muscatine (Iowa) New-Tribune
Nashville American
Nashville Banner
Nashville Daily Union
Nashville Union
National Republican, Washington, D.C.

New Bern (N.C.) Daily Progress
New York Daily Herald
New York Times
New York Tribune
Niles National Register, St. Louis, Mo.
Omaha (Neb.) Daily Bee
Philadelphia Inquirer
Philadelphia Times
Public Spirit, Jenkintown, Pa.
Richmond Dispatch
Richmond Enquirer
Richmond Examiner
Richmond Times-Dispatch
Salem (Ohio) News
Shepherdstown (W.Va.) Register
The Advocate, Buffalo, N.Y.
The Daily Pittsburgh Gazette
The Daily Press, Newport News, Va.
The Daily Republican, Monongahela, Pa.
The Goodhue Volunteer, Red Wing, Minn.
The Jeffersonian-Democrat, Brookville, Pa.
The National Tribune
The Sentinel, Carlisle, Pa.
The Summit County Beacon, Akron, Ohio
The Tiffin (Ohio) Tribune
United Press International
Wall Street Journal
Washington Evening Star
Washington Evening Times
Washington Times

OTHER

"Ashwood: The Polks and the Pillows," Richard Hilary Quin thesis, Middle
    Tennessee State University, 1992
*Ceremonies in Commemoration of the One Hundredth Anniversary of the Birth
    of Abraham Lincoln*, Military Order of the Loyal Legion of the United States
    Commandery of the State of Pennsylvania, Philadelphia, 1909
Historical Vignettes Volume 1 Stafford, Connecticut, 275th Anniversary, 1719-1994
Homestead Manor (Thompson's Station, Tenn.), National Register of Historic
    Places Inventory Nomination Form, April 29, 1977

Impressment of Black Laborers by Union Forces in Franklin; Senate Report Condition and Treatment of Colored Refugees, 38th Cong., 2d sess., S. Ex. Doc. 28 serial 1,209, Dec. 28, 1864.

Meade Post #1, Grand Army of the Republic in Philadelphia minutes, Feb. 26, 1883

Speech of Hon. Benjamin F. Butler, of Massachusetts, in the House of Representatives, Jan. 7, 1874, Government Printing Office, 1874

The George Meade Society of Philadelphia, Meade letter to Captain Sam Ringwalt, Sept. 24, 1864

WEB SITES

American Battlefield Trust (https://www.battlefields.org/)

New York State Military Museum and Veterans Research Center (https://museum .dmna.ny.gov/)

BATTLEOFCHAMPIONHILL.ORG

Matilda Champion: "A Sorrow's Crown of Sorrow," Rebecca Blackwell Drake

Matilda Champion: "I Was in the Cellar During the Fight," Rebecca Blackwell Drake

INDEX